ABOUT THE AUTHORS

Robert D. Hess received his Ph.D. in Human Development from the University of Chicago where he has been Professor of Human Development and of Education, and Director of the Head Start Evaluation and Research Center and of the Urban Child Center. Dr. Hess is past chairman of the Committee on Human Development, a Fellow of the Center for Advanced Study in the Behavioral Sciences, and a contributor of many articles and research reports in the field of human development. Author of Family Worlds (*with Gerald Handel*), Compensatory Education for Cultural Deprivation (*with Benjamin Bloom and Allison Davis*), *and editor of* Early Education (*with Roberta Meyer Bear*), *he is at present Lee Jacks Professor of Child Education in the School of Education, Stanford University.*

Judith V. Torney received her Ph.D. in Human Development from the University of Chicago where, as Research Associate and Project Director, she carried out extensive research on the development of attitudes in children and on political socialization. An important contributor to the literature on child development, Dr. Torney is at present Assistant Professor of Psychology, Illinois Institute of Technology.

The Development of Political Attitudes in Children

The Development of Political Attitudes in Children

ROBERT D. HESS
STANFORD UNIVERSITY

AND

JUDITH V. TORNEY
ILLINOIS INSTITUTE OF TECHNOLOGY

ALDINE PUBLISHING COMPANY / *Chicago*

First published 1967 by
ALDINE Publishing Company
320 West Adams Street
Chicago, Illinois 60606

Library of Congress Catalog Card Number 67-18819
Designed by Bernard Schleifer
Printed in the United States of America

Preface

This book is based upon an analysis of data obtained in a study which began in 1960 at the University of Chicago. It also reflects the outcome of a number of studies of political socialization conducted by Professor Hess and Professor David Easton during the past ten years. These inquiries, which were among the first to be undertaken on this topic, were designed to obtain information about the induction of children into the political life of the United States, to describe the nature of socialization into citizenship roles, and to examine pre-adult political learning and behavior in terms of other implications for the stability of the political system. This research thus had two concerns: (1) the process by which an individual child is prepared to become an adult member of the political community, and (2) the consequences of current procedures of political socialization for the operation of the system.

This book deals with the first of these concerns. It presents the findings of the research in terms of the growth of political attitudes and correlative behavior in individuals. It is particularly centered upon the development in children of a sense of involvement in political life—by which we mean interest, or subjective engagement, and overt or active participation in fulfillment of interest. Other publications, prepared by Professor Easton, will deal with these findings from the view of political theory. In view of his somewhat different theoretical interest in the project, Professor Easton elected not to join us in authorship of this volume.

During the course of this study we had the cooperation and assistance of many colleagues, staff members, students, and personnel in the public schools. Our most important help was given by the children who participated in the project and by their parents, who supported the objectives of the study. We are also especially grateful for the willingness of the public schools to become involved—to the teachers, principals, and superintendents who believe that education in contemporary society can profit from greater knowledge about children and about the processes and patterns that are basic to learning.

A research project of this magnitude requires the efforts of many persons whose assistance, though sometimes limited in time, is as lasting as the effects of the study. We wish to recognize the contribution of these co-workers, particularly Dr. John David Jackson, who served as project director and supervised the field work and data analysis. His role in formulating plans for testing, establishing contacts with school systems, and co-ordinating the project was essential. Dr. Jack Dennis joined the project as a research assistant soon after it began and worked with us until he completed his graduate work in political science and accepted a position at the University of Wisconsin. Joy Zigo took responsibility for producing the final copy of the report to the U.S. Office of Education, upon which this volume is based. She constructed figures, supervised editing, and in general took the production of that report as her personal responsibility. Elliot Simon and Carl Hildabrand handled the specialized, tedious, and exacting problems of urging the data through the computer. Ed Thompson prepared a number of preliminary reports. Sharon Avery and Mrs. Anne Vollmar helped edit the various drafts of the manuscript.

We also acknowledge, with thanks, the contribution of many other staff members who worked with us at various stages of the research: Mrs. Jill Cohen and Mrs. Charlotte Rosen, project secretaries; our interviewers and research assistants, Albert Robles, Reginald Bartholomew, Roger Masters, Mrs. Donna England, Mrs. Patricia Bebout, Mrs. Beverly Rogers, John Fitzgerald, Herbert Haberland, Elliott White, Keith Torney, Mrs. Jean Dames Goodman, Susan Roth, Art Rosner, Tadao Okamura, Frank Smith, Harold Kooden, Paul Waltz, Dan Leatherman, Mrs. Helen Wall, and Anne Niemiec. The staff at the Urban Child Center, particularly Mrs. Ruth Vogeler and Mrs. Nellie Hickman, have been of tremendous help throughout the final phases of manuscript preparation.

The comments of many colleagues have been corrective, encouraging, and always useful. Several have been especially salient in the relevance of their criticism and comments: Professor Donald Fiske, Professor Frederick Frey, Professor Fred Greenstein, and Professor Lawrence Kohlberg. They are not, of course, responsible for whatever faults may remain.

We are grateful for the encouragement and administrative support of colleagues who, in various ways, helped make this volume possible: Dean Francis S. Chase, Dean D. Gale Johnson, Dean Roald Campbell, and Dr. Ralph Tyler (both as colleague and as Director of the Center for Advanced Study). The resources of the Center aided greatly in the final stages of the preparation of the manuscript. Perhaps most important during these studies was the encouragement of Professor Allison Davis, whose long-time interest in social structure and socialization provided the initial orientation toward this study. Also, in many ways the project and the tasks of writing were facilitated by the support, encouragement, and constructive comments of our respective families.

The research reported herein was supported through the Cooperative Research Program of the Office of Education, U.S. Department of Health, Education and Welfare (Project Number 1078). Other than providing financial support, The Office of Education had no responsibility for the direction of the study nor any involvement in decisions about specific topics to be included in the questionnaires, selection of samples to be studied, or conclusions drawn from the findings.

ROBERT D. HESS
JUDITH V. TORNEY

Contents

List of Figures

List of Tables

The
Development of
Political Attitudes
in Children

1

Participation

of Children

in Political Life

"America is the best country in the world, and the President—he's not like a king but he makes all the important . . . well, a lot of important decisions." [1]

Introduction

The child's comment above illustrates the involvement of young children in the political life of the nation. Although the prospect of adult participation is distant, these young citizens develop a view of government, of law and justice, and of the proper role of citizens, and they share some of the excitement of election campaigns long before their interest can have any effect upon the political affairs of the country. These early perceptions, images, and concepts are sometimes trusting and naïve, sometimes cynical, often amusing, and frequently inaccurate and distorted. Yet they are much more than children's playful fantasy—they are characteristic of a period during which children become oriented toward the values, beliefs, knowledge, and opinions of the political culture, and they provide the basis for later behavior as adult citizens.

This book is concerned with this early learning, which we call political socialization. It is a report of a study that included more than 17,000 elementary school children—research designed to gather information about early involvement in political affairs and to describe its nature and the general course it follows from early childhood into the adolescent years.

The feelings that children hold about the distant persons, institutions, and complex activities that make up political life in the United States vary dramatically from one child to another, as these conversations show:

1. Interviews from which these excerpts have been drawn were recorded and transcribed verbatim. The excerpts have not been edited, although deletions have been made for the sake of clarity.

1

"Tommy, what is the government?"

"The government is like the President, but he isn't actually a President. The builders, the street makers, and all these people work for the government. The sidewalks and streets are the government's property, and he lets people walk in them.

"He has a moneymaking machine, and he makes a lot of money. But he doesn't use it. I think he uses money for decoration—some money is put on necklaces with little things.

"He works a lot, like the President does. Maybe the President gives him some directions, and he gives other directions to other people. Maybe he makes the laws of the country. Maybe he tells the numbers on the license plates.

"Probably he works in the capital like the President. He does! He lives in Washington. He doesn't live in the White House. He has his own home.

"He's the judge of the wildlife service. I sent him that letter about banding birds, and he told the wildlife service to send me that pamphlet.

"I've got it! The government is boss of all the governors, probably. Like the President is boss of all the senators. Senators are people from all different states.

"I heard on the radio that he's in charge of the income tax. He can higher it or lower it."

"Tommy, what does he spend the money on?"

"How should I know? Like the government doesn't know what we spend our money on. He spends it for food, clothing, things for his wife, and that sort of thing."

Tommy is seven, in second grade. He is bright, informed, for his age, and imaginative. His conception of the government is specific even when it is inaccurate. It is a highly personalized image—one which includes at the same time the routines of family life and the responsibility for a nation.

In their responses to questions about the role of a citizen and his relationship with government, children often project their ideas of proper behavior onto the political scene, defining an unfamiliar role or describing an unfamiliar person in terms they have learned in their own lives. Nonetheless, they also begin to face some of the more difficult questions about justice and the responsibility of a citizen to his community and they begin to grapple with issues that face the adults around them. George, who is in the fourth grade, gives an example of how some children think about what it means to be a citizen.

"George, who would you say is a good citizen?"

"The President."

"Why?"

"I don't know, but I know he just would make a good citizen."

"Would there be something about him that would be different than those who are not good citizens?"

"Well, you'd have to be polite."
"George, just what is a good citizen?"
"A person whose house is clean and who is polite."
"Is there anyone who lives in this country who is not a citizen?"
"Yeah, some mean people."
"Well, how does that work?"
"Well, they won't be polite for one thing and they just don't get along with others."

"If a person is robbed by a gangster, then told he will be hurt if he tells the police about it, should he tell the police?"
"I would tell. . . ."
"What would make you want to tell?"
"I wouldn't want to get hurt."
"Let's see—you would tell the police, or you wouldn't?"
"I would."
"Even though you might get hurt?"
"But how would he know that I told the police?"
"Well, let's say he had a way of finding out. Should a person still tell the police?"
"Yes."
"Even though you might get hurt?"
"There shouldn't be nobody threatenin' nobody."

"Have you ever heard of a political party?"
"I've heard about parties, but not political parties."
"When have you heard about parties?"
"When it's somebody's birthday."
"Well, have you ever heard about the Democrats and Republicans?"
"Well, yeah, they are some sort of organization . . ."
"Do you think people should belong to that sort of thing?"
"Well, they could or they couldn't."
"What comes to your mind about these organizations?"
"Kennedy. . . ."
"What is that?"
"Well, he was a Democrat."

The emerging concepts are not always reassuring. The system is not always seen as just and responsive. Occasionally a child feels helpless, unable to deal effectively with representatives of government and retreats to passive compliance. Roger, who is a fifth-grade Negro boy 10 years old, expresses these feelings in his conversation with a staff member:

"Well now, Roger, suppose there was a Mr. Jones and he was stopped by a policeman for speeding but the policeman's speedometer was broken, so Mr. Jones really wasn't speeding. What do you think of this?"
"Well, he could ask the policeman to check the speedometer or else he would just have to pay the fine."

"What do you think he should do?"
"I don't know, I believe he'd have to pay the fine."
"Do you think he should?"
"Oh, it wouldn't be fair but there wouldn't be no other way out of it."
"Then you think he should just go along with the policeman?"
"Yes, then he wouldn't have all that trouble."

At a relatively early age many children acquire loyalty to candidates and parties. Especially during periods following elections there is a responsiveness to the competition developed during national contests. Allegiances emerge which are based not so much on specific knowledge about candidates as on personal preferences and identification. Along with this feeling of support, there is often an awareness of the significance of the power and responsibility that follow election to national leadership. Cris, an 11-year-old boy in grade five, offers these opinions about the Presidency:

"Tell me, Cris, have you ever seen the President on TV?"
"Uh-huh."
"What was he doing?"
"Well, he's usually telling speeches."
"What does he talk about?"
"Well, he talks about the satellites and Russia. I never listen that closely to the President talking. Usually we're doing something else, but my Dad and my Mom, sometimes they watch it and usually every time they watch it."
"What does the President do?"
"Well, he has to sign the laws before they go through. You know . . . bills. If he doesn't sign it, why then it doesn't become a law. And, well, he's just like the President of a company; he does good things for the country and shows what he thinks would be best for it. I think he's O.K."
"Uh-huh. Do you know how he gets to be President?"
"No. I know he was a general in the war, fought for our country in the Second World War. He must be an awfully smart man and studied hard while he was in school and a lot of different things."
"What's the difference between the Republican and Democratic party?"
"Hmmm. I don't know."
"Are your parents Republicans or Democrats?"
"Republicans."
"Uh-huh. If you could vote, who would you vote for?"
"I think I would vote for the Republic."
"Uh-huh. What do you think the President could do to be a better President?"
"Oh, I think he could stop sending so much, he's sending, sent some, but not so much foreign aid and I think he could work out the satellites a little more and get to the moon and everything.
"Uh-huh."
"I like that idea."

"I see. Yeah. How do you think the President is different from most other men?"

"Well, I know he is a brave man and he has to be nice so the people like him and will vote for him; he's a higher-class man so he's President, and I think any man could run for President but maybe all of them couldn't do as good a job as he would."

"When you say a higher-class man, what do you mean?"

"Well, he may have studied more in school and he may have gone, well, some men don't get much of a chance to go through their college degrees. Some of them don't run for Master degree or anything, but I think he's studied awfully hard in that field to be something like that . . . a leader."

"Uh-huh. How much education does the President have, do you know?"

"Well, I think he runs up to a Master degree . . . in college."

"Uh-huh. Do you know what he took up? What was his subject?"

"Hmm, hmmm."

"Well, what do you think a President should study if a person wants to be President?"

"Well, oh, arithmetic and science and social studies, being a good leader."

"Tell me, would you like to be President if you could?"

"Well, when I'm older I think I would."

"What would you do?"

"Well, I'd do what the President's job would be."

These excerpts (and others cited later) illustrate something of the emotional involvement of children with their country and its leaders. For both children and adults, this attachment is one of the most profound and complex ties in human experience. All of us are aware of the feelings that develop in this relationship—a sense of national pride in our country's achievements (in sports, say, or the conquest of space), or feelings of loyalty and respect during a ceremonial event such as the salute to the flag. The strength and depth of this attachment are apparent at unusual moments—for example, the widespread and powerful outpouring of emotion in a time of national crises such as the attack on Pearl Harbor a quarter century ago, or the assassination of President Kennedy.

The involvement of the individual citizen is evident also in the dramatic activity of national political conventions and in other features of election campaigns, when millions of persons give effort, time, and money to promote a favored candidate or to support an amendment, school bond, or referendum. All these levels of subjective involvement and overt activity attest to the motivating power of an individual's relationship to his country, its government, and its political processes.

What are the origins of these feelings, motivations, and actions? When do they arise and how are they shaped by experience? What creates attachment or interferes with it? What leads one person to be

more active or more concerned than another? How does involvement
change over time in the life of the individual? In the study described
here, the focus of attention was the growth in children of interest in
the nation and its government and the rise of a desire to participate in
the political process. This emotional engagement and the wish to take
part in the life of the political community will be referred to as
political involvement.

The majority of studies of adult political behavior have concentrated
on interest in election issues and candidates and on decisions basic to the
voting act. Obviously these specific acts and interests are not applicable
to the study of political involvement in children, and as a consequence
little attention has been given to the political beliefs, attitudes, and
activities of children and adolescents. Such a study is justified, however,
by a theory of pre-adult learning which connects the experience of
children with their later political activities as adults. That is, the acquisition of political behavior can be understood from the perspective of a
theory of social learning and socialization—which is useful, although
not precise. *Social learning* and *socialization* refer of course to the
process whereby a junior or new member of a group or institution is
taught its values, attitudes, and other behavior. Socialization may be
regarded as a life-long process, although much of the basic teaching is
apparently accomplished in the early years.

It seems useful to think of this process as one which has both
upward reference to agents (like parents, teachers), lateral reference
to peer groups, and chronological or longitudinal reference to a future
time and status when present socialization may have its most direct
application. From this last perspective, socialization anticipates the adult
behavior with which it is concerned, preparing the individual for a role
which he will exercise more completely at some later time. For example,
in the small child's relationship to his parent, he is not only learning
how to behave as a child but he is also learning about the role of parent
he may eventually assume.

This induction into a social system may be regarded as preparatory
or *anticipatory.* It is useful to distinguish among three types of *anticipatory* socialization. First, there is the acquisition of attitudes and values
about adult roles; although some of these attitudes may have limited
relevance for the child, they are the basis upon which subsequent learning of specific behavior may be built. For example, a small boy may
recognize and accept certain values with respect to the role of father,
such as providing a livelihood for his family, that will later facilitate
his learning the specific behaviors involved. Similarly, he may learn
something about what it takes to be a "worker" from observing his
parent performing an occupational role. He is socialized to accept the

importance of these roles and becomes ready to learn the details more promptly and with less stress when they become appropriate for him.

A second way in which anticipatory socialization may be effective is in the acquisition of specific information which cannot be directly applied until later life. For example, the child learns the significance of stop signs and police sirens long before he learns to drive a car.

Finally, a third type of anticipatory socialization is the learning of both general and specific skills which can be practiced in the immediate childhood situation and which will be called into play throughout life when appropriate occasions arise. For example, suitable classroom behavior such as attentiveness and punctuality are learned by most children in the first grade and are exercised on relevant occasions thereafter throughout the life span. The spontaneous imitating of parental roles, or teacher roles, or sales clerk roles, in which children engage during play is a further indication of the extent of anticipatory socialization to adult roles. Children adopt fragments of adult behavior in fantasy and thereby prepare themselves for adulthood.

There is a great deal of evidence for the existence of continuity between childhood experience and attitudes and adult attitudes and action (Bloom, 1964; Kagan and Moss, 1962). The literature on family transmission of political party preference (Hyman, 1959) presents instances of the relevance of childhood learning for adult political party commitment.

The argument for the importance of childhood learning for the political behavior of adults appears to have considerable validity. Of equal significance is the proposition that the socialization of children maintains basic values of the society. The nature and content of social learning necessarily reflects the structure and values of the group, setting up a circular pattern: the values of the adult society are transmitted through child-rearing and other teaching practices to children who, when they become adults, reinforce and help to maintain the culture in which they live.

The political behavior of adults has childhood origins in attitudes, values, and basic orientation which are broader in scope and which extend beyond the specific acts usually included in studies of adult political involvement. The early learning of the citizen role overlaps with experience in other arenas—the acquisition of a sense of moral justice, an emerging sense of sex-appropriate behavior, and such emotional underlay as passivity or a desire to control the environment.

The view of pre-adult socialization into the political system is more consonant with the role-learning orientation of the sociologists such as Brim (1966) than with the type of socialization which has been studied most frequently by psychologists—adults' attempts to modify the expression of impulses and physiological functions and the effects upon personality of different child-rearing practices. The psychologists' stress upon control over bodily functions follows from Freudian theory, which emphasizes impulses, infant experiences, and parental influence upon children.[2]

In contrast, the focus in this book is upon the origins of political orientations and the development of expectations, norms, and patterns of interaction between the individual and the political system as manifested in the responses of a large number of children at different grades in elementary school. The view of social learning presented here is oriented toward understanding how the individual child is inducted into the complex institutions and systems of a society. Its emphasis is upon the structure of the political system and the role of the individual citizen in relation to it. It reports on one of an increasing number of studies concerned with the child's relationship with a system or institution. The child in school is inducted into the rules, structure, and authority of the educational system, not *merely* into compliance with the particular teacher of his class (Hess and Shipman, 1965). For example, during medical school students are being inducted into roles within the medical establishment as well as absorbing clinical knowledge (Becker, 1961). The concern of this book, then—as we have said— is with the socialization of the child into the political system.

Background of the Study

This book reports on the most recent of a series of studies of political learning in children and adolescents conducted at the University of Chicago during the past decade.[3] The first of these projects was designed to examine the nature and level of attitudes in high-school youth and the changes in attitudes that emerged between the Freshman and Senior years. The rationale for selecting adolescence as an appropriate time for studying growth and development of political behavior was that the teenager is beginning to regard himself as an adult and to experiment with adult roles and identities. It was hypothesized that during the high-school years, the student's interest in political activities would increase and that his attitudes toward political objects and

2. In Child's review (1954) of the state of socialization research and theory, studies are grouped according to types of behavior: *oral, excretory, sexual, aggressive, dependent, achievement,* and others (affection, reproduction, and fear). The categories illustrate the concentration of interest upon socialization as a process of modifying impulses and the absence of studies of the child's increasing participation in systems and institutions of the society.

3. Previous results reported in Hess and Easton (1960); Easton and Hess (1961); Hess and Easton (1962); Hess (1963).

toward himself as a citizen would become more clearly formulated. With this rationale, a questionnaire was constructed covering a variety of political opinions and activities; the questionnaire was then administered to approximately 2,000 students—some from a high school in a working-class neighborhood and some from a middle-class suburb of Chicago.

This questionnaire (for Pilot Study 1) inquired about: (1) interest in political and civic problems and issues; (2) specific political activities such as listening to campaign speeches and talking with parents or friends about elections or current political events; (3) allegiance to a political party; (4) beliefs about the limits within which the government should exercise its power; (5) opinions about who in the country has easy access to governmental officials and who is most likely to have influence upon governmental policy; (6) the behavior expected of a public official, in this case a U.S. senator; (7) how and under what circumstances a senator's role performance might differ from these expectations; and (8) attitudes toward the proper functions and purposes of government.

The results of these testing sessions (Pilot Study 1) failed to support the hypothesis that significant major development and change in political attitudes occurs during the high-school years. On the contrary, the findings revealed that an unexpected degree of political learning and experience had occurred at the pre-high school level. Compared with seniors, the freshman classes were relatively advanced in their attitudes, and they displayed opinions about a wide range of political matters (Tables 1 and 2). It was the extent to which attitudes had been acquired before the Freshman level and their stability during the high-school period that directed our research effort toward the study of political socialization during the elementary school years.

Our subsequent research with younger children began with inter-

Table 1
Changes by Year in High School of Political Party Affiliation

Grade level	N	Democrats	Republicans	Sometimes one, sometimes the other	Don't know
Freshman	307	12.0%	45.6%	36.2%	6.2%
Sophomore	433	17.6	39.7	37.2	5.5
Junior	320	12.5	37.2	44.7	5.6
Senior	290	14.1	37.9	41.0	6.9

Notes.—Item: When it comes to taking sides in politics, which of the two major political parties do you personally favor? (1) Democrats; (2) Republicans; (3) sometimes one, sometimes the other; (4) I don't know. (From Pilot Study 1, middle-class group only.)
  —Significance Unit: 7%.

Table 2

Changes by Year in High School in Report of Political Activities

Grade level	N	Gave out handbills	N	Wore buttons	N	Talked with friends	N	Talked with parents	N	Took sides in election
Freshman	309	33.0%	308	67.8%	309	72.2%	307	77.8%	309	86.4%
Sophomore	435	31.5	435	74.0	435	71.0	433	78.8	434	85.9
Junior	321	31.5	321	69.8	321	76.9	321	78.8	321	84.1
Senior	289	23.2	289	77.2	290	79.7	290	84.1	289	81.7

Notes.—Item: Here is a list of things which persons like yourself have done. Check whether or not each activity is something you yourself have ever done: (1) Given out handbills or leaflets for a candidate at election time; (2) worn buttons for one or another candidate; (3) talked with your friends about politics and public events; (4) talked with your parents about politics and current events; (5) taken sides in elections for one or another candidate for public office. (From Pilot Study 1 questionnaire.)

—Significance Unit: 7%.

views designed to explore perceptions of familiar political figures. These interviews indicated that two figures, the local policeman and the President of the United States, were prominent in the young child's conceptions of governmental authority. They also revealed that the young child was familiar with a number of the symbols of government—the flag and the national anthem, for example—and had some idea of their meaning.

On the basis of these interviews, a questionnaire was devised to obtain the following information: (1) the child's image of the President of the United States; (2) a short essay response to the question, "How can I help make our government better?"; and (3) an essay describing Uncle Sam. Thus the questionnaire provided information about the child's conception of the foremost political figure of the country, his conception of the role the individual citizen is expected to play, and his view of a popular national symbol.

The findings with regard to the child's image of the President have been reported in Hess and Easton (1960), and will be summarized only briefly here. First, the image of the President was very positive, particularly in the early grades. Of 51 second-graders, 60 per cent saw him as "the best person in the world," and 75 per cent said they thought "the President likes almost everybody." Second, there was a developmental- or age-related change in level of response. In some respects, the image of the President became more favorable for older children; in others, it became less positive. Third, the image of the President was differentiated for the older children into a group of attributes having to do with the office or the role demands of the Presidency and into another cluster of personal characteristics such as honesty, friendliness, and the like. The child begins with high esteem for personal qualities of the President not necessarily related to the duties of his office. Subsequently this is modified toward a feeling of high esteem for role qualities essential to the fulfillment of the Presidency.

The results of these studies at the high-school and elementary-school levels led to exploratory studies in several other countries and to the proposal for the national study reported here. Although results of the high-school and elementary-school projects had provided limited information about the attitudes of children and had given preliminary indications of the age changes that might be expected, the larger study was intended to be a descriptive one to establish primary information in a field which had relatively little data or theory on which to base research.

It was from this background that the study grew which this book reports. The study encompassed more than 17,000 children in both pilot and final field-testing phases. For the pilot phase, approximately 5,000 children were interviewed and/or tested in several cities within a radius of 100 miles of Chicago. The field testing which supplied the data of this book took place in eight cities in the four major regions of the United States (Northeast, South, Midwest, and Far West). The details of the method of the study and a description of the cities, regions, and children involved, together with other information about reliability, procedures of test development and instrument format are presented in Appendix A. Included there is an explanation of the methods used to construct the graphs and tables that appear in the following sections.

Patterns of Growth in Emergence of Political Attitudes

The most prominent feature of political socialization is the rapidity with which attitudes change during the elementary-school years. Not all attitudes develop at the same time or show the same types of growth, however. One of the aims of the study was to understand more completely these different patterns of growth and change.

How should we think about this process? One model is offered by Piaget (1947) who in his classic work on the growth of logic conceptualized children's movement away from infantile patterns of thought toward adult thought processes. Perhaps political socialization may be viewed as proceeding along similar lines, assuming that children are moving toward the political concepts, attitudes, and expectations which are characteristic of adults. It is clear from previous work that changes in political attitudes occur as age increases (Greenstein, 1965a; Hess and Easton, 1960); the character of adult participation and the images of government and citizenship prevalent in the adult population are among the most influential forces guiding these changes.

There are several aspects common to the child's and the adult's image of the political systems. The adult holds ideal standards with which to evaluate the political system and its representatives. He also has information about the way the system does in fact operate, and he makes judgments about whether it attains the ideal standards (for example, most government officials are or are not honest; most laws are or are not administered fairly).

The individual also has an image of himself as a citizen: how he *should* act in relation to the government and how he *does* act. There is consensus in the population about most ideals of citizen behavior (for example, citizens should obey laws; they should vote in elections). The particular forms of citizen behavior are also influenced by ideal norms and by other factors (for example, individuals possess varying amounts of knowledge about the most effective ways to channel their influence and about the most fruitful sources of information about candidates).

Children begin early in life to accept ideals about how the system should operate. There is agreement in the society about many of these norms; ideals about government frequently result from a transfer of more general behavior standards, which the child has already applied to himself, onto the political system (for example, children should be honest and public officials should also be honest; rules in children's games should be fair, and laws should also be fair). These ideal perceptions of the system appear to be established easily. In fact, for many children a gap between what is ideal and what is real does not exist; in the child's view of the adult world, what is *ideal* is. The values that encourage citizen activity in influencing the government are not so apparent to the young child, in part because the idea that a citizen should interfere in the operation of a group to which he belongs is a relatively complex concept.

At the present time there is not sufficient information available on the adult population to make precise and careful comparisons between the attitudes of children and adults. However, it was possible as part of the study to assess some of the attitudes of teachers. Although their attitudes are probably not a faithful representation of the attitudes of adults in general, teachers are important representatives of the attitudes toward which children are socialized. In this country, teachers transmit a large share of information about the governmental system, presenting and discussing examples of governmental actions which fulfill or fail to fulfill the accepted ideals. They also transmit ideals of citizen behavior and teach some of the skills necessary to fill these requirements—how to get information for choosing a candidate, how to band together with others in a common cause. While teachers are restrained from partisan controversy, they are held responsible for presenting material about the government's organization and operation and for inculcating norms of citizen behavior. They also play a vital role in organizing many other kinds of experiences which contribute to cognitive development, even though the experiences may not have explicit political content.

PHASES OF EARLY POLITICAL INVOLVEMENT

A study of the child's progressive involvement in the political system of his country could be limited to behavior and attitudes of adults which are appropriate for children—talking about political subjects, reading about political issues, commitment to a party. Much previous research with children and adolescents has described involvement from this point of view (Hyman, 1959), but such an approach leaves unexplored the initial phases of political socialization.

It is useful to consider political involvement starting from the point where no attitudes or cognitions about the political system exist and to define four aspects of engagement with the system. The first is *identification of political objects,* becoming aware of them and recognizing them as part of the political realm. As the child learns more, comes into contact with more aspects of the political system and forms his own opinions about it, he becomes more involved in the system than the child who knows nothing of political objects or processes.[4]

There were great individual differences in the information children in the study had about various aspects of government and political processes. During one interview with a second-grade boy, the following exchange was recorded:

"Jimmy, do you know about the Supreme Court, have you heard anyone mention it?"
"No, nothing at all."
"How about Congress, have you heard of Congress?"
"Nope."
"United States Senate?"
"Nope."
"United States House of Representatives?"
"No."
"County Agent?"
"Nope."
"School Board? City or town government?"
"Nope, nothing at all."

The difficulty encountered in trying to elicit attitudes about political objects from Jimmy is obvious. His responses are in sharp contrast to those of Tommy, whose expansive comments opened this chapter.

Another child revealed impressions of the President and the courts in spite of the fact that his information was exceedingly limited:

"Johnny, what is the United States Senate?"
"I know what the United States is—United States is a country where there is lots of people and presidents. That's all I know—the Senate part makes it too hard."
"What is the United States House of Representatives?"
"You mean the White House?"
"No, not quite the same. How about courts?"
"Courts is a place like a house or something like a building that is big and the man's name is, I can't say his name very well, but you know, he has a cap and he's big. And he sits down on a big desk, and when they want to talk to him, they say—uni– uni—"
"Your honor?"
"Yeah, yeah, yeah."

4. Oeser and Emery (1954) have similarly conceptualized the child's absorption of the country's ideology, measuring it by the number of times questions about political matters are omitted when the child has the choice of answering or leaving out the question.

"Where did you hear about that?"
"Well, a lot of times on television. And this man says to the policeman, do this and do that."
"Oh, I see. How does somebody get to do that, do you think?"
"If they be real good."

"What about the School Board?"
"No."
"The state government?"
"No, I don't know. . . ."
"The White House?"
"Well, I heard that the White House is real big, and it's got a lot of rooms—the teacher told us the number, but it is a big number and I can't even say it. There's a gray room, a gold room, a green room, and the President lives in the White House. . . . It is real big and nice. It is big and has two chairs, and if the King and Queen wants to come and visit, they sit down on the chairs."

From the extraordinary range in level of information revealed in interviews as well as more structured data-gathering instruments, we came to regard the number of attitudes a child is able to express as one index of the amount of his political socialization. Although it touches only one aspect of a multidimensional cluster of attitudes, knowledge, and overt behavior, it is a useful concept, especially at young age levels.

A second aspect of engagement with the political system is the acquisition of more elaborated *conceptualizations* of it, of the norms of appropriate citizen behavior, and of the ways in which the citizen can deal with the system. Interviews with children show their increasing information about the institutions and procedures of government. An exchange with an 11-year-old boy illustrates this awareness of the complexity of the President's activities.

"What can you tell me about the President?"
"Well, the President has quite a direct handling of the country. First, any bill—he can veto just about any bill. I don't really know too much about this. From what I've heard it's correct. He can veto any bill and he has the power—I mean he can make bills. I mean not all of them, but well, they pass, and he has something to do with it. And if he can get the people's support in him—well, that will help the country a lot."

A third aspect stresses emotional or *subjective involvement* with political objects—particularly positive or negative feelings about authority figures and political issues. Subjective involvement is most easily seen in the child's support for a candidate, as in this excerpt from a conversation with an 11-year-old boy:

"I was for Nixon in this past election, but I feel that Kennedy has . . . well, I'm certainly going to give him any support I can give him if I got a chance. I'm sure I probably won't get a chance, out of 200 million citizens, but if I do I'll support him fully. But if there was another election I'd still be for Nixon."

The fourth aspect—step—is that of *overt activity,* which approximates to a limited extent the political activity of adults. These activities include wearing buttons for a candidate, talking with friends about political matters, reading and listening to political presentations, and working for an organization at election time.

The four steps—awareness, conceptualization, subjective involvement, and active participation—indicate the components of political involvement in children. There is some question about the sequence in which these phases occur. From the interviews quoted above, there is clearly a mingling of aspects of involvement in the several excerpts. Possibly some children begin to participate as button wearers before having any real sense of the meaning of elections. Participation without meaning is also typical of other political activities of children—reciting the pledge of allegiance and singing the national anthem. An interview with Billy, age 7, illustrates this point:

> *"What do you do here at school when you see the flag?"*
> "Oh, we say the pledge."
> *"The pledge. Do you know what a pledge is?"*
> "Well, it's a kind of a prayer."
> *"A prayer. And who are you speaking to when you say the pledge?"*
> "To God."
> *"To God. I see. And what are you asking Him to do?"*
> "Take care of people."
> *"Do you ever sing when you see the flag?"*
> "Yeah."
> *"Can you tell me what that song is for?"*
> "Oh, . . . I don't know."

This sort of activity is not the voluntary, self-motivated participation described as the last of the phases above. Rather it might be regarded as *pseudo-participation*—used by adults to teach attitudes and information about the political world. But adult participation in elections and other activities of government and political life can also occur without subjective involvement. Persons may vote without any knowledge of the candidate—as a favor to a friend or relative, in response to urging by an organization or a promise of a bribe. In our view, such activities represent deviant socialization. They obviously affect election outcomes and in this sense must be regarded as political behavior. However, from the standpoint of induction of the individual into behavior appropriate to the system, they are deviant in the normative sense—in that there is evidence that most adults do have a personal concern with political affairs. They are also deviant ideologically, in that the election process assumes a personal preference and interest on the part of the voter. In pre-adults, as with adults, there are frequent instances of participation without subjective involvement. One girl, age 12, expressed it in this way:

> *"Sally, you said you don't think that the teacher, your father, or the postman are as important as senator or judge in making laws. Why?"*
> "Because their jobs aren't high enough—I guess that's all."
> *"What do you mean when you said their jobs aren't high enough?"*
> "Well, like the postman—he doesn't have as much to do as the senator or the President."
> *"These questions are not something you think about too much during the daytime—isn't that so?"*
> "Well. . . ."
> *"Now don't just tell me what you think you should tell me. Right now, what are you really mostly interested in?"*
> "Well, my boyfriend."
> *"Well, now, that explains it. Let's go on. What do you and your friends in class do together?"*
> "Just talk."
> *"Do you talk about politics?"*
> "No."
> *"Did you wear a button or anything like that in the [Presidential] election?"*
> "Yes, but I wore one just for the heck of it. I didn't really care which one."
> *"But most of the time you didn't talk about any of this stuff, huh?"*
> "No."
> *"Did your folks ever mention it?"*
> "Well, just a little bit."
> *"Do you watch the news?"*
> "No."

The interview continues, revealing a good deal of information about current hit records, movie actors and Oscar awards, features on the women's page of the local newspaper. The lack of interest in politics is not part of a more general apathy but is specific.

POLITICAL SOCIALIZATION AS THE
DEVELOPMENT OF RELATIONSHIPS BETWEEN
CITIZEN AND GOVERNMENT

Citizenship is not only a matter of legal status. It is also a pattern of interaction between the individual and the political system. The relative roles played by the citizen and the government and other features of the system are reciprocal. For example, the small child believes that it is his obligation to obey laws, and he usually believes that in return the policeman will protect him. Political socialization can be regarded as the process by which reciprocal relationships such as this are developed.

The term *role* refers to certain specified behavior of individuals within a social system. Roles are defined by the expectations set up by the system (such as rules, laws, and customs) and by the expectations of other individuals. Mutuality is a crucial element in the definition of roles and of role expectations. This has been stated more comprehensively by Parsons and Bales (1955) who used the term *reciprocal role interaction pattern* to indicate roles which are mutually defined by and dependent upon two interacting units or individuals. Reciprocity in these role relationships implies that each partner in the relationship has rights and duties with regard to the other partner (Gouldner, 1960). Social systems are stable and predictable to the degree that persons involved conform to each other's expectations. To produce conformity to reciprocal obligations, there must be strong norms and values which are generally shared throughout the social system.

There are two important aspects in the development of the *citizen role*. First, the child must see his own behavior in relation to that of some other person or institution. Before one's behavior can be regulated by a role, one must learn the expectations of that role—that is, one's rights and duties in relation to the rights and duties of the system. For example, the student's role involves the obligation to study and the right to receive academic credit; the teacher's role includes the obligation to present material for learning and the right to attention from his students. Second, the child, in viewing each social object in terms of reciprocal roles, defines it as an object of his own action or potential action. That is, the child's image of a person or element of a system focuses particularly upon those qualities of the object which are important for the child's interaction with it.

The child is taught expectations and values about political matters in preparation for *future* behavior, not primarily for guiding his current behavior. Given the proper situation and supports, these expectations will orient the child's behavior when he reaches adulthood. For example, a child who develops expectations of his own competence and of the responsiveness of the system to citizen influence, will be likely as an adult to attempt to influence the government when an issue arises which is of concern to him. The concept of reciprocal role relationship also implies that an adult expects different kinds of response from the system than does a child, and the adult acts accordingly; the role relationship between a senator and a voter who writes to him is different from the role relationship between the senator and a school child who writes to him.

Socialization of political involvement proceeds through several phases. At different times in a child's development, different attributes of the national government are salient to him. The initial image of the system and the ground rules for dealing with it comprise the first category for presenting data in the following chapters. Because the data in this book are organized around the child's perception of his relationship with the political system, the second category includes his expectations of the system's response to him as well as his behavior toward it. These two poles of interactive exchange—the child's image of what he can expect from the system and his own attitudinal and behavioral response to this image of the system—will be the bases of discussion.

MODELS OF POLITICAL SOCIALIZATION

Four models are suggested which describe in different ways the acquisition, change, and stabilization of political attitudes. These are not formal explanatory models but devices for examining the attitudes the child brings to the socialization process and the ways he utilizes experience in the development of political roles. Political socialization apparently follows several models: socialization in one attitude area may be understood best by using one model, while socialization in another area or at a different time is best understood in terms of a different conception. The data presented in this and succeeding chapters may be best understood by referring to these four general patterns.

The Accumulation Model. This view assumes that the acquisition of political role expectations proceeds by the addition of units of knowledge, information, attitudes, and activities. Teaching and experience are direct and specific; the units may be small and simple or larger and more complex. Johnny's response quoted earlier ("I know what the United States is . . . the Senate part makes it too hard.") offers an example of this type of learning: some knowledge has been gained but other information is lacking. The basic feature of this mode of socialization is that it involves direct teaching, usually by adults, in which the capabilities of the child and the nature of the materials are assumed to be irrelevant. The child's attitudes, involvement, and behavior are seen as an accumulation of the specific and direct learning which has taken place. These discrete acquisitions are not necessarily transmitted to the child as consistent conceptual systems. For example, the child may fail to see connections among contemporary problems of the civil rights of minorities and the principles of the Bill of Rights (Remmers and Radler, 1957).

Inconsistencies of a similar type appear with some frequency in the data reported in this book; many of the items showed less correlation with each other than would be expected on a priori grounds (Torney, 1965). In the Accumulation Model there need not be any logical connection among the attitudes and information acquired, although there may be consistency. Also, there need not be any particular sequence in which attitudes are learned. This model makes no assumptions about the properties of the child as limiting or facilitating the socialization process. That is, the child's feelings about authority figures in his life (parents, teachers) are not related to his ability to learn about political authority systems. For example, children who mistrust policemen would be equally well prepared to learn about the justice of law and how the courts function as children with more confidence. A teacher who implicitly accepts the Accumulation Model will expect that the information she presents will be absorbed without distortion by the child— that is, the child's own feelings and attitudes will not affect the inflow of information about the political system. This model also assumes that any material may be taught at any age if it is made sufficiently simple. That is, the cognitive equipment and emotional orientations the child brings to the learning situation are irrelevant.

Interpersonal Transfer Model. This model assumes that the child approaches explicit political socialization already possessing a fund of experience in interpersonal relationships and gratifications. By virtue of his experience as a child in the family and as a pupil in the school, he has developed multifaceted relationships to figures of authority. In subsequent relationships with figures of authority, he will establish modes of interaction which are similar to those he has experienced with persons in his early life. For example, as soon as the President has been identified as an authority figure, established patterns of interaction with authority will become relevant. He may see the President's power over the country as similar to his father's power in the family. The child may also see the President as representing ideal authority—benign, wise, helpful, accessible—and embodying other qualities which from his relationship with parents he has come to see as desirable. This does not come from knowledge about the President but from a desire to think about powerful authority figures in this way. Respect for rules in other social systems may also be transferred to feelings about rules or laws of the political system. As interpersonal experience increases and as relationships with persons in the immediate social environment change, the child's approach to more distant authority figures will be modified.

The Interpersonal Transfer Model is primarily useful for explaining affective feelings and relationships with political personages. It speaks to the acquisition of attitude which appears to occur rapidly, sometimes even during the course of an interview. A child begins to consider a question and express an opinion on a topic about which he obviously has little information by finding similarities and relating the unfamiliar to objects and persons with which he is familiar.

Identification Model. This model stresses the child's imitation of the behavior of some significant other person—usually a parent, or a teacher—when the adult has not attempted to persuade the child of his viewpoint. The transmission is thus inadvertent. The child may adopt either small units of behavior or he may take on more far-reaching identifications. This model has been used most extensively to explain the acquisition of political party preference by children who adopt their parents' partisan outlook. The child may have little understanding of the meaning of party identification, and the identification itself may lack consistent relationship with attitudes toward partisan policies. In this model, attitudes toward a given object are imitated directly from another person; in contrast, the Transfer Model assumes that attitudes which have been developed toward one person are transferred so that they apply to a new object.

Cognitive-developmental Model. This model assumes that the capacity to deal with certain kinds of concepts and information sets limits on the understanding that can be acquired of political phenomena. The child's conceptions of the political world are modified by his existing cognitive structure. Unlike the Accumulation Model (which assumes that with proper teaching methods any concept may be taught at any age), this model assumes that it may not be possible to teach a given concept to a child who has not reached an appropriate developmental level: socialization is related to the phase of cognitive development. The child, as he matures, develops progressively more abstract and complex ways of apprehending, classifying, differentiating, and structuring his perceptions and reactions. For example, a young child may be incapable of comprehending an institution as complex as Congress and may have to approach it by understanding the work of a single senator. The developmental progression from concrete to abstract thought, described by Werner (1957), is an example of cognitive processes which may limit the information that a child is ready to receive.[5]

These models apply at different stages of political socialization, as will be evident from data presented in the following chapters. The Interpersonal Transfer Model is most useful for understanding the child's first approach to the political system and the potency during this period of needs and previously derived expectations. The Accumulation Model is insufficient to explain early attachment to the nation and to

5. The concept cognitive-developmental is suggested by the work of Piaget (1947) and has been used by Kohlberg (1966) to discuss the development of sex role in children. See also Schactel (1947).

figures of government but is important in understanding the contribution of the school in building a fund of knowledge about governmental processes. The Identification Model may best explain party affiliation and candidate preference. The Cognitive-developmental Model is most useful in understanding how the child grasps some of the more complex and abstract concepts of political processes.

2

Acquisition of
Attitudes and Attachment
to the Nation

"Sally, would you rather be an American or an Englishman?"
"I'd rather be an American because I like America better, because we
have freedom and I know more people here."

"If it wasn't for the United States, there probably would be a lot of
wars and regular dark ages."

Acquisition of Political Attitudes

The very young child's apperceptive life space obviously includes
no political objects. He is without information, attitudes, expectations,
or behavior toward political institutions and persons, having had no
contact with them. One of the elementary aspects of the process of
adopting behavior appropriate to the role of a citizen is the acquiring
of information, attitudes, and other responses which make it possible
for the individual to participate in the formal and informal operation
of political processes. The notion that we should inquire whether or not
an individual has information and opinions about political affairs is a
particularly significant part of the study of political socialization in children. In order to examine the initial points of contact between the child
and the system, a measure of *attitude acquisition* was developed based
on whether the child expressed an opinion in response to questions
included on the printed questionnaire. This measure was computed by
summing the number of "I don't know" and "I have no opinion"
responses to questions in the instrument to form a DK (Don't Know)
index.[1]

It was discovered that *the acquisition of political attitudes proceeds
rapidly, especially through the fifth grade.* The rate of acquisition is
reflected by a decrease in the number of "Don't Know" responses (Fig.

1. See Appendix C. A similar measure was used by Oeser and Emery (1954).

23

1).[2] The most pronounced change occurred between grades four and five. Fourth-graders, on the average, gave more than eight "Don't Know" responses to the 32 questions which offered a DK option; the eighth-graders gave slightly more than three such responses.[3]

A "Don't Know" response may reflect a lack of information or unfamiliarity with a concept. The word "citizen" is a word which is familiar to all but 4 per cent of second-graders (although the definition of "the good citizen" changes during the elementary school years). Compared to "citizen," the designations "Democrat" and "Republican" are relatively unfamiliar through the fourth grade: 34 per cent of second-graders and 19 per cent of fourth-graders did not know their meaning. Data will be presented subsequently to show that the political parties are poorly conceptualized until late in elementary school.

The rate of attitude development varies in the five attitude areas delineated: (1) attachment to the nation; (2) attachment to the government and to governmental figures; (3) compliance; (4) influence; and (5) elections. There is a sequence in which orientations are acquired as the child progresses from grade two through grade eight. Attachment to the national government and compliance with its rules are focal points of concern before the emergence of the concept that citizens should try to influence the system. However, attachment which is acquired at an early age does not remain unchanged through the age span. Following the acquisition of positive attitudes toward the system, there are modifications in the style, focus, complexity, and conceptual organization of these ideas—elaborations on the basic positive attachment.

Because of these changes in focus within each substantive area, it was important to inquire about the nature of early attitude development *within* each attitude area. Thus, the tendency to respond "Don't Know"

2. The method of presenting data in these figures and the meaning of the *Significance Unit* are described in Appendix A. With the exception of items which have been combined into scales, the original numbers as they were applied to responses on the printed form of the Questionnaire are presented as the scale for the figures. Numbers had *not* been assigned to item responses so that more positive answers would receive higher numerical scores. For this reason, the orientation of the vertical axes in these figures (that is, with the numbers ascending or descending as one reads up the graph) is determined by the purpose of the graph. In many cases the numbers are arranged in descending order as one reads up; thus, points higher on the graph can indicate greater amounts of the characteristic or attitude being described.

The terms "with increase in grade" and "decrease with grade" are used in discussing this cross-sectional data to speak of the consistent differences between group means of children from different grade-levels.

3. Oeser and Emery (1954) reported a similar finding and suggested that before age 10 (grade five) the absorption of political and social ideology is quite limited. Werner and Kaplan (1950) pointed to this same age period as a time when many word meanings are acquired.

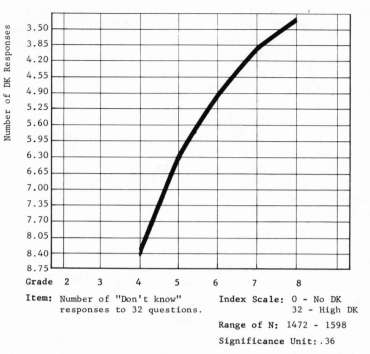

Number of DK Responses

Grade 2 3 4 5 6 7 8

Item: Number of "Don't know"   Index Scale: 0 - No DK
responses to 32 questions.   32 - High DK

Range of N: 1472 - 1598

Significance Unit: .36

Fig. 1.
Comparison of means of grades 4 through 8 in acquisition of
political attitudes.

to specific questions or types of questions *within* each of the five content areas was examined, and proportions of DK responses were compared to determine what *types* of attitudes develop first.[4]

The study showed that children first think of political objects as good or bad; later, more complex information and orientations may be acquired. For example, children at all grade-levels seemed to have very definite ideas when asked for their evaluation of America. A very small percentage answered that they did not know whether America was the best country in the world. Children also appeared to have opinions about Communism as a threat to our country. However, specific information about Communism as a political ideology is acquired more slowly. Children associated the word "democracy" with our nation and valued it highly. However, a more complete definition of "democracy" (other than by association with America) was one of the last conceptual elements to appear. Although definitions of democracy receive substantial attention in the school curriculum starting at grade three (see Chapter

4. See Hess and Torney (1965) for data on which these inferences are based.

Five), children apparently are not ready (in the sense of developmental-cognitive maturity) to absorb this instruction. The attitudes children develop before the sixth grade are typically generalized judgments of good (America and democracy) and bad (communism).[5] The early acquisition of general evaluations on the dimension good-bad was substantiated in other content areas as well.

In summary, the acquisition of information and attitudes proceeds rapidly during the elementary school years. Particularly sizable advances are made between the fourth and fifth grades. Evaluations of political objects in gross good-bad terms are expressed earlier than more differentiated beliefs, probably because of the importance of the evaluation dimension in semantic assessment of objects and concepts and because the child has had more extensive contact with evaluations of his own behavior as good or bad than with any other distinction; he may transfer this interpersonal learning into the political realm.

Growth of Attachment to the Nation

One of the first features of a child's political involvement is his sense of belonging to a political unit. Although it is difficult to obtain evidence on the nature of this early attachment, interview material and early questionnaires indicated that in the United States the young child develops a sense of "we" in relation to his own country and a sense of "they" with respect to other countries.[6] It is not clear whether this sense of a national "we" precedes the perception that the country has a leader or boss. In either case, one of the early foci of involvement is this sense of belonging to a political group which will later be recognized as "my country."

The child's early relationship to the country is highly positive although his conceptualization of it is vague. One of the most remarkable features of the child's initial orientation to America is his positive feelings about his country and its symbols. Nearly 95 per cent of the responding group agreed that "the American flag is the best flag in the world." A similarly high percentage agreed that "America is the best country in the world." This attachment develops despite a fragmentary and incomplete view of the nation and its government. The adult's conception of the United States is associated with specific visual imagery, pictures, verbal descriptions, and maps. In contrast, the young

5. Other writers (Harris, 1950; Osgood, Suci, and Tannenbaum, 1957; Scott, 1963) have suggested that the good-bad dimension is the basic category of thought and that judgments along this axis are the primary and initial elements of attitudes.

6. "America," "the nation," and "the country" are used as synonyms in this book.

child's image is vague and lacks visual conceptualization. The allegiance he develops is to an intangible object. In order for the child to feel a sense of identification with his country, he must be provided with information and clues to elicit and support these affiliative responses. Although he is familiar with a number of figures who work for the government—postmen, policemen, and firemen—they do not represent the nation or government nor do they provide routes of attachment to the country. Although more than 80 per cent of the children studied, in all grades, knew that the policeman works for the government, less than 10 per cent selected him as a symbol of the United States or of the government. Obviously, the child's daily contact with figures performing governmental activities is not sufficient to define for him his country.

Children's rudimentary conception of the nation is not defined by geographical boundaries. Similarly, conceiving of the country as a population bound by common ideas, rules, and loyalties is an unfamiliar concept to the chld. The initial characteristics which he does use to distinguish his country from others were not clearly revealed in the questionnaire data. Interviews suggested that this early differentiation is non-rational and non-political.

A belief in the superiority of one's own country and language appeared frequently in the responses of children in the early grades. One second-grade boy, when asked if he would rather be an Englishman or an American, said:

"Well, I wouldn't like to be an Englishman because I wouldn't like to talk their way, and I'd rather be an American because they have better toys, because they have better things, better stores, and better beds and blankets, and they have better play guns, and better boots, and mittens and coats, and better schools and teachers."

A fifth-grade girl expressed it in this way when asked if she would rather be American or English: "I guess I was just born American and the United States is a nice place to live in." [7]

The readiness to identify with one's country is perhaps an extension of the desire for group association which is exhibited in many facets of life. The child's first group identification is with his family. Feelings of membership in the larger national unit may be generalized from this early experience by a process similar to the Interpersonal Transfer Model. The strength of these feelings for country in adults is best illustrated by the hostility and rejection directed toward anyone who deserts the group and transfers allegiance to another country, particularly to an enemy, as in the case of the "turncoats" during the Korean

7. Meltzer (1941) also reported that children's most popular response when asked why they like Americans best was, "I am one."

War. Public officials, especially those who wish to be re-elected, take every opportunity to demonstrate their patriotic attachment to the country. In the last two decades, probably the most damaging accusation that could be levelled against a U.S. citizen or public official has been that he is not sufficiently hostile toward enemies of the United States. The feeling of national loyalty is not only an individual covenant between the citizen and his country; it is also a bond guarded by considerable group pressures and sanctions. Feelings of allegiance and patriotism reflect a need for group affiliation; symbols to which loyalty can be pledged reinforce this attachment. Although the positive character of national loyalty is usually established at an early age in the United States, there appear to be three stages in the way the nation is conceptualized.

In the first stage, national symbols such as the flag and Statue of Liberty are crucial points of focus for attachment. Since the child's initial identification with his country is supported by so little specific information, symbols provide tangible objects toward which feelings of attachment can be socialized. An illustration of the diffuseness of the conception of the nation and the use of symbols appears in an interview with a second-grade boy whose father is a skilled worker:

"What is a nation?"
"A nation is a state isn't it? Certain places in it that are important."
"Can you name a nation?"
"Washington, New York."
"You see the flag up there? What does the flag mean?"
"Well, I don't quite know. It just stands up there, and you say something to it. We put our hands over our heart and say the pledge of allegiance to the flag."
"What does it mean when you pledge allegiance?"
"Well, we're pledging to the flag."
"What do you pledge to the flag?"
"To give us freedom."
"What does the flag stand for?"
"It stands for freedom and for peace."
"Well, what about the Statue of Liberty? What's that?"
"Well, doesn't he stand to help us and to give us liberty and beauty?"
"Where is he?"
"He's in New York City, not very far out in the ocean. I've never been there."
"Is it alive?"
"I don't think so. I've never seen it, so I don't know."

The link between these symbols and abstract terms like liberty and freedom is also illustrated by the following with another second-grade boy:

"What does the Statue of Liberty do?"
"Well, it keeps liberty."
"How does it do that?"
"Well, it doesn't do it, but there are some other guys that do it."
"Some other guys do it for the Statue of Liberty?"
"The Statue is not alive."
"Well, what does it do?"
"It has this torch in its hand, and sometimes they light up the torch. If the Statue was gone, there wouldn't be any liberty."

At all grade-levels except the second, the modal choices of "the best pictures to represent America" were the Statue of Liberty and the flag. There were minimal changes with age in choice of these symbols.[8] Attachment to concrete national symbols and to vaguely understood but highly valued "America" apparently occur simultaneously.

National symbols are vital unifying forces in the process of socialization. Warner (1959, p. 233) commented in discussing rituals and symbols, "Complex societies . . . need a general symbol system that everyone not only knows but *feels.*" Symbols of this type are necessary not only to the society as a whole but particularly to young people who must be initiated into allegiance to America.

The attitudes of national attachment which are established are permanent, as indicated by relatively stable age patterns in response to items concerned with the flag and "our country." There was no change with age in high endorsement of the item, "America is the best country in world." A pilot study item, "Other countries have freedom, but it is not as good as the freedom we have in this country," also received a high level of agreement at all grades, as did choice of the American flag as a symbol of the country.

This process of orienting a young child toward a symbol or ritual and making him aware of its significance precedes the comprehension of the symbol in any real way. Even at older ages, children occasionally feel that such patriotic acts as saying the pledge of allegiance are lacking in the meaning that is usually associated with national pride. An eighth-grade girl is candid in expressing her feelings on this point:

"Betty, how do you feel when you say the pledge of allegiance?"
"Well, in first and second grade we said pledge of allegiance to the flag

8. This information comes from a supplementary questionnaire administered in the Chicago area (N = 811) two years after the nationwide study. One purpose of testing was to determine whether children made a distinction between the country (America) and the government. In the nationwide testing, the flag and the Statue of Liberty were chosen as the best representatives of *government* by less than 20 per cent of the sample. In the supplementary testing, the question required a choice of the two best pictures of *our country*. The flag and the Statue of Liberty were chosen as the most appropriate symbols of America. Clearly, then, children do distinguish between the government and the country.

and nobody really knew what that was, and in second grade up to eighth grade we say it every morning and I never think about it. I always think about what I'm going to do that day because it's just a routine. We do it every day just like we say the Lord's Prayer. When you just pray by yourself you say something, like a prayer for your country at night, and you do it in your own way and you think about it more. But in the morning when everybody is just kind of fresh out of bed, we're just standing up there and reciting and I don't think anybody thinks about it very much."

In the second phase, the concept of the nation acquires cognitive substance, including abstract qualities and ideological content. Concrete objects and symbols become less important. There is an increase across the age range in ideological components of national pride. The question, "What makes you most proud to be an American?" elicited "freedom" and "right to vote" as increasingly popular answers (approximating responses of teachers by grade eight). In contrast, "beautiful parks and highways" and "our President" decreased as sources of pride after the second grade. When asked in interviews why they preferred being American to being another nationality, older children referred more specifically to freedom and democracy; they placed less emphasis upon concrete, material aspects of our country and more on those ideological features emphasized in school. An interview with a fifth-grade boy expresses this:

"What is freedom?"
"Well, to be free, you could vote any way you want. Like Khrushchev makes everybody vote for him, because he uses force. And in America, in a free country, you can do whatever you want. Free speech, I guess that's what it means."

Younger children simply evaluated the United States as "good" and Russia as "bad." The evaluation of the fifth-grader had more substance, and he thought of the United States and Russia as representing different political systems. In some children, who are between the first and second stage, concepts such as freedom maintained an ethnocentric character and retained qualities of magic. Many fourth-graders, for example, said that freedom prevents war.

In the third phase, our country is seen as part of a larger, organized system of countries. The child's view gains a perspective which includes many other nations and our relationships to them. The most dramatic example of change in perception of the United States' relationship to the rest of the world is shown in Table 3, in response to the question, "Who does most to keep peace in the world: the United States or the United Nations?" At grade two, the choice was overwhelmingly "the United States"; by grade eight, the choice was just as decidedly "the United Nations," a response approximating that of teachers.

Table 3
Changes by Grade in Perception of Relative Influence of United States and United Nations in Preventing War

Grade level	N	United Nations keeps peace	United States keeps peace	Don't know
2	1630	14.4%	70.7%	14.9%
3	1646	27.3	62.3	10.3
4	1727	48.9	40.2	10.9
5	1786	68.2	27.3	4.5
6	1742	78.8	16.5	4.7
7	1717	84.6	12.5	2.9
8	1689	86.9	10.2	2.8
Teachers	369	87.0	13.0	a

Notes.—Item: Which [picture shows the] one of these [which] does most to keep peace in the world?
—Significance Unit: 3%.
a. No DK alternative.

Early attachment to the nation, then, is basic to political socialization and to subsequent learning and experience. It is interesting that feelings of attachment do not call for a response; the citizen does not expect something from the country in return for his allegiance. It is when the relationships with persons in the government and the political system become established that reciprocal role relationships become important.

3

Attachment to Government and Regard for Law

"Mike, what is the government?"
"Well, the government is a man. . . ."

"George, what do you know about the President?"
"The President is the most important in running the country because he guides our country and he tries not to make war and things."
"In what way?"
"Like if someone is poor, he usually gives money and tells the people to give special money or something . . . so they could buy food and what they need."

"Judy, do you know of anyone in the United States government?"
"Well, the President."
"What do you know about the President?"
"Well, that a . . . oh, dear . . . he . . . ah, makes laws and a . . . and ah . . . well, he tries to do good."

Attachment to Government

CONCEPT OF THE SYSTEM

It is difficult for a child to comprehend a complex political institution. Although there are symbols of Congress, the Supreme Court, and other institutions of government, these are not used with the same frequency and ritual as the flag and pledge of allegiance are used as symbols of the nation. It seems likely that complex social and political systems are initially conceptualized as *persons* to whom the child can relate. Through attachments to these persons, the individual becomes related to the system. In short, to the child, the government is a man who lives in Washington, while Congress is a lot of men who help the President. During the developmental period when a child begins to build a positive regard for institutions and becomes subject to their sanctions, complex social systems must be represented by personal figures who can act as sanctioning agents and objects of attachment.

The importance of personal symbols to a young child is congruent with discussions by Kelley and Krey (1934) and Wesley and Adams (1952), who classified persons, events, and other tangible objects as the social concepts which are most easily acquired. Relationships among groups, social codes and standards, and interactions between the society and groups are much more difficult for children to understand and must be symbolized by material associations or symbols to be grasped.

The second- or third-grade child's image of government is largely confined to persons. In interviews, these young children referred to government as "the man who signs the checks," "the state and city governments are different men, but they both are governments," or "the government is a nice man." On a pretest questionnaire, 60 per cent of a group of fourth-graders expressed agreement with the statement, "The government is a man." [1]

Data from a question asking children to select the two pictures that "showed best what the government is" are presented in Table 4. Pictures of President Kennedy and George Washington were chosen by 46 per cent and 39 per cent respectively of the second-graders. For older children, choices of these personal figures, particularly Washington, dropped off sharply. Congress and voting, which represent government as an institution and a process, were chosen by less than 10 per cent of the second-graders. Eighth-graders (between 45 and 50 per cent) found these impersonal aspects of government to be more appropriate symbols. This approached the 72 per cent choice by teachers. Selection of Congress increased at an earlier grade-level than did voting. This suggests that the conceptualization of government is tied to personal figures for young children, then to institutions, and finally to political processes for older children.

Parallel developmental trends occur in the child's conception of the origin of laws and governmental administration. As children grow older, they come to believe that Congress is more important in law-making than the President. In the second grade, 76 per cent chose the President and 5 per cent the Congress when asked "Who makes the laws?" By eighth grade, 85 per cent chose the Congress and only 5 per cent the President. The most striking change occurred between grades four and five (Table 5). Younger children were also more likely to say that "the President runs the country" (Table 6).

Unlike the marked shift with age on the item dealing with legislative functions (Table 5), the response to questions about the administrative functions of Congress and the President (Table 6) remained relatively constant; a differentiation with increasing age does occur in the chil-

1. Pilot Study 5.

Table 4
Changes by Grade in Choice of "The Best Picture of Government"
(Children were asked to choose two alternatives)[a]

Grade level	N	Policeman	George Washington	Uncle Sam	Voting	Supreme Court	Capitol	Congress	Flag	Statue of Liberty	President	Don't know
2	1619	8.2%	39.4%	15.6%	4.3%	4.5%	13.6%	5.9%	15.7%	12.1%	46.2%	15.7%
3	1662	4.1	26.8	19.0	8.4	6.4	16.1	12.9	16.5	14.3	46.8	12.9
4	1726	5.7	14.2	18.0	10.8	10.2	16.6	29.0	13.3	12.9	37.2	13.2
5	1789	2.7	6.9	19.4	19.2	16.8	11.6	49.0	11.6	11.2	38.5	4.9
6	1740	2.4	4.9	16.8	28.0	16.8	9.9	49.7	11.4	17.1	30.3	4.7
7	1714	3.0	3.4	18.3	39.4	13.5	9.4	44.2	12.8	18.6	27.9	3.0
8	1689	1.7	1.7	16.4	46.8	15.9	6.9	49.1	11.8	19.6	22.9	1.5
Teachers	390	1.3	1.3	4.6	71.8	12.8	5.1	71.0	6.2	8.5	15.1	.2

Notes.—Item: Here are some pictures that show what our government is. Pick the two pictures that show best what our government is.

—Significance Unit: 3%.

a. Percentages do not always sum to 200 per cent for any grade because some children chose only one alternative or chose "I don't know."

Table 5
Changes by Grade in Perception of Source of Laws

Grade level	N	Congress makes laws	President makes laws	Supreme Court makes laws	Don't know
2	1627	4.8%	75.6%	11.5%	8.2%
3	1648	11.4	66.1	17.0	5.5
4	1723	27.5	44.1	21.1	7.3
5	1793	57.4	19.4	19.8	3.4
6	1743	65.1	13.2	18.3	3.4
7	1712	72.1	8.9	16.4	2.6
8	1690	85.3	5.4	7.9	1.4
Teachers	384	96.4	.5	3.1	a

Notes.—Item: Who makes the laws? Put an X next to the [picture of the] one who does most to make laws.
—Significance Unit: 3%.
a. No DK alternative.

Table 6
Changes by Grade in Perception of "Who Runs the Country"

Grade level	N	Congress runs country	President runs country	Supreme Court runs country	Don't know
2	1627	3.9%	86.3%	3.3%	6.5%
3	1662	6.7	85.4	3.1	4.7
4	1725	13.2	77.0	3.4	6.5
5	1796	20.0	71.8	3.8	4.3
6	1744	24.9	66.2	4.5	4.4
7	1711	27.8	64.0	5.3	2.9
8	1683	35.1	58.4	3.6	2.9
Teachers	383	61.4	35.8	3.0	a

Notes.—Item: Who does the most to run the country? Put an X in the box next to the [picture of the] one who does most to run the country.
—Significance Unit: 3%.
a. No DK alternative.

dren's conceptions, and they tend to see the administrative functions as divided between the President and the Congress. At grade eight, 58 per cent believed that the President ran the country.

A young child's image of the national government is confined mainly to the President. He is the figure about whom children believe they know most. They reported seeing him on television, and 95 per cent of the second-grade children knew his name. The President is a source of national pride, and is seen as serving a vital function in protecting and representing the nation and watching over its administration. The following excerpts from an interview with a third-grade boy, the son of a teacher, give a fairly representative impression of the younger children's image of the President, although these responses are more complete and articulate than those of most subjects this age.

"Have you ever seen the President?"
"I've seen him on television, and heard him on the radio, and seen him in newspapers."
"What does the President do?"
"He runs the country, he decides the decisions that we should try to get out of, and he goes to meetings and tries to make peace and things like that."
"When you say he runs the country, what do you mean?"
"Well, he's just about the boss of everything. . . ."
"And what kind of person do you think he is?"
"Well, usually he's an honest one."
"Anything else?"
"Well, loyal and usually is pretty smart."
"Usually, but not always?"
"Well, they're all smart, but they aren't exactly perfect [pause] . . . most of them are."
"Who pays him?"
"Well, gee, I don't know if anybody pays him, he probably doesn't get too much money for the job—I don't even know if he gets any money."
"Why would he take the job?"
"Well, he loves his country and he wants this country to live in peace."

The President is not a noble, salient figure to all children. For some he is visible but apparently not very important. Bobby, a fourth-grade boy, shows something less than enthusiasm in his comments about the President:

"Bobby, have you seen the President on TV?"
"Yes."
"What kind of things does the President do in his job?"
"Well, he goes on trips, and . . . I don't know."
"What does he do when he goes on these trips?"
"I dunno . . . he has speeches and all that stuff."
"Have you seen him make speeches on TV?"
"Yes."
"What does he talk about?"
"I dunno . . . Ma always watches it."

The child subsequently develops a more impersonal and institutionalized conception of the government. Interviews provide clues to the development of this view. Responses such as the following are given by older children: "The government is made up of representatives that the people elect," or "The government is just an organization that the people formed to rule themselves." Instead of focusing on one person, these children emphasized a group of persons elected by the citizens. Perceiving government as synonymous with the President is a simple way for young children to organize perceptions of the political world. The school is important in fostering the more refined, complex picture of government which develops later. Our evidence indicates, however, that schools put equal and concurrent emphasis upon the President and Congress (see Chapter Five).

The importance of the President in young children's conceptualization of government is not determined primarily by classroom learning but by the child's tendency to focus upon a personal representative of the system. This phase of socialization may be understood best in the context of the Cognitive-developmental and Interpersonal Transfer Models (see Chapter One). The child is not conceptually ready to understand the government as an abstract institutionalized entity, and he transfers the approach to personalized authority which has been useful to him in coping with other social systems (such as the school). This pattern of induction to systems through personal authority is applicable to a range of other social systems. The small child's view of the medical profession centers around the doctor, the nurse and the specifics of his interaction with them; his image of the church is initially one of human and super-human figures; his understanding of the school is not concerned with policy, finance, or administration, but with the teacher and the principal.

CONCEPT OF THE CITIZEN'S ROLE

The initial conception of a "good citizen" is largely one of the "good person." Interview responses suggest that second- and third-grade children made little distinction between a good person and a good citizen.[2] They stressed the image of general goodness, although concern with the country was of some importance. An interview excerpt from a conversation with the fourth-grade son of working-class parents illustrates this point:

"Well, what is a good citizen?"
"A person whose house is clean and who is polite."

A second example is from a fourth-grade, working-class child:

"How could a citizen help his country?"
"Well, follow the laws, don't get in accidents, and do practically everything as hard as he can."

2. In one city where a clean-up campaign had recently been conducted, 62 per cent of the children agreed that keeping the city clean was one of the citizen's major duties.

Children in this study chose from seven alternatives the two which they believed characterized the good child citizen and the good adult citizen. Seventy-four per cent of second- and third-grade children reported that the "boy who helps others" is the best citizen. Choices of personally oriented alternatives declined with age for both child and adult citizen, to be replaced by a conception of the citizen in more specifically political terms—voting (for the adult citizen) and showing interest in government (Table 7). The absence of distinctions between personal goodness and politically oriented citizenship exemplifies the low level of differentiation in children's thinking, the assimilation of the political world to personal experiences, and the transfer of rules from the personal to the political realm (Interpersonal Transfer Model).

THE CHILD'S RELATIONSHIP TO THE SYSTEM

The child's first relationship with his government is with the President, whom he sees in highly positive terms. This indicates his basic trust in the benevolence of government. Young children relate to the President as they do to figures they know personally, expressing strong emotional attachment to him and expecting protection from him. They believe that the President is intimately involved not only in momentous decisions concerning the fate of the country but also in more mundane decisions that affect them and their neighborhood: how much meat will cost, whether people must remain in jail or be freed, what the traffic laws are. A strong sense of trust is evident in their responses; they think that the President is personally responsive to children's wishes and believe that they could even go to the White House and talk to him.

The child's conception of the President's concern for the individual is also indicated by responses to the item, "If you write to the President, does he care what you think?" (Table 8). Seventy-five per cent of second-grade children felt that the President would care about their ideas if they wrote to him. The mean response to this item declined, but eighth-graders also believed that the President would pay considerable attention to their opinions.

Young children also believe that the President personally would help them if they needed it (Fig. 2). The average second-grade child in the sample reported that the President would be nearly as helpful to him if he were in trouble as the policeman or his father. For students in grade eight, the mean score for these figures diverged; the President was rated similarly to impersonal and distant agencies such as the Supreme Court and government.[3] The child's early approach to the system is highly personal; he expects from personal representatives of the politi-

3. Greenstein (1965a) also reported that spontaneous references to the President's benevolence declined with age.

Table 7

Changes by Grade in Perception of Qualities of the Good Citizen (Adult)

(Children were asked to choose two pictures) [a]

Someone who:

Grade level	N	Works hard	Everybody likes him	Votes and gets others to vote	Helps others	Interested in way country is run	Always obeys laws	Goes to church	Don't know "citizen"
4	1719	13.5%	7.0%	26.4%	47.8%	28.2%	44.3%	23.6%	2.0%
5	1780	11.3	8.5	29.8	42.1	41.8	42.0	20.6	.6
6	1736	10.7	9.0	35.8	35.4	50.5	37.4	16.0	.6
7	1710	11.1	8.3	35.9	34.2	57.7	32.7	14.6	.2
8	1674	10.0	8.1	44.6	26.3	65.0	29.0	11.8	.7
Teachers	392	7.9	3.6	51.5	31.6	72.4	22.4	3.8	2.3

Notes.—Item: If the President came to your town to give prizes to the two grown-ups who were the best citizens, which grown-ups would he choose? Put an X beside [the pictures of] the two he would choose as the best citizens.

—Significance Unit: 3%.

a. Percentages do not always sum to 200 per cent for any given grade because some children chose only one alternative or chose "I don't know."

Table 8

Changes by Grade in Belief The President would Care what Citizens Thought if They Wrote to Him

Grade level	N	President would care a lot	President would care some	President would care a little
2	1639	75.2%	19.6%	5.1%
3	1664	68.5	26.0	5.5
4	1738	56.4	36.3	7.2
5	1795	51.5	39.8	8.7
6	1744	46.3	42.3	11.4
7	1710	45.0	43.9	11.2
8	1686	43.1	43.0	13.9
Teachers	385	47.3	44.7	8.0

Notes.—Item: Which do you think is the most true? (Choose one) If you write to the President, (1) . . . he cares a *lot* what you think; (2) . . . he cares some . . . . ; (3) . . . he cares a *little*. . . .
—Significance Unit: 3%.

cal system the same help and nurturance he receives from his parents.

In one pilot study [4] the percentage of children choosing the alternative, "The President is about the best person in the world," declined from approximately 52 per cent at grade two to 10 per cent at grade eight. This illustrates the charismatic quality in second-graders' relationships to the President (Davies, 1954; Weber, 1946). Davies, in analyzing charisma in the 1952 campaign, suggested that it was the result of insecurity generated either by unstable upbringing or by situations of national crises. We have suggested that idealization of the President as an authority figure is a technique children utilize in dealing with feelings of vulnerability and powerlessness (Hess and Easton, 1960; Torney, Hess, and Easton, 1962).

Since government is perceived as personally responsive to the individual, the second- or third-grade child might be expected to be attached to the President in the same manner he is attached to his father; indeed, a positive feeling was reflected in ratings of the President as a personal favorite (Fig. 3). The age trends and relative positions of father and President on these ratings resembled those on the item dealing with helpfulness. Expressions of this type of emotional attachment to the President declined most rapidly between grades two and five.

Although the senator would be appropriate as a personal link between the child and the system, children do not develop a high level of regard for him. At all grade levels, the senator was rated below all other figures in willingness to help. He was also less well-liked than the

4. Pilot Study 3.

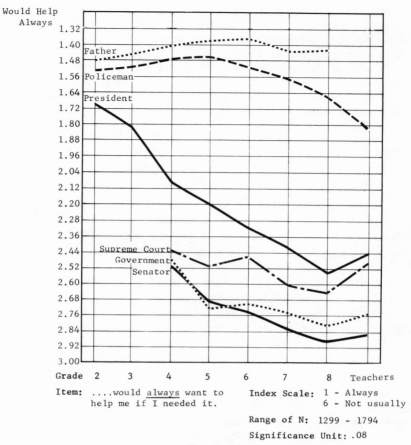

Fig. 2.
Comparison of means of grades 2 through 8 in rating the responsiveness of figures and institutions.

President.[5] Interviews indicated that children know little about the senator; references to his function were vague—". . . to help the President when he asks them."

The Senate and senators are not clearly etched in the child's image of political institutions. A fifth-grade boy described a senator as ". . . a man in the House of Representatives that's gone up so far he's become a senator so he can run against the Vice-President. Only the senator and Vice-President can run for President."

An eighth-grade girl also shows a good bit of misinformation about the role of senator:

5. Data reported in Hess and Torney, 1965.

"What's their job—the Senate and the House of Representatives?"

"Well, I think . . . I don't know, but my opinion is that they have more part of the government than anyone else because that's where most of the bills originate . . . and the laws."

"What's the difference between the House of Representatives and the Senate?"

"Well, isn't the Senate Democratic and the House of Representatives Republican? I mean . . . ah . . . what do I mean? Democrats and Republicans, that's right . . . I'm not sure."

"How does a Senator get to be a senator?"

"Well, he's probably a member of the Senate first and then they would vote a . . . a senator . . . oh, wait . . . he's elected by the state which he represents."

There were many children, of course, who have more information about the Senate and about the role of senator. There was little evidence, however, that individual senators, as persons, are salient in the child's mind. This may be because of the lack of visibility and publicity given to senators in the public press and, apparently, in classroom instruction. It may also derive from the number of persons in the Senate, resulting in a diffusion of individual importance in the child's view. It also seems possible that the executive and administrative functions are more visible, more dramatic, and more easily presented to children, while the significance of senators often gets lost in the teaching process.

The reciprocal nature of children's attachments is illustrated by children's expectation that the President would be concerned with their welfare: they reciprocate by extending loyalty and affection. This is the essence of a role relationship, one of the most basic personal attachments: protection reciprocated by love.[6] The recognition of these personal feelings toward the President contributes to an understanding of the strength of early attachment and its implications for the stability of the political system.

As children grow older they learn to distinguish between the personal characteristics of the President and the abilities he needs to perform his job. They like him less as a person but have more respect for his executive abilities. Interviews indicated that children often saw the President's most important duty as being an administrator of the country, making decisions which affect the nation and the world. Mean ratings of the President on these aspects of performance classified him as knowing more and working harder than most people, always a leader, making important decisions all the time. These ratings were reasonably constant from the fourth through eighth grade, and ratings of his deci-

6. The extent to which adults also feel personally close to the President is documented by reactions to President Kennedy's assassination. Greenstein reported that college students compared the event to deaths within their immediate group. (Greenstein, 1965b).

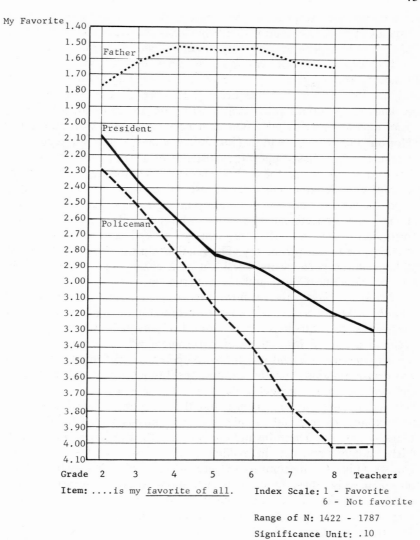

Fig. 3.

Comparison of means of grades 2 through 8 in attachment to figures.

sion-making role increased (Figs. 4, 5, 6, 7). Teachers and eighth-graders differed only slightly.

The policeman and father were rated lower than the President on all of these attributes. Apparently, leadership, working hard, being knowledgeable, and making decisions are defined, even by younger children, as Presidential qualities. These characteristics clearly differentiate his role from that of other authority figures. With increasing age, children see the President as one whose abilities are appropriate to the demands of his office [7] and whose behavior is shaped by these demands, rather than as a personal authority directly related to the child.[8]

The average senator was rated as much less responsive than the President. This suggests that the relationship existing between the child and the President is possible because the President's name and face are known. Children's relationships with him are comparable to *para-social* interactions that television audiences experience with performers (Horton and Wohl, 1956). This intimacy and perceived reciprocity of relationship is based upon the existence of a living, visible person— President Kennedy for these children—not a composite figure such as Average U.S. Senator. The clearest distinction children make in judging responsiveness is between the figures in their immediate environment (father and policeman) and those who are not known personally (institutions, senator). The President, for second- and third-graders, is intermediate to this dichotomy. The relationship with him is para-social. Older children perceive the President as a distant figure similar to the senator, Supreme Court, and the government.

The older child perceives institutions of government as powerful and infallible. At the same time that the child forms opinions about the President's role qualities apart from his personal attractiveness, he becomes aware of institutions of government which do not have personal representatives and which are competent in performing leadership and decision-making functions. These institutions are regarded by older children as more dependable than the President. For example, at the later grades the Supreme Court and the government are regarded as more knowledgeable and less likely to make mistakes than the President (Figs. 4 and 8). These institutions and the President are perceived as fairly equally important in making decisions by seventh- and eighth-graders (Fig. 7). In contrast to perceptions of the President, children do not perceive these impersonal institutions to be highly protective or helpful (Fig. 2). In summary, eighth-graders distinguish between persons and institutions that are highly knowledgeable and make many important decisions (President, government, Supreme Court), and figures who are not noted for either superior knowledge or decision-making (senator, father, policeman).

The infallibility of figures and institutions is a particularly important

7. "Office" is used here as it is defined by Hughes (1937): a standardized group of duties and privileges which are consciously fulfilled and which form the basis of an institution.

8. Being elected to the Presidency confers an aura of competence in itself. Other authors (Paul, 1956) have called this the *fait accompli* effect. In pilot data, within three months after he took office, Kennedy was rated equal with Eisenhower on a number of dimensions and much more favorably than Nixon (even by middle-class children who, presumably, were pro-Nixon at election time).

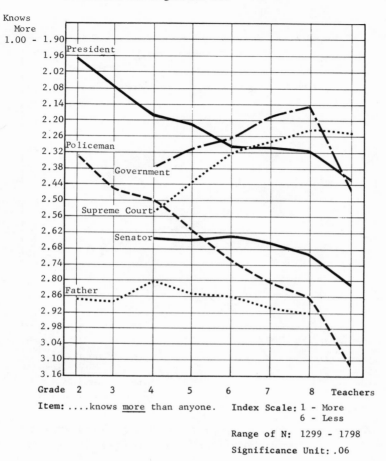

Fig. 4.
**Comparison of means of grades 2 through 8 in rating role
performance (knowledge) of figures and institutions.**

aspect of children's perceptions. At later grades, all personal authority
figures were judged more fallible than institutions; this suggests that
institutionalized role, independent of an individual's whim, is perceived
as more legitimate. Early belief in the benign qualities of political
authority sets a level of expectations that is never completely abandoned.
As a maturing child becomes aware of the fallibility of persons in
authority, he looks to institutions for the protection he formerly sought
from parents and personal figures. Mean ratings given by teachers
accentuate the distinction between the Supreme Court and all other
figures and institutions.

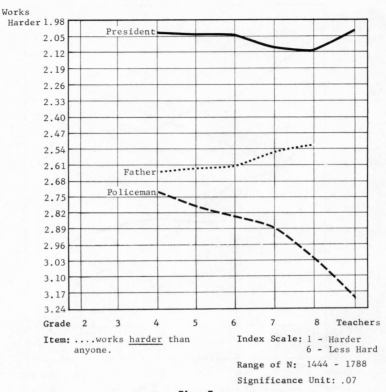

Works
Harder 1.98

Fig. 5.
*Comparison of means of grades 4 through 8 in rating role
performance (hard work) of figures.*

DISCUSSION

   Presumably, the child's attachment to figures and institutions of
government is typically maintained into adulthood. If this is so, this
confidence in government is an important source of stability in the
system. In societies where this trust in officials is not maintained, as in
the amoral Italian society described by Banfield (1958), long-term
planning and cooperative improvement of living conditions seem difficult if not impossible.

   Attachment to the government—affiliation with the system—is
mediated by a relationship with a personal figure: the President of the
United States, with whom children feel they have a particularly strong
relationship. The chief executive serves as a "living symbol" [9] and a
basis from which the child later progresses to awareness of other ele-

   9. A term used by David Truman (1963) to describe the President.

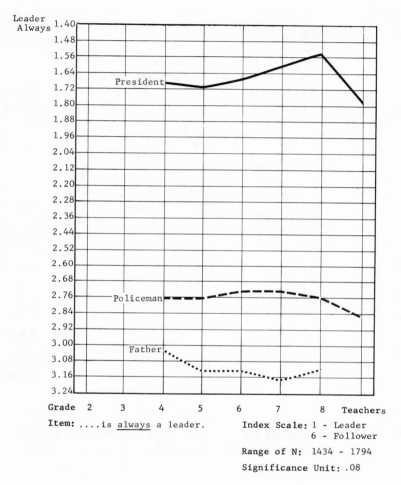

Leader
Always

Grade   2   3   4   5   6   7   8   Teachers

Item: ....is <u>always</u> a leader.   Index Scale: 1 - Leader
                                                         6 - Follower

                                             Range of N: 1434 - 1794

                                             Significance Unit: .08

Fig. 6.
*Comparison of means of grades 4 through 8 in rating role
performance (leadership) of figures.*

ments of the political system. Impersonal and institutionalized role systems into which children are socialized must be represented initially by
individuals—persons that children know—who can be objects of affection and agents of punishment, either in reality or fantasy. This attachment is not developed through the school curriculum but emerges with
relatively little specific information. Attachment to the President is
based upon knowledge that there is a very powerful "boss" of the
United States; this awareness or belief may be the basis of children's
perceptions of powerful figures as benevolent—as their way of dealing

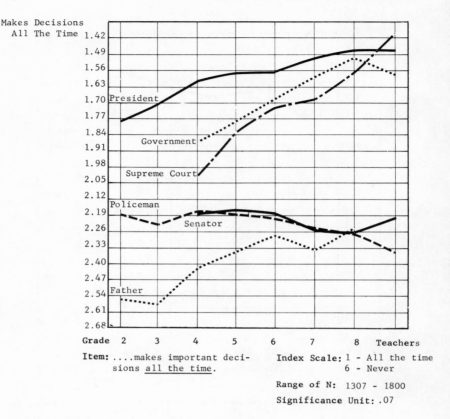

Makes Decisions
All The Time

Grade 2   3   4   5   6   7   8   Teachers

Item: ....makes important deci-   Index Scale: 1 - All the time
      sions <u>all the time</u>.   6 - Never

                                       Range of N: 1307 - 1800
                                       Significance Unit: .07

Fig. 7.

**Comparison of means of grades 2 through 8 in rating role
performance (decision-making) of figures and institutions.**

with their own feelings of powerlessness. In the early school years, the
relationship between child and chief executive is highly particularistic,
echoing many characteristics of the child's family relationship. Children
expect the President to be personally concerned for their welfare, and
in turn they accord him respect and affection.

In the early school years, the President as an individual and the
office of the Presidency are not separated in the child's mind.[10] The
maturing child learns to distinguish between the role and its occupant
and develops respect for institutions of government which do not have

10. Hartley and Krugman (1948) have reported that young children frequently see an individual as identical with and limited to the single role in
which he is momentarily observed.

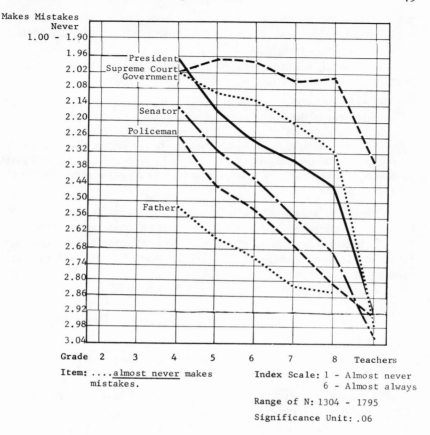

Fig. 8.
*Comparison of means of grades 4 through 8 in rating infallibility
of figures and institutions.*

personal representatives. The increase with age in regard for the office
of the Presidency and for institutions composed of offices whose incumbents are unknown is an example of relationships with roles rather
than persons. The necessity of maintaining stable support for offices,
even when incumbents change, is the reason that socialization to roles
and institutionalized offices (rather than to personal figures) is
important.

Davies (1954) asserted that strong, institutionalized patterns which
limit government are the major forces for minimizing the charismatic
relationship between candidate and voter. For this reason, a system of
institutional structures must be accepted by citizens as the most legiti-

mate mechanism for the realization of values. One of the functions of socialization is to modify object attachment to include these roles, organizations, and principles.

The role of affective ties to the governmental system in adult political involvement is discussed by Verba:

> The political system can offer some satisfaction for the individual's affective needs through emotional attachments to the symbols of the state, to a charismatic leader, or to some "cause" for which the state stands. But the specific demands that the larger system places upon the individual and the distance of the center of authority from the individual makes it difficult for the system to satisfy his affective needs adequately (1961, p. 56).

Small groups in which the adult has direct involvement must substitute for these strong personal ties to the nation and government, modifying them so that positive regard is not lost but is effectively channeled into active involvement combined with critical consideration of issues and candidates.

Authority and Compliance: Response to Law

"If we had no laws it would be a mess, and we wouldn't learn anything."

The compliance system, as that term is used here, is a network of laws, persons, and institutions vested with authority to enforce their demands. Induction into the compliance system is a complex process which will not be discussed in detail.[11] In this study the two dimensions of concern were the child's view of the power of authority figures to punish non-compliance, and the trust he has in the good intentions of rules and their justice. Although the qualities of power and positive intent are logically distinct, children frequently appeared to associate power and benevolence. Benevolent qualities, attributed both to authority figures and to the system of laws, offer a basis of positive regard which justifies and encourages compliance. Attachment to government leaders motivates personal obedience in hope of reward.[12] A child also trusts the system of laws, believing that all laws are fair and that those who enforce them do so in order to protect citizens.

The young child views law as helpful and protective. The children

11. See Hess and Minturn (in preparation).
12. "Reward" is used here as in theoretical discussion of identification. A child experiences positive reinforcement when he behaves as his model does, even when the model does not directly reward him. The same kind of process is important in all situations where the child emulates an ideal.

tested perceived laws as positive forces in society, seeing their major functions to keep people safe and, increasingly with age, to help run the country. Statutes are not intended primarily to punish wrongdoers (Table 9). Interviews showed that a sense of being protected by law is important to the child's acceptance of the legal system. An excerpt from

Table 9
Changes by Grade in Perception of Functions of Laws

Grade level	N	To punish people	To run country	To keep people from doing bad things	To keep people safe
2	198	16.2%	6.6%	16.7%	60.6%
3	217	7.4	14.3	14.7	63.6
4	211	6.6	14.7	13.3	65.4
5	210	3.3	20.0	10.5	66.2
6	233	3.9	27.0	14.6	54.5
7	226	4.0	28.3	8.0	59.7
8	89	2.2	34.8	9.0	53.9

Notes.—Item: Why do we have laws? Put an X beside the one that is most true. (From Pilot Study 14 questionnaire.)
—Significance Unit: 10%.

an interview with a kindergarten girl illustrates this point:

"What is law?"

"If someone steals something or that . . . it's a law and the policeman had to go looking for it. And when they find him they put him in jail and lock him up and then the law is done."

"Do you think laws are a good idea?"

"Yes, because so far no one has stealed anything from us."

A second illustration comes from an interview with a third-grade girl:

"Well, what do you think about laws? Do you like them?"

"Well, it's for us to obey; it's for our safety. They're fair, and people who make them think of the people."

"Could there be bad laws?"

"I don't think there are any laws that would be cruel."

The young child's conception of laws and law enforcement is undifferentiated. Children often do not distinguish rules at home and school from the more formal laws of government, though they know that all rules are important. Responses given by a fifth-grade boy from a middle-status home illustrate this confusion:

"Will you tell me what a law is?"

"A rule that a city makes up."

"Can you name a law?"
"School or government law? Well, like don't run down the stairs and don't slide down the bannister."

The young child sees laws as just and unchanging. Positive orientations toward laws and faith in their absolute justice apparently characterize the attitudes of young children. Figure 9 shows the rapid decline with age in agreement that "all laws are fair." The mean response at grade two was closest to strong agreement. Frank (1949) suggested one reason why children regard the law as infallible. "The Law—a body of rules apparently devised for infallibly determining what is right and wrong and deciding who should be punished for misdeeds—inevitably becomes a partial substitute for the Father-as-Infallible Judge" (p. 18). The individual seeks stability in his world by attributing absolute virtue to the legal system. Kohlberg (1963), reviewing Piaget's theories of moral development, suggested that conceiving rules as sacred and unchangeable results from two cognitive defects in children: egocentrism (the inability to see moral values as related to persons other than oneself) and realism (the conception that rules are not subjective phenomena). Though implicit trust in law decreases with age, it establishes the criteria a child may use later in assessing the performance of all authority figures. If, at a later age, he discovers that laws are not always just, he may nevertheless believe they should be; if he has experience with authority figures who enforce law arbitrarily, he may be disillusioned yet hold to the principle of fair administration of laws. These early and changing conceptions of the justice of laws seem to be an example of the operation of the cognitive-developmental model.

Young children believe laws are unchanging as well as just. At grade three, 24 per cent of this group selected the alternative "no laws will change" when asked to predict alterations in the legal system during the next decade. Choice of this alternative declined rapidly, so that by grade five, only 6 per cent of the research population subscribed to this statement, and at grade eight less than 2 per cent agreed. Young children also perceived most laws to have been made in the distant past, with the permanence and weight of tradition already behind them (see Appendix D, Fig. D.01). Fifty-four per cent of second-grade children strongly endorsed the statement, "Most laws were made a long time ago"; at grade five, 22 per cent; and at grade eight, 9 per cent strongly agreed. Eighth-grade children more commonly perceived law-making to be a continuous process.

Induction into the compliance system is through visible authority figures—the President and the policeman. To the young child, political authority figures and institutions appear to be highly powerful. They both make and enforce laws and rules. A child's first contact with the

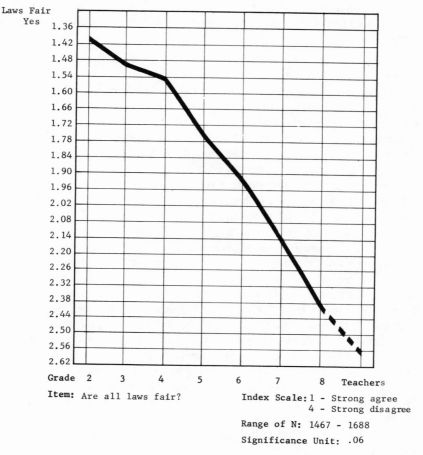

Fig. 9.
*Comparison of means of grades 2 through 8 in
belief that laws are fair.*

system of laws is mediated by specific authority figures, particularly the President, who is perceived as author of the laws (Table 5).[13] Children attributed omniscience to the President as a law-maker. A fifth-grade girl from the working class expressed this feeling:

"Well now, suppose Mr. Jones said he would not obey the law because it is a bad law. What kind of law do you think that could be?"

"Well, it might be something that the citizens don't like, and it may be

13. Interviews suggest that small children view Congress, the Supreme Court, and senators as the President's assistants and helpers. The concept of checks and balances is foreign to the child, who has difficulty understanding that there may be more than one valid side to an issue.

just his opinion of just a bad law. The President okays them before they're obeyed, so I guess if it is good enough for him, it is good enough for anybody."

The President is also perceived by young children as the figure most capable of decisive action. His power to "make other people do what he wants" was rated greater than that of the policeman and markedly superior to that of the father (Fig. 10). The policeman and President were equally respected for their authority by older children. Fourth-graders also perceived the President as approximately equal to the policeman in ability to "punish anyone" (Fig. 11). The senator was seen by older children as having narrower ranges of authority, eighth-graders having little more respect for the senator's power over people than for that of their own fathers. Eighth-graders attributed much more authoritativeness to the government and the Supreme Court than to either the President or the senator. By the eighth grade, institutions are seen as most powerful; the policeman and the President have inter-mediate amounts of power, while the senator and father have least.

Children's respect for the power of the policeman is moderately high and relatively stable across grade. The policeman was judged to be nearly as concerned for the child's welfare as his own father (ex-pressed by the policeman's desire to be helpful), a perception which was also stable with age (Fig. 2). The judgments of power and helpful-ness were the only three items in which the policeman was rated high and where this rating remained stable over age. On elements of general role competence—leadership, infallibility, decision-making, working hard, knowing a great deal—the policeman was perceived considerably below the President (Figs. 4, 5, 6, 7, 8).

Children have dual role expectations for the policeman; he will enforce laws but he will help the child when necessary. Table 10 indicates the importance to children at all grade-levels of the police-man's ability to make people obey laws, and the increasing importance of his helping people in trouble.

What will be the child's response to his perceptions of the police-man? Compliance is clearly evident, particularly in responses of young children to the question, "If you think a policeman is wrong in what he tells you to do, what would you do?" Only 6 per cent of a pilot test group stated, "I would not do it." [14] Non-compliance in a face-to-face encounter with the policeman is an untenable idea to young children; only the extent to which compliance is questioned may vary (Table 11). A very small percentage of children would do what the policeman said and tell him they thought he was wrong. A more popular alterna-

14. Because there were so few responses of non-compliance, and because the inclusion of this alternative was disturbing to some children and teachers, it was eliminated from the final instrument.

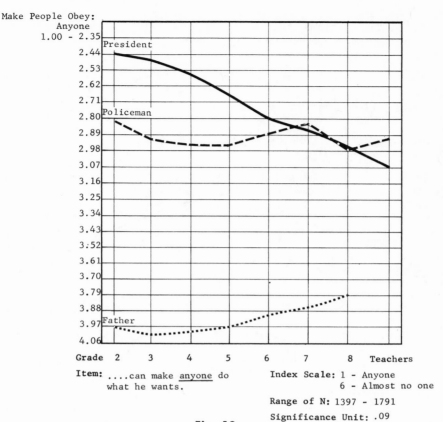

Make People Obey:

Item: ....can make <u>anyone</u> do
what he wants.

Index Scale: 1 - Anyone
6 - Almost no one

Range of N: 1397 - 1791

Significance Unit: .09

Fig. 10.

**Comparison of means of grades 2 through 8 in rating
coercive power of figures.**

Table 10

**Changes by Grade in Perception of Most Important Aspect
of Policeman's Job**

Grade level	N	Make people obey the law	Help people who are in trouble	Catch people who break the law
4	1526	38.3%	23.0%	38.7%
5	1787	42.4	29.6	28.0
6	1731	42.8	32.5	24.7
7	1709	44.5	34.0	21.5
8	1680	41.6	39.6	18.8
Teachers	382	50.3	38.5	11.3

Notes.—Item: Which is the most important for the policeman to do? Choose one.
—Significance Unit: 3%.

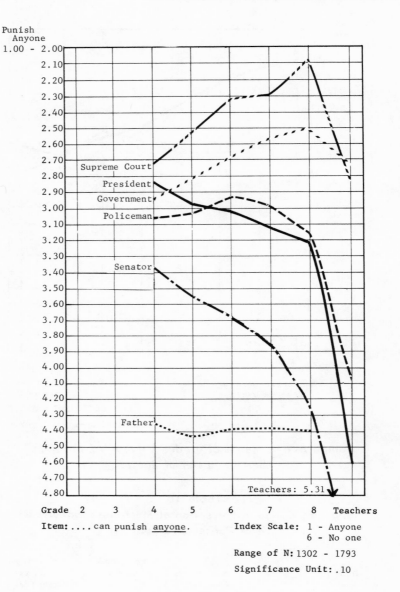

Punish
Anyone

Fig. 11.
**Comparison of means of grades 4 through 8 in rating punitive
power of figures and institutions.**

Table 11
Changes by Grade in Child's Response if He
"Thinks a Policeman Is Wrong"

Grade level	N	Do what he tells you and forget about it	Do what he tells you but tell your father	Do what he tells you but ask the policeman why	Do what he tells you but tell him he is wrong
2	1635	19.6%	45.5%	24.0%	10.9%
3	1663	20.8	41.8	27.8	9.5
4	1729	17.0	38.7	34.3	10.0
5	1791	17.3	33.1	37.9	11.7
6	1740	15.4	24.9	48.1	11.6
7	1708	13.4	23.0	52.5	11.1
8	1677	11.5	17.3	58.4	12.8

Notes.—Item: If you think a policeman is wrong in what he tells you to do, what should you do? Put an X beside the one that tells what you would do.
—Significance Unit: 3%.

tive for young children is to obey but "tell your father." Asking the policeman to explain an unjust command, a more common response among older children, represents an increasing tendency to question authority within a framework of compliance. Perhaps the idea of confrontation with a policeman is so threatening to a child that almost any alternative seems preferable. Recall George's comments on the opening pages of Chapter One. Children may feel the desire not to comply which they suppress rather than becoming engaged in conflict with law-enforcing agents, even when they feel they have been unjustly treated.

The young child believes that punishment is an inevitable consequence of wrongdoing; this view declines with age. Children's assessment of the likelihood that criminals would be apprehended was probed by the question, "Do people who break laws: (1) always get caught; (2) usually get caught; (3) usually get away; or (4) always get away?" Fifty-seven per cent of second-graders believed that punishment inevitably follows crime. This certainty declined, however, with only 16 per cent of eighth-graders choosing this alternative. Only 2 per cent of teachers agreed with this statement. The same type of age change appears in perceptions of the system of laws. Older children have learned, perhaps from their own experience, that punishment is not the inevitable consequence of misdemeanor and they generalize this conclusion to the legal system.

Children believe that the policeman helps people in trouble, but they have no strong personal feeling for him (Figs. 2 and 3).

There was much less personal liking for the policeman than for father, and somewhat less affection for him than for the President. Only the senator was less esteemed than the policeman. Mixed feelings concerning the policeman are illustrated by an increase with age in the number of children who saw the policeman's major function as helping people in trouble, accompanied by a decrease in the number of children who reported that they liked the policeman. Most responses to interview questions about the policeman were positive; however, there were some which showed ambivalent feelings. An interview with a fourth-grade, working-class girl illustrates this point:

"Do you like the policeman?"
"I don't know. They help, and they give you tickets. I don't like them. I like to obey my own rules. I listen to them, but I don't like them."

Children have learned that policeman may help but also may punish them.

To children, the policeman represents the authoritative ruling order; more than 80 per cent of the total group knew he worked for the government. The policeman is also a well-known figure; a second grader knows the postman and policeman better than other government figures. Children expect their behavior to be directly influenced by the policeman and anticipate suffering the consequences of disobedience. Although schools probably present a nurturant image of the policeman, children learn from an early age that one of the policeman's major responsibilities is to capture (and they believe also to punish) lawbreakers. Because children's first contacts with law are through observations of its enforcement, mixed feelings about its representatives are very important in determining perceptions of law.[15]

Not all attitudes toward the system of law shift toward moderation with increased age. Norms concerning how the system should operate are distinguished from attitudes regarding the way it actually operates. The item, "The policeman's job is to make people obey laws," is stable across the age range, although children's belief in the inevitability of punishment declines. Agreement with the statement that "laws are to keep us safe" is stable, while agreement that "all laws are fair" shows a marked decline with age. Ideal statements of how things ought to be tend to be more stable than perceptions of the way the system actually functions. This discrepancy may be the basis for cynicism.

The origin of orientations toward the compliance system is four-fold: first, the fund of positive feeling for government, particularly the

15. Only compliance to law and commands from an authority figure were assessed. Broader social compliance was not a primary concern of this study.

President, which is extended to include laws made by governmental authorities; second, the core of respect for power wielded by authority figures, particularly the policeman; third, experience in subordinate, compliant roles, acquired by the child at home and school; fourth, the normative belief that all systems of rules are fair. These elements are central to a young child's induction into the compliance system.

4

Strategies for Exerting

an Effect upon

the Political System

"Larry, how do you think the Congress works?"
"Well, people from the different states have representatives in the Congress and if they want something to go to Congress, they write their representatives."

"Steve, who is it that has the say about what happens in this country?"
"Well, out of the civics book it would say 'The voters,' but who are they? What group? I'd say on the whole the people, really, except in some of these political matters there is a little wheeling and dealing. . . ."

"Richard, if the President did something that people didn't like, what could they do?"
"The people can't do anything. They can't go to the White House and tell him what to do because he makes all the decisions. If people don't like it, too bad for them."

"Jane, are there some people in America who have more power than the rest of us?"
"Well, I'd think Congress does, but we also give them ideas and they carry them out for us."
"How do we give them ideas?"
"Well, if you wrote a letter or made a petition. If they thought this was a very good idea and it would help your country, they'd talk to the rest of the Congress and they'd decide whether they should make it a law or whatever it was supposed to be."

Influencing Government Policy

The franchise is a central feature of a democratic government, and the preparation of children to exercise this right as adults is one of the key elements of the socializing process. In the relationship between a citizen and his government, the right to vote is the power to effect change and to exert control.

A major role is open to the individual: watching over the government's conduct and attempting to influence its actions.[1] Because a citizen votes, he may also play an influential role in the period between elections. His power is largely based upon this right to vote and his ability to influence the votes of others. The vote is one expression of a fundamental relationship between the citizen and his country, but the act of casting a ballot is not sufficient evidence that the citizen comprehends or will implement his right to influence the governing process. This orientation involves a view of oneself as effective, a view of the system as responsive, and a knowledge of the procedures and techniques of influence required to implement this intent.[2]

To try to intervene in the government's actions requires an assertiveness contrasting sharply with the submissiveness of the subject's role. This assertiveness must not destroy compliance with the law nor proceed beyond structures which regulate dissent. The power to regulate the government—which the child will share as citizen—is unlike any relationship children experience. The readiness to become actively involved must be developed during childhood by teaching attitudes based on trust in the system and compliance to it. Trust in the system motivates attempts at influence, assuring that effort will not be futile. Failure of socialization may foster apathy or it may lead to the emergence of influence techniques which are antisocial or illegal. The citizen's place in the compliance system limits and constrains the techniques of influence, keeping them within legal bounds.

Two types of influence are available to the individual citizen—the power to affect decisions and actions of the government (including noncompliance and passive resistance), and the power to influence government by changing elected representatives. Although the techniques involved in these different types of action are not identical, the under-

---

1. Almond and Verba (1963) referred to this as the "citizen's role," an active one, and contrasted it with the passive "subject's role."
2. Although many citizens are politically inactive, feelings of political competence are characteristic of adults in the United States. Seventy-five per cent of the sample interviewed by Almond and Verba felt that they could do something to modify or prevent the passage of an unjust or harmful law being considered in Congress:

> Much of the influence that our respondents believe they have over government probably represents a somewhat unrealistic belief in their opportunities to participate. It is likely that many who say they could influence the government would never attempt to exert such influence; and it is likely as well that if they tried they would not succeed. . . . If an individual believes he has influence, he is more likely to attempt to use it. . . . And if decision makers believe that the ordinary man *could* participate . . . they are likely to behave quite differently than if such a belief did not exist (1963, pp. 182-183).

lying orientations are essentially the same. The acquisition of attitudes in this critical area is complex and begins early in life. The intricacies of personal involvement in political behavior have been presented by Smith, Bruner and White (1956) and by Lane (1959) in extensive case histories. Possibly one of the most difficult tasks of political socialization is to teach the individual citizen to engage in action (through community groups and other organizations) which he recognizes may have a very delayed effect or possibly no discernible effect at all.

The processes of government—passing and enforcing laws, making and implementing decisions—are too complex for children to comprehend. To develop the capacity and motivation necessary for intervening in governmental process requires a complex pattern of attitudes. First is a belief that citizens should participate—bring about changes in governmental policy which they think desirable and maintain standards of integrity in government officials—in order to protect their own self-interest. This opposes the belief that government is perfect and that citizens fulfill their role by remaining silent and complying with law. The belief that the status quo is satisfactory acts to deter active citizen participation. Second, a citizen who wishes to influence government policies must learn the most efficient ways to make his opinion felt. This problem is complicated by the schools' emphasis upon the formal structure of governmental process, and the underemphasis on the role of group structures and interactions which constitute a pluralistic society. David Truman has summarized this:

> So strong is our awareness of the standardized, formal aspects of government . . . that we easily fall into the error of a simplified, stereotyped picture of the process: the legislature adopts policy, the executive approves and administers it, the courts adjudicate controversies arising out of it (1963, p. 262).

The influence of interest and pressure groups upon government policy is apparently often ignored in public discussion of congressional action and in school curricula. Admittedly it is not easy to teach children that groups who promote their own interests rather than the public interest may be effective, even decisive, in the legislative process. But the citizen could act more realistically and effectively if he had such information.

One ideal of American democracy has been that each individual should be able to make *his* opinion count, as it did in the town meetings of early America. Banfield contrasted the American and British government in this regard: "The British . . . still believe that the government should govern. And we . . . still believe that everyone has a right to 'get in on the act' and to make his influence felt." (1960, pp. 61-77)

CONCEPT OF THE SYSTEM AND THE CITIZEN'S ROLE

The following discussion is oriented about these questions:

1) Do children see government as so perfect that the citizen's only legitimate responsibility is to obey its commands and not interfere with its pronouncements? Do they allow other individuals the freedom to criticize the government?

2) Do children have knowledge of extra-legislative, informal processes of government and the legitimate channels of influence which are open to them as citizens?

3) Is stress placed upon individual participation or upon the goal of incorporating individuals in group action?

The concept of government as an object which will respond to citizen protest on issues is the most crucial aspect of this relationship of citizens to government. Young children have a highly idealized acceptance of the system as a whole—an attachment both to their country and to the figures and institutions of government. Operation of the democratic system, however, demands that citizens have reservations about particular facets of public policy. Without abandoning his positive attachment to government, to the rules of law, and to the structures designed to regulate dissent, the citizen must be watchful over the government's actions. He must learn to separate particular government policies from his allegiance to the government as a whole.

Most children have implicit trust in the wisdom and benevolence of government. This is documented by agreement with the item, "What goes on in the government is all for the best" (Fig. 12). At grade three, 90 per cent of the respondents agreed with this statement (excluding those who did not respond or who did not know). At grade eight, 76 per cent of the students agreed. (Among teachers, the agreement rate dropped to 46 per cent.)

The idealized perception of government by children is further documented by pilot-study responses to the question, "The United States government knows what is best for the people." [3] Between 80 and 90 per cent of students at all grade levels agreed with this statement. Children accept a system which "knows what is best for its citizens," just as their parents presumably know what is best for them. These data confirm the trend presented in Fig. 8, concerning the perceived infallibility of governmental decisions.

Accepting the supreme authority of government obviously does not mean that an individual is prepared for action in pursuit of his own goals. The age changes in the item regarding perception that the govern-

3. Pilot Study 11.

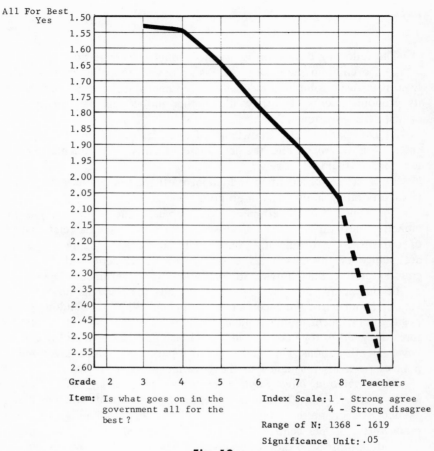

All For Best Yes

Grade 2   3   4   5   6   7   8   Teachers

Item: Is what goes on in the government all for the best?

Index Scale: 1 - Strong agree
4 - Strong disagree

Range of N: 1368 - 1619

Significance Unit: .05

Fig. 12.
Comparison of means of grades 3 through 8 in belief that government is "all for the best."

ment is "all for the best," show that a somewhat more realistic view of government is acquired with increasing experience. The discrepancy between eighth-graders and teachers was very large, however; the experience acquired by adults, who see many governmental decisions with which they cannot agree, leads to expressions of discontent which may stimulate political activity.

Information about school curriculum also suggests that in the second through fourth grades teachers emphasize positive aspects of their social studies material, or at least present the material impartially (see Table 12). Teachers see their role as forming the child's lasting positive

Table 12
Teachers' Report of Their Presentation of Curricular Material

Grade level taught	Number of teachers responding	Critically, point out bad aspects as well as good	Favorably, emphasize good aspects	Impartially, without value judgment
2	22	18.2%	54.5%	27.3%
3 & 4	32	31.2	31.2	37.5
5 & 6	38	44.7	36.8	18.4
7 & 8	22	68.2	13.6	18.2

Note.—Item: I usually try to present material about the country, (1) *Impartially*, giving no value judgment; (2) *favorably*, emphasizing the good aspects; (3) *critically*, pointing out bad aspects as well as good. (From Curriculum Questionnaire.)

attachment to the system. Teachers of seventh- and eighth-grade classes, in contrast, reported that they tried to present material including less favorable aspects. The principle that our government is good but that it is not infallible on certain issues is a very subtle idea and one difficult to communicate even to eighth-grade students. Presentation of controversial issues for discussion in the classroom and the child's increasing experience with actions of a political system which do not meet his standards modify the feeling that governmental activity and power are beyond question.

Children believe that democracy is "rule by the people," but they have limited understanding of how this rule is exercised. Children hold certain norms about the operation of democracy. "A democracy is where the people rule," is clearly among a democracy's most important definitions (Table 13). An interview with a sixth-grade, lower-status boy illustrates his limited understanding of such rule by the people;

"Oh, in the United States the people are supposed to rule the government—well—I—the people make up the government. They are not the officers; the government supposedly rules, but the people have command over the government. . . . Well, I'd say really the people rule, because the people have charge over the government; it's just an organization that the people are trying to keep order. So really the people would rule, but that is kind of complicated because the government rules over the people, and the people tell the government. It is kind of mixed up, but it's a good set-up, but yet there's no real good rule. Everybody has power; that is, everybody's power is limited. Well, it is like an organization; if the majority doesn't like this—why then—it doesn't go. If the majority does, it's all the majority— the majority rules—nobody rules—but the majority rules. . . ."

Children have a limited knowledge of the role of pressure groups in making political policy. Their understanding of the role pressure

Table 13
Changes by Grade in Concept of Democracy
(Percentages answering "Yes" for each definition)

Grade level	The people rule	No one is rich or poor	All grown-ups can vote	All have equal chance	You can say things against the government	If most agree, the rest should go along
4	26.0%	19.4%	39.4%	35.8%	15.4%	29.9%
5	35.9	24.3	52.4	50.2	23.0	35.5
6	51.9	27.1	69.0	66.4	39.1	35.2
7	64.3	24.2	75.4	76.8	48.6	28.2
8	76.4	22.7	75.3	82.8	53.5	27.6
Teachers	98.4	7.5	76.5	88.3	55.0	67.6

Notes.—Items: What is a democracy? (In each of the following questions, choose one: (1) Yes; (2) No; (3) Don't know.) (37) Is a democracy where the people rule? (38) Is a democracy where no one is very rich or very poor? (39) Is a democracy where all grown-ups can vote? (40) Is a democracy where everyone has an equal chance to get ahead? (41) Is a democracy where you can say anything against the government without getting into trouble? (42) Is a democracy where if most of the people agree, the rest should go along?
—N ranged from 1530 to 1787 for students; for teachers, from 373 to 375.
—Significance Unit: 3% for all items.

groups play in government is indicated in Table 14. Until the seventh grade, children rated the policeman's influence in law-making as higher than that of any other individual or group except the President and labor unions. Although ranks differ slightly, an examination of the means shows that children did not distinguish among the power of big companies, churches, rich people, and the average voter. Labor unions were attributed much higher power; they seemed to exemplify the concept of "pressure group" for respondents.

As a clear illustration of the strength of the American ideal of the importance of the individual, the average citizen's influence on law-making was perceived as equal or superior to the legislative power wielded by churches, persons of wealth, and newspapers. Perhaps this ideal distorts the child's view. Teachers differed greatly from eighth-graders in their perceptions, rating the influence of unions, newspapers, companies, and rich people nearly equal and at a level much higher than they rated that of the average citizen. Stable age curves from grade four through eight, followed by a sharp divergence of teachers, suggest that this facet of governmental process is not handled by the school either directly or indirectly.[4] Schools concentrate on formal aspects of

4. Pressure groups are perhaps the most publicly devalued part of our government process. Remmers (Remmers and Radler, 1957) reported that in a high-school sample only 25 per cent agreed that pressure groups are a useful and important feature of representative government.

Table 14
Changes by Grade in Ranking Influence of Officials, Pressure Groups, and the Average Citizen
(Rankings)

Grade level	Rich people	Unions	President	Newspapers	Churches	Average person	Policeman	Big Companies
4	5.5	2.5	1	7.5	5.5	7.5	2.5	4
5	7	2	1	8	5.5	5.5	3	4
6	5.5	2	1	7.5	7.5	5.5	3	4
7	6	2	1	6	8	6	3.5	3.5
8	5	2	1	5	8	3	7	5
Teachers	5	3	1	3	7	6	8	3

Notes.—Items: How much do each of these people help decide which laws are made for our country? (1) very much; (2) some; (3) very little; (4) not at all; (0) Don't know.

—Mean ratings given to each influence source were ranked within each grade group. N upon which means were based ranged from 1141 to 1773 for students; for teachers, from 368 to 376. The lower the ranking, the greater the perceived power. Rankings with decimals indicate ties.

the government, teaching that Congress makes the laws but not recognizing the influence of interest groups.

Perception of the different channels of influence which the citizen may adopt does expand with age. Agreement that "Voting is the only way people like my parents can have any say about how the government runs things" dropped with age. In a pilot study, recognition that "Everyone can write to his Congressman to say what laws he wants passed" increased with grade.[5] On another pilot instrument, however, the average citizen was rated as only slightly less influential than "people who write to their Senators."[6]

Responses to the three questions posed at the beginning of this section seem fairly clear, even from this brief analysis. Many children believe that the government provides for all citizens in such a way that they need not be alert or responsible for its conduct. Children's evaluation of pressure groups is generally negative, and knowledge of the most efficient channels of influence is limited. They believe in *individual* access to power—an unrealistic viewpoint, particularly in a rapidly expanding society.

Older children stress interest in politics and current events as part of the ideal citizen's obligation. Part of the citizen's responsibility, in the

5. Pilot Study 11.
6. Pilot Study 12.

mind of an older child, is to be interested in the government. The choice of this aspect of the citizen's role as important increased dramatically with age, eighth-graders being quite similar to teachers (Table 7). The belief that citizens should be interested is socialized, even though motiviations for this interest and the channels through which it can be expressed in action are not clearly defined. It is obvious to children, however, that many citizens do not meet this obligation of interest. More than half of a pilot sample agreed that, "Politics are interesting, but not as interesting as sports or dancing for most people." [7]

THE CHILD'S RELATIONSHIP TO THE SYSTEM

The young child's conception of the government emphasizes its unity and protectiveness; he expects personal responsiveness from the President when he is in trouble. What is the older child's perception of the government's responsiveness to demands that people like himself and his family might make on it? Does he believe that his actions or interest would be influential? [8]

Children's sense of the efficacy of citizen action increases with age. The sharpest increase occurred between grades four and five (Fig. 13). The questions were focused on individual action, although group cooperation was not excluded. Teachers and eighth-graders received similar mean efficacy scores, suggesting that expectations of governmental responsiveness become highly socialized during the elementary-school period.

By the end of elementary school, most children have acquired some interest in the government and have participated in discussions about its policies. In response to the consideration which they expect the government to show individuals' opinions, the seventh- and eighth-graders reported a relatively high level of active involvement, although they did not approach the amount of activity reported by teachers. Although children believe that citizens *should* be interested in government, there was a slight decline with age in reports of their own interest (Fig. 14). [9] The discrepancy between eighth-graders and teachers may represent, on the children's part, a low level of interest which will increase in adulthood or, on the teachers' part, a high level of interest relative to that of other adults.

Table 15 documents the rapid increase with age in reports of discussions with friends and family about political matters (candidates and

7. Pilot Study 11.
8. SRC Efficacy Scale, modified to make statements about the child and his family, and people like the child's family, was used. See Appendix C.
9. The high level of interest reported at grade two must be evaluated in light of the facts that second-graders equate the government with the President, and that these children reported interest in this personal figure.

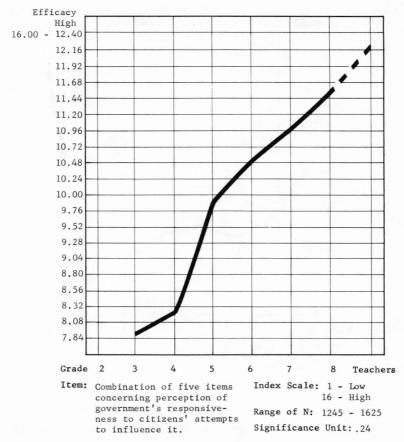

Grade 2   3   4   5   6   7   8   Teachers

Item: Combination of five items
concerning perception of
government's responsive-
ness to citizens' attempts
to influence it.

Index Scale: 1 - Low
            16 - High

Range of N: 1245 - 1625

Significance Unit: .24

Fig. 13.
Comparison of means of grades 3 through 8 in
sense of political efficacy.

certain problems facing the country). In this item, also, the most rapid
change occurred between grades four and five.

Analysis of the questions which compose this index illustrates the
importance of candidates and elections in stimulating discussion. The
question, "Who will be elected?" mobilized the children's interest more
quickly than more abstract problems. Informal discussion, outside the
schoolroom, may be a major source of attitudes toward cooperative
group participation in politics which Almond and Verba (1963) made
the focus of their study. Politics is not an activity which can be pursued
alone, and this index indicates that older children have had some
experience in discussing political matters with their peers and parents.

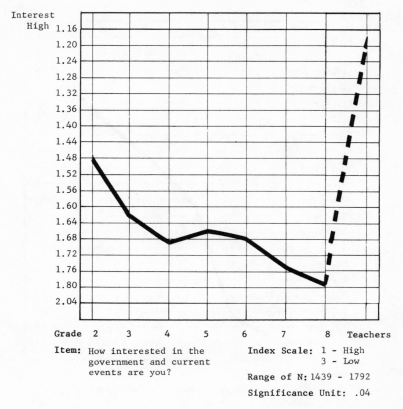

Fig. 14.

Comparison of means of grades 2 through 8 in political interest.

The Index of Concern with Political Issues asked whether children had discussed five national issues and, if so, whether they had taken sides on the issues in their discussion (Fig. 15). This involvement demands both willingness to tolerate conflict with another's opinions and an assertive approach on the child's part. Analysis of the six issues which were part of the original questionnaire showed that the space race (at the time of the testing) was the issue which mobilized the children's interest at the earliest age.[10] Children remembered discussing the United Nations more than most other issues, but they did not take sides in these discussions, probably because the United Nations is not presented as a controversial issue in the schools. Other national issues mobilized children's interest about equally. Sizable increases with age

10. Because of low correlation between this item and the other five, it was not included in the index.

Table 15
Changes by Grade in Participation in Political Discussion
(Percentage answering "Yes" for each type of discussion)

Grade level	N	Talked with parents about country's problems	N	Talked with parents about a candidate	N	Talked with friends about a candidate
3	1651	57.1%	1655	52.4%	1658	49.0%
4	1733	58.8	1732	61.6	1732	57.4
5	1794	66.2	1800	77.2	1798	75.5
6	1740	71.4	1745	80.3	1744	80.8
7	1711	72.5	1719	84.2	1713	86.9
8	1687	71.7	1688	85.0	1690	89.0
Teachers		a		a	378	96.0

Notes.—Item: Things about government, politics, and candidates that you have done: (36) I have talked with my mother or father about our country's problems—(1) Yes; (2) No.
(37) I have talked with my friends about a candidate. (39) I have talked with my mother or father about a candidate.
—Significance Unit: 3%.
a. Item not included in teachers' questionnaire.

in the Index of Concern with Political Issues can be accounted for by increases in the number of children reporting they took sides on these issues. Teachers represented a striking increase in concern with political issues, when compared with eighth-graders. This index represents one of the largest student-teacher discrepancies in this study.

Despite different levels of interest in discussing issues, there is surprising congruence between children's and teachers' assessment of *importance* of problems facing America (Fig. 16). Communist Russia was perceived as the most important challenge, and throughout the age span, this external threat was seen as more crucial than domestic problems such as civil rights. The increasing interest, with grade, in economic problems such as unemployment, and the decline of aesthetic concerns such as beautiful cities, is congruent with previously discussed findings on the movement of interest from personal, close-to-home issues toward more abstract and distant problems.

SUMMARY

The emergence of attitudes, norms, and capacities necessary for active involvement in the political process and the growth of a belief that citizens' responsibility extends beyond attachment and compliance are prominent in elementary school political socialization. An active

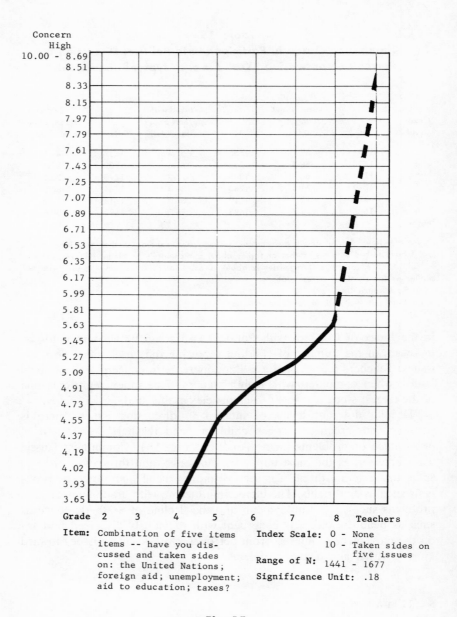

Concern
High
10.00 - 8.69
        8.51
        8.33
        8.15
        7.97
        7.79
        7.61
        7.43
        7.25
        7.07
        6.89
        6.71
        6.53
        6.35
        6.17
        5.99
        5.81
        5.63
        5.45
        5.27
        5.09
        4.91
        4.73
        4.55
        4.37
        4.19
        4.02
        3.93
        3.65

Grade 2   3   4   5   6   7   8   Teachers

Item: Combination of five items   Index Scale: 0 - None
       items -- have you dis-   10 - Taken sides on
       cussed and taken sides   five issues
       on: the United Nations;   Range of N: 1441 - 1677
       foreign aid; unemployment;   Significance Unit: .18
       aid to education; taxes?

Fig. 15.
**Comparison of means of grades 4 through 8 in concern
about political issues.**

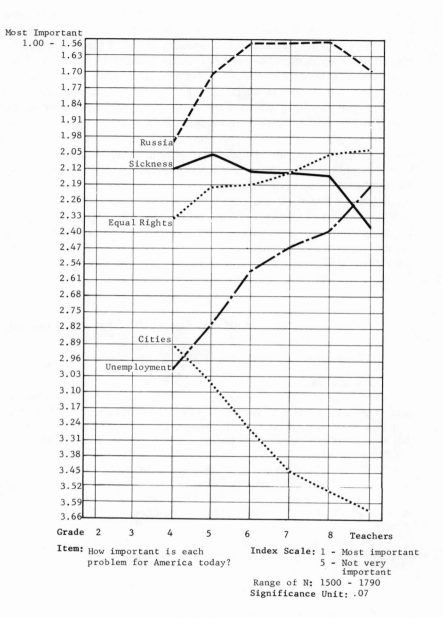

Most Important

| Grade | 2 | 3 | 4 | 5 | 6 | 7 | 8 | Teachers |

Item: How important is each   Index Scale: 1 - Most important
problem for America today?   5 - Not very
                                                      important
                                      Range of N: 1500 - 1790
                                      Significance Unit: .07

Fig. 16.
Comparison of means of grades 4 through 8 in rating
importance of national problems.

citizen-government relationship is unimportant to second- and third-graders; they believe that citizenship requires only personal goodness. By the eighth grade, children have acquired norms which make interest obligatory; they accept the notion of citizen control over government and they expect citizen action to be effective. They engage in less activity than teachers, as might be expected. There are also aspects of children's perceptions which may have negative consequences. For example, the effectiveness of individual effort is overemphasized, while the advantages of group cooperation in political action are often not recognized. Too, the unrealistically positive image of benevolent government power in all its activities and the underevaluation of pressure groups as significant forces in the formation of government policy deprive the individual of access to one of the most potent sources of influence. Although political parties express conflict which is difficult for a child to accept, the mere visibility of the parties and the positive value attached to party membership define parties as legitimate influence groups. Children devalue other pressure groups and perceive them as non-legitimate channels of influence.

Participation in the Process of Elections

"Andy, how do we choose our President?"
"We elect them."
"What does that mean?"
"Well, it means like this little piece of paper with some names on them and these little boxes and you put a little check mark in it, and then you put it, you do it in a little booth. And you bring it to the person who is holding this place where you're doing it at, and you stick it in a little box."
"Could anybody be President?"
"Well, no. There are a lot of men who want to be President, so they select of all those men, two, and those two are the ones that they try out. See, everybody votes for one of the people that they think that they want, and the two that get the *most* votes are the ones that are going to go for President."
"Can a rich man be President?"
"Well if he wants to, but he has to be elected."
"Can a poor man?"
"Yes, if he's elected."

"Danny, how do parties pick a candidate?"
"Well, a lot of times I think the different parties will bribe some one person to come to their side. He has to have a name. . . . I mean you don't just draw or pick one person from someplace that nobody else knows about. . . . Everybody has to know about him. They [the political party] try to

make it sound like they could get him to be President easier than the other party and they could make it easier for him to get elected. . . ."

"Wally, did you see the TV debates (between Nixon and Kennedy)?"
"Some of them. I thought they were very good. It gave you a chance to see what's going on while they're running for President."
"Were you interested before?"
"No, but after the debates I just wanted to see if Kennedy wins."

In this section, two aspects of political influence will be discussed: orientations toward voting, a constitutionally defined element of the system, and attitudes toward political parties, an informal element of the system. Attitudes toward voting and partisan commitment mingle when a citizen becomes involved in an election contest.

VOTING — CONCEPT OF THE SYSTEM AND THE CITIZEN'S ROLE

During the elementary school years, an increasing number of children recognize the importance of voting. In the early grades, voting was rarely selected as a symbol of government (4 per cent at grade two). By the eighth grade, however, it had become one of the system's most significant symbols, being chosen by 47 per cent of the students tested (Table 4). The same trend was observed when children were asked to choose the source of their pride in being Americans. This emphasis upon voting extends to the conceptualization of democracy in terms of voting privileges.[11] Children chose the right to vote as a characteristic of the United States, differentiating it in this respect from other countries, especially those associated with the Soviet Union.

Children see political candidates and elections in positive terms. Negative concepts, such as possible corruption in the operation of the voting system or in the actions of politicians are present in only a small number of the student group. In a pilot study, more than 70 per cent of children at all grade levels believed that "Most elections in the United States are fair." [12] Students' regard for the motives and qualities of "people who try to get elected" was assessed by ratings of honesty, altruism, reliability, intelligence, and power (Table 16). Esteem for the power and intelligence of politicians was relatively stable across grades. Ratings of honesty, unselfishness, and promise-keeping, however, declined with age. But in all these evaluations the politician was seen

11. As shown in Table 13, children most frequently rated these three definitions of democracy as most appropriate: "A democracy is where all grown-ups can vote," ". . . where everyone has an equal chance to get ahead," and ". . . where the people rule."
12. Pilot Study 6.

fairly positively even though erosion of his image was evident after grade seven. He was rated less highly than were prominent elected officials (the President) or institutions such as the Supreme Court. On those items where comparison was possible, "people who try to get elected" were rated similarly to the "Average U.S. Senator." This is further evidence that political roles which are not associated with a particular individual are probably indistinguishable to children. Teachers rated "people who try to get elected" considerably more negatively than did eighth-graders. These ratings of candidates for public office are another example of young children's positive feelings about elections and persons in public life.

One item inquired into children's beliefs about the motivations of candidates. Why would someone want to run for public office? The question was presented in this form: "Many people would like to be President, a Senator, or a Mayor. Why do you think these people would like to have these jobs?: (1) They want to change things that are not

Table 16
Changes by Grade in Ratings of "People Who Try to Get Elected"

Grade level	More honest than anyone or than most people	Less sneaky than almost anyone or than most people	Always or almost always keep promises	More powerful than almost anyone or than most people	Less selfish than almost anyone or than most people	Smarter than almost anyone or than most people
4	60.8%	53.0%	56.4%	29.6%	57.7%	45.6%
5	59.0	55.8	51.7	30.2	54.1	45.1
6	55.8	50.9	44.6	29.3	48.7	46.8
7	48.6	44.8	36.9	26.4	41.7	42.8
8	39.5	39.1	25.5	24.3	30.7	35.1
Teachers	18.2	34.0	8.5	19.3	14.2	13.3

Notes.—Items: People who try to get elected . . . (Circle the number of your choice in each item).
—N ranged from 1403 to 1735 for students; for teachers, from 345 to 364.
—Significance Unit: 3%.
—Percentages do not add to 100 because the six columns represent the percentage of ratings in the two most positive alternates on six different scales.

good in the government; (2) They want to make a lot of money or be important; (3) They want to keep things as good as they are in the country." Only a few respondents (15 to 20 per cent in grades three through eight) perceived candidates as primarily motivated by selfish desires to make money or to be important. Age changes in this item were reflected most clearly in the alternatives, "To change things that are not good," chosen by 15 per cent of third-graders and 37 per cent of eighth-graders; and "To keep things as good as they are," chosen by 67 per cent of third-graders and 43 per cent of eighth-graders. There was, with age, increased recognition of candidates' expressions of discontent with the status quo. This is commensurate with a decline in the belief that "What goes on in the government is all for the best." Seventh- and eighth-graders recognized politicians as representing the need and desire for change. This was accentuated in teachers' responses, where reform was selected as the motivation for candidacy by 59 per cent of the respondents.

To young children, voting and elections are important democratic activities. The conflict which is present in every campaign is minimized. Throughout the age span there typically is a positive attitude toward candidates: they are viewed as concerned more with the public welfare than with selfish gain. Elections are perceived as crucial to the goals of the democratic process even though they may result in removal of incumbents for whom the child feels personal attachment.

Elections are part of the government's structural organization and are esteemed by children as much as offices and roles of the government. Voting is a legitimate procedure for changing the role occupants, but emphasis is placed on the *role* and change is limited to the incumbent. Observing elections may, in fact, facilitate the distinction between roles and those occupying them. Children who remember more than one Presidential incumbent may be better able to separate the President's office from its occupant's performance in this office than those who know only one incumbent. The high value placed upon the election process may also encourage the acceptance of a newly elected President. Though the campaign winner may not be his personal favorite, a child's trust in the election process assures him that any person chosen by election will be capable and trustworthy.

Paralleling the growth of attitudes toward voting is an emerging morality regarding the election process and the behavior appropriate to candidates. The behavior which these children would condone during a campaign is predictable from their image of the system and their generally positive attitudes toward all candidates.

Children's conceptions of campaign rules were explored by a number of pilot-study items. Children in grades three, five, and seven were asked, "Mr. Jones and Mr. Smith are running for an important government office. Mr. Jones finds out something bad about Mr. Smith. What should he do? (1) Tell all the voters right away that he has found out something bad about Mr. Smith; (2) Wait until Mr. Smith says something bad about him, then tell the voters; (3) Keep it to himself and not tell anybody." [13] Less than 15 per cent of the children in each of

13. Pilot Study 8.

the grades chose the alternative, "Tell all the voters right away. . . ."
Children in all grades tested felt that this kind of personal attack upon
an opponent should not be introduced into a campaign.

Children believe that unity and cohesion should follow election
conflicts; this belief increases with age. What should be the behavior
of a politician following his defeat? How do children handle the divisive
nature of an election contest? Even children in the middle grades are
aware of adult norms which sanction unity, cohesion, and cooperation
once the contest has been decided. In grade five, 55 per cent of the
children believed that a defeated presidential candidate should "help
the winner to do a good job," and in grade eight, 75 per cent of the
children chose this alternative. Less than 1 per cent of the children
in each grade thought the defeated candidate should withdraw from
public life or verbally attack the winner. This conclusion is supported
by another item, "The man who loses in an election should ask his
followers to help the winner." [14] Eighty per cent of the children in
grades four, six, and eight agreed with this statement. Norms supporting
unity and cooperation are socialized at an early age and aid in the transfer of power following an election. These prescriptions also apply to
voters. More than 85 per cent of a pilot sample agreed that, "You have
to go along with the man who was elected even if you didn't vote
for him." [15]

In viewing politics, children minimize conflict. This desire to preserve the appearance of unity may distort a child's perception of the
realities of a political campaign. Many young children saw the 1960
Presidential race as free from conflict. This view was expressed in
response to a pilot-study item inquiring about the behavior of Kennedy
and Nixon during the Presidential race.[16] The item had these alternatives: (1) they said bad things about each other because they were
enemies; (2) they said bad things about each other because they did not
agree about everything; (3) they were just pretending when they said
bad things about each other; (4) they never said anything bad about
each other.

Seventy per cent of the children in grade three chose the alternative,
"they never said anything bad about each other." This refusal to
recognize disagreement declined with age, and the alternative ". . . they
did not agree about everything" was chosen more frequently (15 per
cent in grade three, 60 per cent in grade eight). Many young children
denied the existence of conflict in the campaign. Others, though recognizing conflict, deplored it. A seventh-grade girl, daughter of a skilled

14. Pilot Study 6.
15. Pilot Study 5.
16. Pilot Study 12.

worker, discussed the 1960 election campaign and expressed these feelings:

"What sort of thing do you remember, the things that impressed you?"
"How Kennedy and Nixon both promised many things. And the morning of the election when Kennedy was elected, and Nixon said that Kennedy would be a nice President. Kennedy said how sorry he was that Mr. Nixon wasn't elected. He would have been just as good a President as he was himself, and that he wished they could both be President together. I would have liked them to go together instead of going through this big thing that they go out in the streets and talk to all the people and giving the impression that they got a better impression than the other one. It would have been easy if they both went together. Then there wouldn't have been much quarreling and fighting. Usually during election time in school they wear their pins and quarrel which man is the better."

The preservation of our system requires strong adherence to norms about the value of elections and to the belief that once an election is decided, unity of support must be the focus. These norms are taught very early by the school and they color the child's perception of elections. Conflict is minimized by children, and consensual aspects are focused upon instead.

By grade eight, virtually all children accept the importance of voting. Children's perception of the citizen's role in an election is that he should vote. Interviews provide evidence that an understanding of what voting entails occurs simultaneously with the knowledge that only adults may vote. Related to this knowledge is a growing sense of obligation that every adult *should* vote. The extent to which this norm is accepted by children in elementary school is indicated in Table 7. Older children identify the best adult citizen as, "A person who votes and gets others to vote." This is a normative attitude which the schools support and with which teachers concur.

During elementary school, socializing agents stress certain consensus values regarding the importance of elections in a democracy, rules of morality surrounding them, and the reconciliation of differences and expressions of solidarity behind a winning candidate. These norms, along with recognition of the citizen's duty to vote and the criteria by which his voting choice should be made, are the elements stressed in elementary-school civics.

CONCEPT OF POLITICAL PARTIES AND THE CITIZEN'S ROLE

Though political parties are not constitutionally established in our system of government, they have a well-defined position in American political culture. Political parties and the dramatic conflicts occurring within and between them represent cleavages in the political culture of our nation. They offer an opportunity to examine the socialization of attitudes toward division and antagonism within a system and the development of norms permitting such conflict and providing for its resolution. Political parties offer the citizen an organization through which he may actively influence the government. They also offer the group support for political action necessary to maximize return from an individual's effort.

While the image of political parties develops late, and differences between the parties are not clearly defined, attitudes toward elections and voting are acquired early. There is consensus about their importance. The nature of the division or difference between political parties is somewhat unclear to children. The national sample, however, answered a series of questions asking which party does most for the country, most to keep us out of war, most for rich people, most for people out of work, most to protect the rights of citizens, and most to help their own families. The children chose one of the four alternatives for each issue: (1) Democrats; (2) Republicans; (3) Both about the same; (4) Don't now which does more. Most striking is the overwhelming response that both parties do about the same things and contribute equally to national and personal welfare. This was the modal response *to each question* (40 to 50 per cent) for children *at every grade level.* Clearly, children do not see striking differences between the two major political parties, nor does the ability to differentiate between policies of the parties appear to increase markedly during elementary school.

Table 17 compares the relative percentage of those who chose Democrat and Republican for each issue. Associating a particular economic group with a party did not appear until grade eight. At that time, 21 per cent of the children saw Republicans as helping the rich and 10 per cent saw Democrats as serving this group. Conversely, 24 per cent believed that the Democrats help people out of work, while only 9 per cent saw this as part of the Republicans' role. The teachers, confirming adult findings, magnified this trend. Forty-one per cent of them claimed that Republicans help the rich, while only 4 per cent saw the Democrats in this role. Forty-eight per cent attributed aid for the unemployed to the Democrats, and 2 per cent attributed this to the Republicans. These items present strong evidence that an understanding of party differences on specific issues usually does not begin before grade eight, and that when it does appear, it includes only those issues on which partisan cleavage has historically been most apparent. The differences between teachers and pupils on this item were exceedingly large and point out

Table 17

Changes by Grade in Attributing Specific Contributions to Democratic and Republican Parties

Guess who does more to:

Grade level	HELP RICH		HELP UNEMPLOYED		HELP MY FAMILY		HELP KEEP US OUT OF WAR		PROTECT CITIZENS' RIGHTS		FOR UNITED STATES	
	Rep.	Dem.	Rep.	Dem.	Rep.	Dem.	Rep.	Dem.	Rep.	Dem.	Rep.	Dem.
4	10.4%	7.9%	14.8%	12.3%	17.7%	12.5%	15.8%	12.1%	15.5%	11.3%	17.6%	13.1%
5	10.1	8.7	12.4	13.9	14.8	13.2	14.4	13.8	13.8	13.9	14.3	13.5
6	12.8	9.9	11.6	16.7	13.3	16.1	13.7	15.6	13.2	13.9	11.8	15.5
7	13.7	11.1	10.0	17.7	11.2	17.2	10.7	15.7	10.7	14.7	9.2	16.2
8	21.3	10.1	9.3	24.2	9.9	19.4	11.2	15.1	9.4	16.5	9.3	16.6
Teachers	40.8	4.3	1.9	47.7	9.9[a]	[a]	13.6	10.4	3.5	12.1	4.3	12.3

Notes.—Items: Here are some "guess who" questions about the Republicans and the Democrats. Put an X in the box beside each question to show your guess. Alternatives, (1) Republicans; (2) Democrats; (3) Both about the same; (4) Don't know.

—N ranged from 1443 to 1788 for students; for teachers, from 372 to 375.

—Significance Unit: 3%.

   a. This item not included in teachers' questionnaire.

once again that there is often a lack of understanding of the role of conflict and cleavage in children at the end of the eighth grade.

Political parties are first associated with candidates who are identified as Democrat or Republican. Just as children's first contact with government is the President, so their first understanding of political parties comes when they label Presidential candidates or incumbents as either Democrats or Republicans. The percentage of children who can correctly identify the party to which the President belongs is surprisingly high—surprisingly, since political parties are relatively unfamiliar to young children (see Appendix E, table E.01). Children perceive little difference between the parties in their handling of issues, but political candidates are seen as very different from each other. Socialization of attitudes toward political parties apparently occurs in conjunction with the description or labeling of a candidate.

Some children use political party as a convenient concept for categorizing persons connected with the political world. The organizations standing behind these candidates, the different positions taken by the parties, and the population groups to whom they appeal have little importance in childrens' perception. Because they equate a party with its candidates, young children believe that parties are different. The slightly older elementary-school child sees very little difference between the parties in regard to their position on issues. He does not believe that they espouse different ideologies or cater to primarily different groups, and he denies conflict between them. A few eighth-graders can distinguish the Democrats' traditional position as supporter of the working classes from the Republicans' support of upper classes, but this is not true for the majority of children at that age. This ideological split does not show clearly except in the data from teachers.

Judgments of the value of conflict and differentiations between the parties are presented in Fig. 17. Conflict between parties is as undesirable as conflict between candidates. The national sample not only denied party conflict but also believed that it would be injurious to the nation. This view was not identical with that of teachers, who were better able to tolerate conflicting viewpoints. The discrepancy on this item is one of the most marked pupil-teacher differences in these data. This demonstrates with particular forcefulness the child's need to see the political world as one in which unity and harmony prevail. Perhaps the comments of an eighth-grade girl illustrate this view of the lack of difference between the parties:

"How do the parties differ?"
"Well, basically they both want the same things—just peace and happiness and want our country to be free. And as far as some decisions are, I think they have different opinions. Basically they are the same."

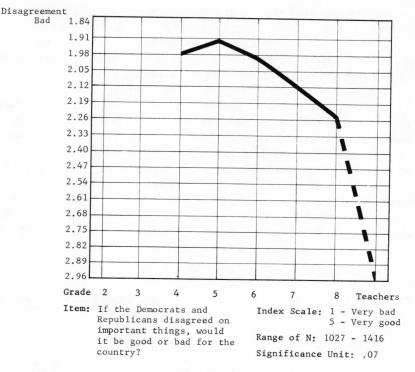

Disagreement
Bad

Grade 2   3   4   5   6   7   8   Teachers

Item: If the Democrats and
Republicans disagreed on
important things, would
it be good or bad for the
country?

Index Scale: 1 - Very bad
5 - Very good

Range of N: 1027 - 1416

Significance Unit: .07

Fig. 17.
**Comparison of means of grades 4 through 8 in attitudes
toward interparty disagreement.**

This tendency to see little differentiation also holds for children who do
not attribute such benign intent to the objectives of the two parties, as
Danny's comments, quoted at the beginning of this section, illustrate.

Children believe that partisan commitment should be deferred until
adulthood. Belief that it is important for adults to belong to political
parties is widespread and changes very little with age (Appendix E,
Fig. E.02). Teachers, when compared with eighth-graders, believe that
it is slightly *less* important for adults to belong to parties. It is also
clear from responses to the question, "When should someone make up
his mind which party to belong to?" that many children believe partisan
political activity should be postponed until adulthood. Less than 25
per cent of the children at all grade levels believed that this choice
should be made before high-school graduation. Teachers replied they
would encourage children to put off this choice until after they are old
enough to vote.

The ambivalence of children's beliefs about political parties is evident from the kind of political party support they advocate. Although parties are good things and adults should belong to them, this commitment to a party is not sufficient reason for straight-ticket voting. Confusion is produced by the conflict between choosing candidates on independent grounds and supporting the party of one's choice. The children in this research group were simultaneously socialized toward independence and toward the desirability of partisan commitment. When asked whether the good citizen should "Make up his mind to be a Democrat or a Republican and always vote the way his party does," or "Not join either the Democrats or Republicans and vote for the man he thinks is best," older children selected the latter response (Table 18). Among fourth-graders, these two choices were of roughly equal popularity; by grade eight, three children in four selected the candidate-oriented response. Eighty-seven per cent of teachers also chose this response. To older children, voting is an idealized quality of our system and should be untainted by partisan concerns.

Table 18
Changes by Grade in Basis of the Good Citizen's Candidate Preference

Grade level	N	Join party and always vote for its candidate	Not join party; vote for men he thinks are best
4	1035	48.8%	51.2%
5	1321	40.6	59.3
6	1556	35.3	64.7
7	1591	34.1	65.9
8	1588	26.4	73.6
Teachers	350	12.6	87.4

Notes.—Item: Which of the following is the best citizen? Put an X beside the sentence that describes the best citizen: (1) He makes up his mind to be either a Democrat or a Republican and always votes the way his party does; (2) He doesn't join either the Democrats or the Republicans and votes for the man he thinks is best.
—Significance Unit: 4%.

Some additional evidence of our group's candidate orientation comes from an item on the pilot study, "How a candidate will run the country is more important than which party he belongs to." [17] In grades six and eight, most of the children (80 per cent) agreed with this statement. The children are socialized, possibly by teachers, away from a belief in partisan guidance and toward the belief that it is each citizen's responsibility to judge the merits of all candidates.

Children come to believe that family loyalty is not an appropriate basis for deciding which party to support. There is a drop in agreement

17. Pilot Study 6.

with the statement, "It is better if young people belong to the same political party as their parents" (Table 19). This is most striking when teachers are compared with eighth-graders.

Table 19
Changes by Grade in Choice of Parents as Models for Party Choice

Grade level	N	It is better to choose same party as parents	It is not better to choose same party as parents
3	1452	60.9%	39.1%
4	1537	67.2	32.8
5	1788	66.1	33.9
6	1740	62.9	37.1
7	1712	55.3	44.7
8	1654	48.5	51.5
Teachers	373	17.6	82.4

Notes.—Item: It is better if young people belong to the same political party as their parents. Choose one. (1) Yes; (2) No; (3) Don't know.
—Significance Unit: 3%.
—Children who chose "Don't know" were excluded from the computation of percentages.

Another question in the national questionnaire inquired directly about the appropriate sources of *information* about voting. Children were asked where they would search for advice about whom to vote for if they could vote. The alternative, "Make up my own mind," received an increasing number of choices with age—31 per cent at grade four, 53 per cent at grade eight (Table 20). The percentage who would look to parents as models for their choice of candidates decreased with age. No other source received more than 10 per cent of the choices at any grade level. Children are apparently socialized to believe that although one may at some time vote as his parents, teacher, or minister vote, one should make up his mind independently.

The source of basic information which these children intend to use to find out the candidates' stands on issues is unclear; the mass media (television, newspapers, etc.) were not highly valued as sources of voting information, though their valuation is beginning to increase at grade eight. Teachers apparently socialize the ideal that rational assessment of issues and candidates is important, but are not successful in teaching children what sources are most useful in obtaining information about candidates or in providing them with realistic criteria to use in making a judgment.

The cluster of attitudes surrounding political independence is present in the majority of children only after the middle elementary-school years. Young school children believe that all the world is divided into Democrats and Republicans, that the parties are identified by their support for a particular candidate, that one's parents are adequate models for partisanship, and that partisan commitment is a legitimate basis for making voting decisions.

Table 20
Changes by Grade in Choosing Source of Advice about Candidates

Grade level	N	Father	Mother	Mother and father	Teacher	Make up my own mind	Peer	Minister	Radio and TV	Magazines and newspapers
4	1231	7.8%	3.1%	46.8%	1.3%	31.0%	1.3%	3.7%	3.2%	1.7%
5	1644	6.3	2.7	44.3	1.2	36.4	1.2	2.4	3.4	2.1
6	1643	4.6	2.1	32.0	1.0	47.3	.6	2.6	5.2	4.8
7	1634	5.8	1.8	26.6	.9	49.3	.7	3.0	4.4	7.6
8	1589	4.5	1.4	20.8	1.6	52.7	1.1	1.8	4.7	11.4

Notes.—Item: If you could vote, where would be the best place to look for help in making up your mind who to vote for? Choose one.
—Significance Unit: 3%.

PARTICIPATION IN ELECTIONS

Elections are highly visible events in the child's experience. A pilot inquiry revealed that voting was seen as the most influential activity by 48 per cent of fourth graders, 59 per cent of sixth-graders, and 65 per cent of seventh- and eighth-graders.[18]

The awareness that voting privileges are limited to adults does not mean that children believe it necessary to postpone interest and activity in politics entirely. Some children participate in political activities as early as the third grade, and there is a gradual increase through the eighth grade in the number of children who report these activities. Although non-voting activities open to children in campaigns are limited, this research group reported participation in the areas which are appropriate. Table 21 and Fig. 18 present data from three questions asking whether the child has participated in activities around the time of elections. Reading about candidates in the mass media showed the sharpest increase with age (probably as children's reading skills improve). Exposure to the image of candidates in these publications was

18. Pilot Study 10. Frey (1966) in his studies of other nations suggests many contrasts to the data presented here on the United States.

reported by more than 90 per cent of the students in grades six through eight, and by 100 per cent of the teachers. Wearing a campaign button to proclaim the candidate of one's choice was less frequently reported

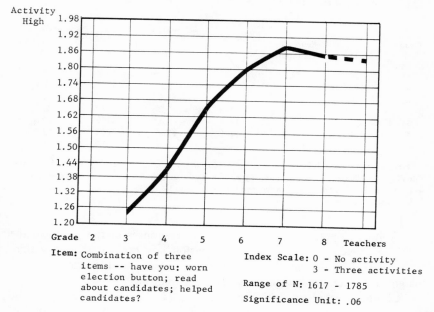

Item: Combination of three items -- have you: worn election button; read about candidates; helped candidates?

Index Scale: 0 - No activity
3 - Three activities

Range of N: 1617 - 1785

Significance Unit: .06

Fig. 18.
Comparison of means of grades 3 through 8 in political activity.

as an activity, though it also increased in a cumulative fashion.[19] Approximately 60 per cent of eighth-graders reported this activity. Giving out handbills or buttons was reported least frequently, as one might expect, and it showed only a slight increase during the elementary grades. These three items have been combined into Fig. 18, an index of political activity. (See Appendix C.)

Taking sides in an election is a prominent aspect of children's political behavior. An important indication of the involvement of children in the political life of the United States is the degree of interest displayed in national contests at election time. The field testing of the national study took place a year and a half after the 1960 Presidential election,

19. Another national test item which showed no age changes inquired why the subject thinks boys and girls wore campaign buttons. The alternative which received more than 60 per cent of the choices at all grades was "because they thought it would help their candidate win." Wearing a campaign button is a politicized activity even for children.

Table 21
Changes by Grade in Participation in Political Activities
(Percentages answering "Yes" for each type of activity)

Grade level	N	Read about candidates	N	Wore a campaign button	N	Handed out buttons and handbills
3	1651	59.7%	1645	43.5%	1646	21.6%
4	1734	75.0	1735	45.9	1735	20.9
5	1798	87.5	1797	56.8	1792	22.4
6	1743	91.9	1743	62.2	1737	26.1
7	1717	95.1	1715	65.4	1717	28.6
8	1690	95.0	1688	63.4	1689	26.9
Teachers	380	100.0	377	49.3	372	34.7

Notes.—Items: (34) I have worn a button for a candidate, (1) Yes; (2) No. (35) I have helped a candidate by doing things for him—such as handing out buttons and papers with his name on them; (38) I have read about a candidate in newspapers or magazines. —Significance Unit: 3%.

providing an opportunity to examine the responses of the group to the partisan aspects of this contest. Television coverage of the campaign, particularly the debates between Kennedy and Nixon, made the campaign and election struggle a uniquely visible one.

Children's concern with the outcome of the election matches the reactions of adults in its emotional tone (Table 22). A very small and constant proportion, ranging between 14 and 18 per cent, claimed they were not interested in the election outcome. Most children did choose sides. At all grade levels, the proportion who reported that they were "happy" when Kennedy won was considerably larger than the proportion who reported that they were "unhappy." Few teachers reported they were unconcerned with the outcome, and they were somewhat more equally divided between positive and negative reaction than the children. As stated earlier, students believe that one must support the elected candidate even if one did not vote for him. This may have led to a more positive recollection of the election than justified by the actual feeling at the time. In summary, it appears that the election itself had a strong impact on many children and may in itself have been a socializing experience.[20]

Party affiliation is usually not acquired until late in the elementary school years; the proportion of children who report that they would vote independently of partisan affiliation is large and increases with age. A more abstract kind of side-taking involves the child's perception of

20. The tendency to become emotionally involved in the election has a definite association with other types of involvement (see Chapter Nine).

Table 22
Changes by Grade in Emotional Responses to Kennedy's Election

Grade level	N	Very happy	Happy	Didn't care	Felt bad	Felt so bad I almost cried
3	1445	49.7%	12.9%	14.5%	17.8%	5.1%
4	1537	42.9	13.5	18.0	20.4	5.2
5	1591	39.1	14.0	17.7	24.8	4.3
6	1513	37.4	18.4	14.9	24.2	5.1
7	1496	35.0	17.8	14.4	28.8	4.1
8	1606	33.4	21.8	14.1	26.2	4.6
Teachers	331	23.9	28.4	9.7	32.9	5.1

Notes.—Item: When I heard Kennedy won the election over Nixon . . . (mark the one which is closest to the way you felt at that time).
—Significance Unit: 3%.

himself as a member of one of the major political parties rather than merely supporting the candidate of his choice at election time. Information reported earlier indicated that children do not believe that party commitment is appropriate for them until after high-school graduation. However, the child was asked to *imagine* himself an adult of voting age: "If you could vote, what would you be. . . . ?" Party preferences for all grades are shown in Table 23.

Two features of these data are of particular interest. First, 55 per cent of the second-graders either did not know what "Democrat" and "Republican" are, or did not know what party they would choose. This proportion fell to 15 per cent at grade eight. Political party divisions are quite unimportant to a child when he thinks about the other children in his classroom. More than 55 per cent of the children in all grades said they did not know which party was supported by most of the children they knew. There was no increase with age in sensitivity to partisan affiliation of classmates.

The second aspect to be noted is the increasing proportion of children who reported independence of party loyalty. The belief that one will not be committed to a single party when one is an adult, and lack of feelings of commitment to a party during childhood probably reflect socialization by the school. The 32 per cent of this sample who reported political independence of this type is slightly larger than the largest of the recent estimates of the number of independents in the adult population (Agger, 1959). The 55 per cent of teachers who reported that they were not committed to a single party (but were sometimes Democrats, sometimes Republicans) is also large.

Adults very frequently report they follow the party which their

Table 23
Changes by Grade in Party Preference

Grade level	N	Republican	Democrat	Sometimes Democrat, sometimes Republican	Don't know which	Don't know what Democrat and Republican mean
2	1639	22.4%	13.4%	9.4%	21.1%	33.7%
3	1668	24.8	17.2	10.2	19.8	28.1
4	1738	30.1	19.0	15.0	16.9	19.0
5	1794	30.0	25.2	21.5	14.5	8.8
6	1744	28.2	28.8	26.0	12.6	4.5
7	1715	24.5	31.9	28.6	12.5	2.6
8	1685	20.5	32.5	31.6	13.8	1.6
Teachers	383	19.8	23.8	55.4	1.0	a

Notes.—Item: If you could vote what would you be? Choose one.
—Significance Unit: 3%.
a. No DK alternative.

parents supported (Hyman, 1959). In the pre-final testing, conducted with second- through eighth-graders in two cities, questions not only about the child's party commitment but also his perception of his parents' political partisanship were included. Between 30 and 55 per cent of the children at all grade levels reported that their father was committed to the same party they had chosen. This correspondence rose slightly with age. A very small percentage, never more than 8 per cent and clustering around 4 per cent, reported that their father belonged to the Democratic party while they belonged to the Republican party, or vice versa. With age, an increasingly large percentage reported either they and their father were independent in party orientation or that their father was committed to a party while they were independent. Although these children did not think they should choose a party on the basis of their parents' choice, more than half were in fact committed to the same party as their fathers, while a very small percentage were aligned with the other party.

These data suggest that the Identification Model is probably accurate to account for the partisan preference of the majority of children. This identification with parental party seems to be accomplished without the simultaneous acquisition of consistent beliefs about what stands a political party takes on issues; there is no increase with grade in the consistency between a child's partisan commitment and his belief about which party does most for the country.[21] There is an increase with

21. Torney (1965) presents a more complete discussion of the meaning of partisan consistency and differentiation based on the data from this project.

grade, however, in consistency between one's party affiliation and one's feelings about the results of the election (Torney, 1965). This is a further indication of the important linkage between the perception of candidates in elections and the acquisition of a meaningful partisan affiliation.

SUMMARY

The pattern of age changes during the elementary-school years is clear evidence that much of the process of political socialization occurs at the pre-high school level. In each of the five areas, there is a characteristic pattern of change in children's attitudes from grade two to grade eight.

The child's relationship to the country is established early and depends heavily on national symbols such as the flag and the Statue of Liberty. The child's attachment to the governmental system is achieved through attachment to personal figures, particularly the President. This feeling of positive regard is later transferred to institutions of the system as these objects become more clearly defined. Changes in the child's conceptualization of the government parallel the perception of his own relationship to it.

Induction into a pattern of compliance with authority and law occurs through visible authority figures—the President and the local policeman. The young child believes that punishment is an inevitable consequence of wrongdoing, but this view declines with age in favor of a more realistic opinion. In general, children have a positive image of the policeman and see him as helpful; however, they also see him as a somewhat more fear-inspiring figure than parental authority.

Information about the rights of citizens and a consequent sense of efficacy develop relatively late in the elementary-school years. The basis for this emerging sense of efficacy is probably the implicit trust that children have in the benevolence of government. However, many types of influence are unfamiliar to the child. He knows little about the role of pressure *groups* in legislation and formation of policy and has a very high opinion of the power of the *individual* citizen. Older children see citizen involvement as important; this is matched by an increasing tendency for children to enage in political activities as they grow older. By the end of elementary school, most children have acquired some interest in government and have participated in discussions about its policies.

Increasingly with age, children see voting as the most central feature of our governmental processes and recognize the citizen's obligation to vote. Their understanding of the role of political parties in elections is vague and tends to develop relatively late, probably because of a lack of instruction in the schools. The child's party preference most frequently matches his family's and is apparently facilitated by the child's identification of favored candidates as belonging to one party or the other. However, the majority of children believe that firm commitment to a party should be deferred until adulthood. The proportion of children who report that they would vote independently of party affiliation is large and increases with age. Children begin engaging in political activities, such as wearing campaign buttons, in the early grades; the number of politically active children increases through the eighth grade.

Several models of socialization are required to explain these patterns of age change. Some age trends fit the Accumulation Model, especially the growth in the number of attitudes about the system, indicated by the decrease in "Don't Know" scores. The development of other clusters of attitudes, such as affiliation with the President, cannot be explained by an Accumulation Model; nor can the child's attachment to the nation be seen in terms of an accumulation process. The young child holds strong feelings about these objects without much information about them. Also, the changes with age are in the direction of less positive feeling. These feelings are modified downward (negatively) as they approximate the adult pattern. These growth curves appear to be explained more appropriately by the Interpersonal Transfer Model. The Identification Model is most appropriate for understanding the acquisition of political party preference. Other attitudes, such as the conceptions of institutions and processes of government, are too abstract for most young children to grasp and probably could not be taught at an early age. Growth in the importance of these conceptions is perhaps best explained by a Cognitive-developmental Model, which underscores the child's increasing ability to deal with abstractions.

5

The Family and
the School as Agents
of Socialization

In the complex process of acquiring the behavior of the adult community in which he is reared, the child is influenced by several groups and individuals who do not necessarily agree in their attitudes toward political figures or public policy issues. There are some issues on which almost all groups in the community are united (such as respect for the flag, obedience to law, loyalty to country), but there are other issues on which a variety of views is presented to the child. Socialization of political behavior produces diverse attitudes on most of the topics with which this study dealt. The previous chapter dealt with variations in these political attitudes observed in children of different ages. There were also wide response differences among children within each grade group. It is the purpose of this chapter and the next to present evidence of variation in children's perceptions at any given age period and to describe some of the systematic influences which bring about this range of response.

Not all changes and individual differences occurring in children's political attitudes can be traced to direct socialization pressure. Socialization contexts are of three general types. The first type includes *institutions* of well-defined structure and organization—the family, the school, and the church—which influence children by direct teaching of political attitudes and values (Accumulation Model). Such institutions also induct them into the behavior and roles appropriate to family, school, or church membership. These values, behavior, and roles may then be generalized to attitudes toward the political life of the community and nation. A role may mediate between one situation or system in which learning takes place and another in which that learning is directly or indirectly applied. Particularly because a child does not have direct experience in the political arena, his experience in non-political roles is an important influence upon the later development of role relationships within the political system, assuming that transferral occurs. For example, parents teach children regard for authority and the rules of the family group, which are then translated into respect for law and political authority figures. This is illustrated by the tendency for children in early grades to confuse such family-imposed rules as, "Brush your teeth every morning," with more formal laws. Early experience in the family orients the child toward authority and law and in this way anticipates political socialization. Similar illustrations apply to the child's experience in the school and church, where both formal teaching of values and concrete experience of participation give the child orientations which are transferred to behavior in the political system. This type of indirect learning follows the Interpersonal Transfer Model presented in Chapter One and is especially significant in the formation of attachment to governmental figures and in compliance to laws.

The second type of socializing influence occurs in larger social settings. The most important of these social contexts are social class, ethnic origin, and geographical region. They are diffuse in the sense that the specific elements and experiences connected with them are numerous, subtle, and difficult to measure precisely. The social-class context has been described by several social scientists (Bronfenbrenner, 1958; Davis, 1948; Hess and Shipman, 1965; Kohn, 1959, 1963; Miller and Swanson, 1958; Warner, 1959) some of whom have analyzed the way in which social class influences behavior. This presentation assumes that a broad categorization, such as social class, is not a variable in the usual sense, but rather a general category indicating and subsuming several more specific influences, attitudes, interpersonal experiences, and types of roles. Because of the diffuse nature of the social class influence, the various models of socialization are all represented in the learning process.[1]

A third type of influence in the socializing process derives from the child's personal characteristics. These *individual characteristics* influence socializing efforts of the family, school, and other agents and limit the extent of learning. Socialization is not exerted upon a passive receptive object. Each child's emotional, intellectual, and physical properties modify the images, attitudes, and information transmitted to him by adults. The most salient influencing factor is intelligence. Much of political socialization occurs in school; the child's mental capacity mediates his comprehension of material presented in the classroom. Personal needs also play an important part. Individual differences in compliance and dependency needs may alter the child's perception of government's role in assisting and protecting the citizen. Children differ in character-

1. The socializing influence peculiar to a geographical region or to membership in an ethnic group is also diffuse, resulting from an interplay of many variables. Obviously, traditions and historical events are very powerful, as in differences within this country over the issues of integration and states' rights. The reasons for omitting discussion of differences between regions and between ethnic groups in this report are covered in Appendix A.

istics which mediate their understanding of the world. Intelligence limits their comprehension of what is taught in school; sex role mediates other experiences.

Comprehensive examination of the ways in which a child transforms and selectively accepts teachings would require intensive case studies, such as those by Lane (1959) and by Smith, Bruner, and White (1956). Their studies illustrated and elaborated on the importance of internal, dynamic elements of personality in the socializing process. This project had somewhat different objectives; data were based on self-report and were drawn from relatively large research groups in order to examine group trends and differences. Hence, information about children's individual qualities is somewhat limited.

Systems Acting as Agents of Socialization

ROLE OF THE FAMILY IN POLITICAL SOCIALIZATION

Introduction. Students of personality development and human behavior frequently regard the family as the most important agent of socialization, a unique context in which children acquire values and behavioral patterns. This view may be valid within certain areas of behavior, but it is not adequate as a model for the development of attitudes toward political objects or the growth of active political involvement. The data of this study raise several questions about the efficacy of the family as contrasted with other socializing agents, although there is certainly some family influence.

The family unit, especially the parents, participates in the socialization of political perceptions and attitudes in three ways. First, parents transmit attitudes which they consider valuable for their child to hold. The family may operate as one of several teaching agents imparting attitudes or values which reflect community consensus; that is, the family reinforces other institutions. Since the attitudes imparted are similar or identical to those transmitted by other groups and institutions, it is difficult to determine accurately the family's influence compared to that of other agents. Some attitudes which children acquire in these areas of high consensus are well known and perhaps taken for granted— feelings of loyalty, respect for the symbols of government (especially the flag, Statue of Liberty, and Uncle Sam), and the kind of behavior expected of the citizen (especially compliance to law). Also, the family transmits attitudes which represent differences of opinion existing within the community. In some cases this involves taking a position on a current issue (for example, civil rights, federal aid to education). In transmitting a position on a current issue, a family competes with some agents holding different views and is supported by other agents. This type of attitude transmission promotes and maintains the disagreement and division characteristic of our political life. The family may also transmit idiosyncratic attitudes; that is, those which do not correspond to any recognized or defined division within the community. All of these types of attitude acquisition correspond to the Accumulation Model.

The family also presents examples that children may emulate (Identification Model). Probably the most significant socialization of this kind involves parental affiliation with a political party. Despite some variability in reported data, there is evidence that the family exerts an important influence upon the child's party preference (Hyman, 1959). Remmers and Weltman (1947), in studying preferences of high school youth and their parents, reported correlations of .8 and .9. Socialization of partisan preference is apparently well-established before voting age, and frequently follows that of the parents. These results are supported by retrospective studies of parent's party preferences which report the child's tendency to identify with his parents' party—or at least to report that he has done so (Campbell, Gurin, and Miller, 1954; Hyman, 1959; Maccoby, Matthews, and Morton, 1954). These results reaffirm the hypothesis that children follow the party preference of their parents in at least three-fourths of the cases in which both parents are affiliated with the same party. Also following the Identification Model, children may become politically active if their parents are active. Children may learn to value modes of political involvement which they observe in their parents (see Stark, 1957). Adults vary markedly in the extent of their political activity, a majority of them performing only the voting act and displaying little interest otherwise (Woodward and Roper, 1950). Children may therefore have only limited opportunity to observe their parents in political pursuits.

A third possibility is that expectations formed from experience in family relationships are later generalized to political objects (Interpersonal Transfer Model). The home provides the child's first and most lasting experience with interaction in a hierarchic social system. Through this experience, children develop relationships, expectations, and behavior patterns. A child becomes attached to the family unit through attachment to its individual members, relates to the hierarchy of authority and learns compliance to its regulations, thus establishing a frame of reference by which to approach systems he will later encounter.

The structure of family power not only influences the child's relationship to the system (Bronfenbrenner, 1961; Hoffman, 1961; Kagan, 1958) but also mediates class differences in personality and attitudes (Kohn, 1959, 1963). Families in which the father plays a strong, dominant role encourage in the child a different attitude toward authority than do mother-dominated families. Investigations of families from which the father is absent for long periods of time have indicated that personality differences may be expected, particularly in boys (Bach, 1946; Tiller, 1958). Here, the nature of transmitted attitudes and values does not necessarily differ, but specific experiences with an authority system do affect later relationships to governmental authority.

Data. The following types of analysis were performed to assess family influence on political socialization: (1) comparison of the attitudinal similarity among siblings with that occurring in pairs of unrelated children matched by social class and grade; (2) examination of the effect of absence of the father on attitude development; (3) analysis of the relationship between the children's perceptions of the family power structure and characteristics and certain political variables.

In examining these data, two questions were considered: (1) What evidence is there that the family socializes non-consensus attitudes, such as those toward a Presidential incumbent or party affiliation, by presenting models of partisan affiliation or political involvement? (2) What evidence is there that family structure or characteristics are important in creating orientations toward political affairs or political authority?

ROLE OF THE FAMILY IN SOCIALIZATION OF DIVISION

Responses of sibling pairs were studied to assess the accumulated effect of family in transmitting attitudes. If the similarity between siblings was greater than that in pairs of children not from the same family, matched on relevant characteristics, it would be evidence for the effect of family influence. Sibling similarities should be particularly obvious in those attitudes which reflect well-defined variation between families (for example, party and candidate preferences). In areas where the family teaches attitudes shared by the community, the expectation was that siblings would not resemble one another more than they resembled unrelated children of the same grade, sex, social class, and school as their sibling.

Using school records, all the sibling pairs were identified among children tested in two cities of the study. The younger child of each pair was also matched with an unrelated child of the same school, sex, grade, and social status as his older sibling. To avoid confounding age trends with possible dissimilarities based on family teaching, the groups of siblings and random pairs were subdivided into four categories: sibling pairs with small age difference formed one group, those with large age difference another; this was done with the unrelated pairs as well. These groups were also subdivided by social class to control the possible difference in family influence attributable to parents' educational level or other class-related factors.

Similarities among children in the same family are confined to partisanship and related attitudes. Responses of the pairs in these groups were correlated for each of the 113 scaled items. The median coefficient for the total groups of siblings was .05, and that for the randomly chosen group was .01 (Table 24). For the total sibling group, only five correlations of .21 or above appeared; the sibling correlation on the item which inquired about feelings concerning Kennedy's election was .50.

From the perspective of political socialization, the family's primary effect is to support consensually held attitudes rather than to inculcate idiosyncratic attitudes. The presence of some family effect of a general nature upon attitudes is indicated by the relatively greater number of sibling correlations that exceeded chance expectations. The number of correlations that appeared between matched unrelated pairs was close to the number expected by chance, over a series of such comparisons. The number of correlations appearing in the sibling pairs, while not large, nevertheless was consistently greater than the number in the unrelated group.

Table 24
Sibling Resemblances in Political Attitudes

Group	No. of pairs	Proportion of significant correlations [a]
Total sibling pairs	205	12.6
Total randomly matched pairs	205	2.7
Low status sibling pairs	100	8.9
Low status randomly matched pairs	100	7.1
High status sibling pairs	100	12.5
High status randomly matched pairs	100	5.7
Sibling pairs with small age difference (two grades or less)	135	16.1
Random pairs with small age difference	135	3.6
Sibling pairs with large age difference (more than two grades)	65	10.7
Random pairs with large age difference	65	5.4

a. Based on 113 items; significance level $p < .05$. This analysis was done early in the study and did not include those indices on which later analyses were based.

In one area the family does appear to transmit its own attitude. In four of the five groupings, the sibling correlation was .48 or above for the item which asked about feelings after learning of Kennedy's election.[2] This sibling similarity supplements other evidence that many children identify with their parents' party. The responses to this item reveal a familial similarity that goes beyond party affiliation to include competitive and emotional involvement with a candidate in a national election. The effect of this commitment on political attitudes is described elsewhere in this chapter and the next.

INTERPERSONAL TRANSFER AND MODELING:
THE INFLUENCE OF FAMILY STRUCTURE
AND POWER CHARACTERISTICS

Family structure. Data concerning the direct effect of family structure upon socialization are limited and will be reported briefly. The testing instrument included an item inquiring about the presence or absence of a father or mother in the home. In very few families was the mother absent, but 12 per cent of the children came from homes without fathers. On the hypothesis that attitudes toward authority stem, in part, from experience with paternal authority, children from father-absent homes were compared with children from homes with both parents present. This comparison showed no difference between the two groups that could not be attributed to chance.

Perceptions of the family. It is apparent from extensive research (summarized by Schaefer, 1961) that two major dimensions order relationships within the family: attachment or support, and power or control. These also form the basic outline of the political relationships presented in this book. A factor analysis of correlations between the scale ratings of family and non-family figures was performed. An affect or attachment grouping of items (including "I like him," "He protects me," "He is my favorite") and a grouping of power items (including "Can make anyone do what he wants," "Can punish anyone," and "Makes important decisions") appeared clearly for ratings of the father. These item sets represent the separation of supportive and affective qualities from qualities of power and control. Similar item groupings appeared in the correlations of the scales for the President and the policeman. The child apparently learns to judge family members along these two dimensions of power and affection; he transfers these *dimensions of relationship* into perceptions of his relationships with figures of the larger political system.

Does the child transfer or generalize the content and direction of specific judgments of his father to perceptions of members of the political system? Does he relate to the President as he relates to his father?

2. No item inquiring directly about partisan affiliation was included in these correlations.

Correlations of the father ratings with ratings of other figures indicate that the father items co-varied among themselves to a much greater extent than they co-varied with perceptions of other figures. This and other evidence (Torney, 1965) support the conclusion that there are essentially two groupings in the child's world: the family figure (father) and all non-family political figures. Although they are judged on the same basic dimensions, non-family political figures are viewed as considerably more similar to each other than they are viewed as similar to family figures.

Comparison of the father items with items for other figures, however, revealed that children who rated their father high also tended to rate non-family figures high. These differences must be interpreted cautiously because of the possibility that some children used the extreme response alternatives excessively. Because there was little difference among children in their attachment to their fathers (between 60 and 70 per cent at all grade levels said that their father was their favorite of all), relationships are reported only between perceptions of the father's power and items of political orientation. This dimension was also chosen because there were four sources of information about fathers' power and the home atmosphere: the child's rating of whether his father "can make anyone do what he wants"; perception of who is "Boss in the family"; perception of the amount of interest his family has in current events; and perception of who teaches him most about citizenship.

Children from high-status families see their fathers as more powerful in the family and as more instrumental teachers of citizen attitudes than do lower-status children. The ratings of the father showed pronounced social-class differences; for example, lower-status children rated their fathers lower on ability to make others do what they tell them than upper-status children (Fig. 19).[3] This may result from the child's knowledge about his father's occupational role—an awareness that middle- and upper-class jobs carry more prestige and power. Perception of the parents' interest in government also varied by social class (Fig. 20). Children from homes of lower and middle social status viewed their parents as less interested in government and current events than did children from higher-status homes. These findings indicate differences in the home atmosphere in different social classes, particularly in the perceived political involvement and interest of the parents and the perception of the father's authority. Children of lower social status also tend to be oriented toward the school (represented by the teacher) as the agent of citizenship training, rather than toward the home (represented

3. The relatively small number which represents the lower limit of the Range of N in certain figures in this chapter and the next results from two factors: some questions were not administered at grade 3; the correlation between some independent variables meant that some group sizes were reduced. For all graphs, group sizes cluster at top not bottom of reported Range of N.

by the father; Fig. 21). Not only does the lower-class child perceive his father as lower in status (of lower power and less interested in politics), but these children do not regard their fathers as potential sources of information about politics and citizenship.

What other associations do these items show with political behavior and attitudes? Briefly, the child who has a strong father tends to be more attached to figures and institutions in the political system, particularly the President and the policeman, than the child whose father is relatively weak. A set of items in the area of political participation and involvement also was related to these aspects of family atmosphere. In most cases, these political items also showed some social-class divergencies. The differences in family structure which are characteristic of the various classes may be one of the most important mediators of differences between socioeconomic groups.

Children who see their fathers as powerful tend to be more informed and interested in political matters. The citizen's role as a force in the political system is influenced by adult models within his family. Evidence for this is summarized in Table 25. The congruence of these trends, based on three different items used as indicators of family structure, shows that having active and powerful male role models is important in the development of active political involvement (particularly for boys). Having a father who asserts himself in family matters makes children more able to perceive themselves as active in the political world. More information about family perceptions is presented in Figs. 22 and 23. Children who rated their fathers low and family interest low tended to give more "Don't Know" responses. That is, they had acquired fewer political attitudes. Families in which parents are distinctly uninterested in political affairs and where there is no active male figure have children who do not develop political orientations as rapidly as other children.

COGNITIVE PROCESSES IN POLITICAL SOCIALIZATION: ROLE OF THE SCHOOL

Teachers' evaluation of the politically relevant curriculum. The public school appears to be the most important and effective instrument of political socialization in the United States. It reinforces other community institutions and contributes a cognitive dimension to political involvement. As an agent of socialization it operates through classroom instruction and ceremonies. It is important, therefore, to assess the impact of the school by an analysis of teachers' views of the civics curriculum and of its effects on the children whom they teach.

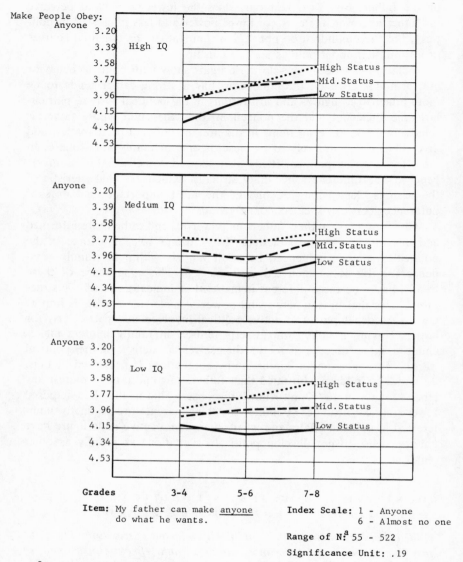

Fig. 19.

Comparison of means of social status groups in rating coercive power of fathers, within IQ and grade.

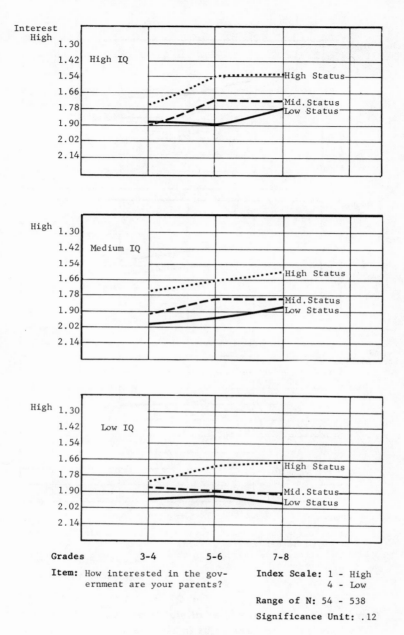

Fig. 20.

Comparison of means of social status groups in reported amount of parents' political interest, within IQ and grade.

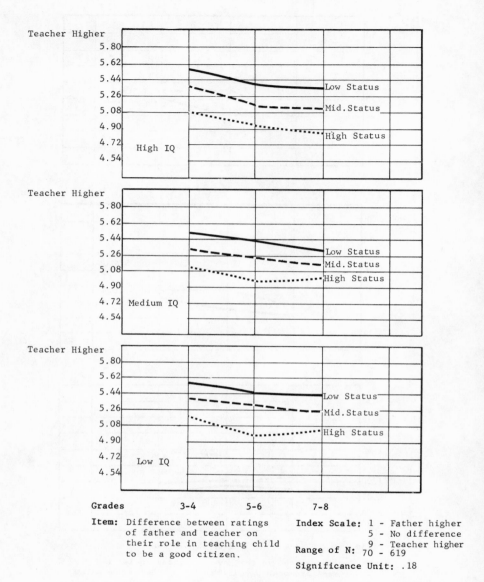

Fig. 21

Comparison of means of social status groups in differentiating fathers' and teachers' roles in citizenship training, within IQ and grade.

Table 25
Relation of Family Characteristics to Report of Political Involvement

RELATIVE POSITION ON INDICES

Family characteristic	Sense of efficacy	Political interest	Participation in political discussion	Political activities	Concern about political issues
Mother dominant [a]	Lower (in boys only)	Lower (in boys only)	Lower (in boys only)	Lower (in boys only)	Slightly lower (in boys only)
Father low in power [b]	Slightly lower (in both sexes)	Lower (in both sexes)	Lower (in both sexes)	Lower (in both sexes)	Lower (in both sexes)
Family interest low [c]	Lower (in all social classes)	Lower (in all social classes)	Lower (in all social classes)	Lower (in all social classes)	Lower (in all social classes)

a. Item: Who is the boss in your family?
b. Item: Think of *your father* as he really is: Can make people do what he wants.
c. Item: Are your parents interested in current events and what happens in the government?

SOCIALIZATION OF LOYALTY

The schools reinforce the early attachment of the child to the nation. This reinforcement of patriotism is accomplished in a number of ways in the schools in which we tested—displaying the flag, repeating the pledge of allegiance, and singing patriotic songs.[4] In addition, in the majority of classrooms, pictures of historical figures, such as Washington and Lincoln, and of historic monuments or other symbols and sites of national interest were displayed. Many classrooms also contained a picture of Kennedy. The percentage of teachers who displayed these symbols and utilized these procedures as part of their daily classroom practice is shown in Table 26. It is interesting that rituals surrounding the flag and the pledge of allegiance are frequent throughout elementary school, while patriotic songs are less often a daily activity in classrooms for older pupils.

What is the effect of these patriotic rituals upon the young child? A typical first-grader does not understand the meaning of many words in the pledge of allegiance or the "Star-Spangled Banner." The questionnaire responses showed that a number of second-grade children believed the pledge of allegiance was a prayer to God. Whatever the child sees as the purpose of these daily routines, it is clear that they are highly valued by adults. (This is particularly evident whenever any group, such as Jehovah's Witnesses, refuses to pledge to the flag and in recent

4. The analysis of curriculum practices is based on responses from 121 teachers in the cities in which testing was done.

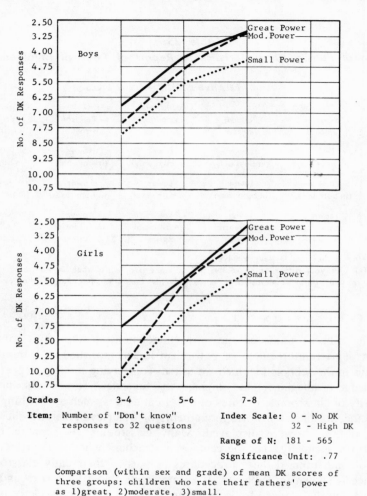

Item: Number of "Don't know"   Index Scale: 0 - No DK
      responses to 32 questions   32 - High DK

Range of N: 181 - 565

Significance Unit: .77

Comparison (within sex and grade) of mean DK scores of
three groups: children who rate their fathers' power
as 1)great, 2)moderate, 3)small.

Fig. 22.
Coercive power of father and acquisition of political attitudes.

incidents of flag burning.) The feeling of respect for the pledge and the
national anthem are reinforced daily and are seldom questioned by the
child. In addition to this basic tone of awe for government, two other
elements are important. The first is the attitude of submission, respect,
and dependence manifested in the gestures and words surrounding these
acts, and the second is the group nature of the behavior. These rituals
establish an emotional orientation toward country and flag even though
an understanding of the meaning of the words and actions has not been
developed. These seem to be indoctrinating acts that cue and reinforce

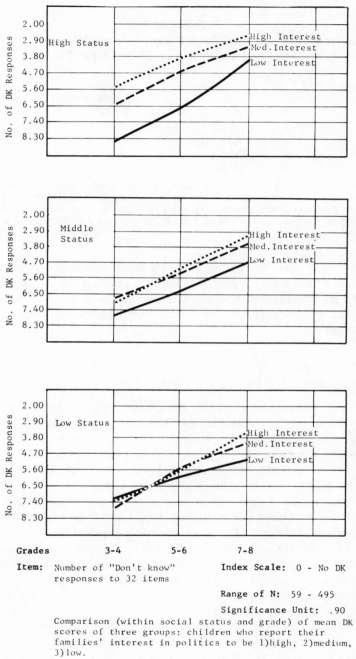

Grades   3-4   5-6   7-8

Item: Number of "Don't know"   Index Scale: 0 - No DK
         responses to 32 items

                                          Range of N: 59 - 495

                                          Significance Unit: .90
         Comparison (within social status and grade) of mean DK
         scores of three groups: children who report their
         families' interest in politics to be 1)high, 2)medium,
         3)low.

Fig. 23.
Family interest in politics—acquisition of political attitudes.

Table 26
Comparison of Teachers of Each Grade in Their Display of National Symbols and Participation in Patriotic Rituals

Grade-level taught	N	Display flag permanently	N	Pledge allegiance to flag daily	N	Sing patriotic song daily
2	24	100.0%	23	95.7%	24	58.3%
3-4	33	100.0	34	87.9	33	60.6
5-6	40	98.5	40	95.0	40	32.5
7-8	22	100.0	23	86.9	21	14.3

Note.—Items: In my classroom, we display the flag (choose one), (1) Permanently; (2) Only on special occasions; (3) Rarely or not at all. In my classroom, we say the Pledge of Allegiance (sing a patriotic song such as the "Star-Spangled Banner" or "America the Beautiful") (Choose one), (1) Every day; (2) Almost every day; (3) Once in a while; (4) Never.

feelings of loyalty and patriotism. This early orientation prepares the child for later learning and stresses the importance of loyalty for citizens of all ages. The process of socialization in later years can best be understood in the context of this early establishment of unquestioning patriotism.

SOCIALIZATION OF ORIENTATIONS TOWARD GOVERNMENTAL FIGURES AND INSTITUTIONS

The emphasis which teachers place upon topics other than patriotic observance is indicated in Fig. 24. The importance assigned to topics dealing with governmental persons (President, mayor, senator) and institutions (Supreme Court, Congress) is of particular interest. Both topics were ascribed more importance by teachers of grades five and six than by teachers of younger children. According to their reports, the stress upon these topics was even greater at grades seven and eight. While teachers placed increasing importance at higher grade levels upon the child's regard for the President, children's personal feelings about the President declined with age, and the rated attributes of the President's role increased only slightly. In addition, teachers of grades five through eight attributed approximately equal importance to teaching about the President and the senator, but children at all grade-levels expressed much less respect for the senator than for the President. Also, teachers of all grades viewed persons and institutions as approximately equal in importance as curriculum topics. Again, this did not coincide with children's orientations and attitudes as reported on the questionnaire. In contrast to the teachers' similar assessment of persons and institutions, older children attached greater importance to political institutions and a decreasing importance to persons. This disparity between children's responses and the importance teachers placed upon these subjects may indicate the role that the child's level of development plays in socialization (Cognitive-development Model). On another point, there is also

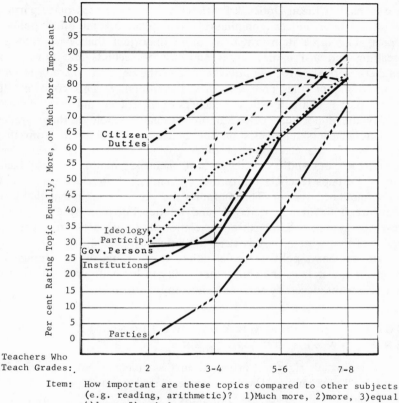

Item: How important are these topics compared to other subjects
         (e.g. reading, arithmetic)? 1)Much more, 2)more, 3)equal,
         4)less, 5)much less.

Fig. 24.

Comparison of teachers of different grade-levels in view that political topics are at least as important as other subjects taught in their classrooms.

some disparity between the young child's interest in political figures and the teachers' relatively low emphasis upon these figures in the curriculum. This suggests that teachers do not recognize these figures as useful aids in teaching about the operation of the political system.

SOCIALIZATION OF ATTITUDES TOWARD DUTIES OF CITIZENS

Compliance to rules and authority is the major focus of civics education in elementary schools. The significance which teachers attach to inculcating the obligations of the citizen is illustrated in Fig. 24 by the line labeled "Citizen Duties." Teachers of young children place particular stress upon citizen compliance, de-emphasizing all other political topics. The three items rated as more important than basic subjects (reading and arithmetic) by a majority of second- and third-grade teachers were *the law, the policeman,* and the child's *obligation to conform* to school rules and laws of the community. This concern with compliance is characteristic of teachers of all grades and parallels most closely the importance placed upon national symbols at these grades.

The teachers' emphasis on the policeman is different from their treatment in the classroom of other governmental figures (President, senator, mayor) and is concurrent with their presentation of the citizen's duties. Perhaps teachers utilize the policeman to introduce the child to the compliance system. This supports the previous argument that children are initiated into behavior and relationship to a system (in this case, the system of laws) through relationships with personal representatives of that system, in this case, the policeman.

In summary, political socialization at early age levels emphasizes behavior that relates the child emotionally to his country and impresses upon him the necessity for obedience and conformity.

SOCIALIZATION OF CONCEPTIONS OF RIGHTS AND POWERS OF CITIZENS

The citizen's right to participate in govenment is not emphasized in the school curriculum. The importance placed upon the citizen's active participation (his power, right to express opinion, effectiveness, voting) shows a pattern different from the emphasis placed upon attachment to country and compliance to law. The citizen's power to influence government is stressed very little until the fourth grade and is not given equal emphasis with the citizen's duties until the seventh and eighth grades. The role of political parties and partisanship receives less attention in the elementary school than any other topic. Orientation toward parties and politicians was considered less important than academic subjects by all second-grade teachers and by more than 85 per cent of third- and fourth-grade teachers. There was a slightly greater emphasis in later grades, but its importance at grades seven and eight was still lower than any other area of political socialization.

The tendency to evade some realities of political life seems to be paralleled by the school's emphasis upon compliance with respect to both itself and the community—although teaching children to obey is certainly an important function of the school. For some children, the combination of complacency and compliance may contribute to political inactivity and the failure to progress from early levels of involvement (attachment to nation) to a more vigilant, assertive involvement in political activities.

The teacher as a model for identification and imitation. Teachers' evaluations of the importance of various political topics reveal their orientation toward teaching certain materials but do not indicate their own attitudes in these areas. In order to obtain information about the teachers' own orientations, teachers responded to the same questionnaire filled out by the children. This provided a group of adult attitudes against which to compare the children. Particularly in matters dealing with partisan conflict and disagreement, the teacher is obliged to refrain from expressing opinions to students in the classroom. The beliefs of the teacher in other attitude areas may be more readily apparent to the children in her class from direct expression of opinions and from indirect and subtle indications of feelings. The processes of identification and imitation apply to the transmission of political attitudes in the classroom; teachers' opinions play a role in the socialization of children's attitudes, even though evidence on the amount of such attitude transmission is neither readily available nor precise.[5]

The major question to be answered is whether school children come to share their teachers' attitudes before they graduate from the elementary school. These data show both the mean level of teacher responses, and attitude differences between teachers and the total group of eighth-grade children. Indirectly, they show the extent to which political socialization has been completed by grade eight. Conclusions drawn from these data must be tentative. Teachers, as an occupational group, are not representative of the general population and may be expected to hold dissimilar views in several important respects. Even in those areas of opinion which show the greatest similarity between teacher and

5. The teacher group which completed the children's questionnaire overlapped with that of teachers who evaluated the importance of various parts of the curriculum. Those completing the attitude questionnaire, however, constituted a larger group and included teachers in a majority of the classrooms where the the questionnaire was administered to children. Although this group did not represent a random sampling of teachers, it was one in which considerable diversity of opinion existed. There was relatively little difference in teachers' viewpoints between the several cities represented, however, except on a small number of topics which have particular regional significance. Other differences could easily be attributed to differences in political party preference. Differences between male and female teachers were relatively small. The most significant reason for using this group, of course, is that these teachers are responsible for teaching the children from whom we have gathered attitudinal data about political objects.

pupil, there is no assurance that subsequent changes will not be made by these young people before they reach voting age.

These qualifications expressed, the results of the comparison show that eighth-graders hold attitudes highly similar to teachers on most items in the questionnaire. The magnitude of differences in mean response between eighth-graders and teachers on the rating scales for persons (including the President, policemen, and senators) for example, is very small. (Figs. 2, 3, 4, 5, 6, 7, and 10; Figs. 8 and 11 are exceptions). In most cases, the difference which does exist is not larger than that existing between any two adjacent grades on the same items. These similarities occurred on the majority of items which expressed the child's attachment to persons, his beliefs about the role qualifications of these persons, and his statements about the power of these people to punish or to exercise control. The orientation of eighth-grade children to governmental figures is very similar to that of their teachers; the socialization accomplished by the school in this area appears to be completed by the eighth grade. The same is true for institutions; that is, attitudes concerning the Supreme Court and the more general conception of "the government" showed more marked similarities than differences between teachers and eighth-grade students.

Conceptions of the government showed somewhat less similarity between teachers and students (Tables 4 and 6). One striking difference in response level between grade eight and the teacher group occurred in the choice of Congress or voting as giving the best picture of government, indicating that considerable change occurs in the conception of government between the eighth grade and adulthood. Although teachers have effectively imparted general orientations toward authorities, the greater appropriateness of institutions as symbols of goverment seems to have been less effectively communicated.

The ideal citizen's role was viewed in a similar fashion by eighth-grade children and teachers (Table 7). Despite marked age changes across grades, children grow to resemble their teachers in this area. This was especially true for the following qualities of citizens: "obey the laws," "is interested in the country," and "votes." These norms are learned even though children themselves are not necessarily as interested as their teachers, nor do they have the right to vote. Normative statements about the importance of adult party membership also showed similarity between teachers and children.

Teachers are more interested in political affairs and express less absolute trust in the operation of the political system than eighth-graders. A group of items dealing with global aspects of the political system and with parties in particular show marked differences between teachers and eighth-grade children. A number of items indicated greater cynicism on the part of teachers about the political system: considerably *less* tendency to agree that "people who break the laws always get caught," that the government is "all for the best" (Fig. 12), that people run for political office in order "to keep things as good as they are in the country," and lower rating of the infallibility of government and its representatives (Fig. 8). In each of these items, children were more trusting and willing to vouch for the goodness of the system and for the status quo. A second area where student-teacher differences were marked concerned the perception of the influence of pressure groups, lobbies, and certain special interests on legislative processes (Table 14). Although the mean ratings given to pressure groups (unions, newspapers, churches, etc.) are rank-ordered similarly for teachers and children, teachers consistently assigned these groups more power in affecting legislation than did the children. Teachers attributed somewhat more power to these groups than to "the average citizen," which indicates their greater grasp of the realities of political life. In a third area, teachers tended to ascribe more positive value to conflict or disagreement between the political parties than children, who said that if the political parties disagree about many things it is "very bad" for the country (Fig. 17). Teachers, apparently, see the function of disagreement between the parties as promoting instructive dialogue in the political world.

In the sphere of political parties, teachers felt that independence, late choice of political party, and free choice with regard to alignment with parents' political party are ideal (Tables 18, 19, and—in Appendix Table E.02). Although the differences in proportions of eighth-graders and teachers choosing these alternatives were marked, eighth-grade children tended to agree that independence is desirable and that one should vote for the best man rather than for the political party. Forty-three per cent of teachers felt that children should postpone choice of political party until after attainment of voting age; eighth-graders did not agree, only 25 per cent endorsing this alternative. The figures on alignment with parents' political parties indicate that while a majority of teachers felt that students should not be committed to choosing their parents' party, eighth-graders did not agree (Table 19). There is considerable evidence that similarity in party commitment between parents and children is very great. It is conceivable that parents consciously or unconsciously attempt to socialize their children into partisanship, but that this is counteracted by teachers' socialization of independence.

In the area of political activities, teachers showed much more interest, more participation in political discussion, and demonstrated a more pronounced tendency to take sides on issues than did eighth-graders (Figs. 14 and 15, Table 15). This is in contrast to two other indices of overt activity—sense of efficacy, and specific political activities—which showed very few differences between eighth-graders and teachers (Figs. 13 and 18). Specific factors in the indices themselves may account for this. The political activities inquired about did not include voting. Other types of activity—reading about current events, wearing buttons for candidates, and passing out literature—may reach a peak by the eighth grade (see also Table 21).

A listing of items on which teachers and eighth-graders are in relatively close agreement and of those where they are not would show that clear dissimilarity appears on few items. This result calls for an explanation of two features of the data—the meaning of this high degree of similarity and the significance to be attached to those topics on which disagreement is clear.

The extent of congruence in responses supports the conclusion that the school is a powerful socializing agent in the area of citizenship and political behavior. It also provides evidence that much of the basic socialization of political attitudes has taken place before the end of the elementary school years. While there is no doubt that attitudes and behavior change in some ways in the years following the eighth grade, from these data it may be argued that many of the basic orientations are established in the pre-high school years.

What of the areas in which this seems not to be true? Presumably not all of the sectors in which teachers and eighth-graders differ were tapped by this questionnaire. Within the attitude areas covered by this project, however, the dissimilarities may represent testing problems (items that may have been interpreted differently by teachers than by children), areas in which the school has less effect as a socializing agent, or behavior that shows great differences between adult and child levels. Where dissimilarities occur, there is likely to be specific participation by socializing agents and institutions of the community other than the school.

One of the items where teachers and eighth-graders are dissimilar can probably be explained on the ground of response appropriateness. The item dealing with the punitive power of authority figures, asking whether they could "punish anyone," may evoke a different interpretation of the word punish from the two groups. Teachers also have a different frame of reference concerning the prerogatives of authority figures to punish and may give answers affected by their own professional training and constraints upon their punishment of children. This is the only item where a case can be made for differences in the interpretation of an item.

The other items where teacher–eighth-grader dissimilarity is greatest fall into three areas: 1) trust *vs.* cynicism concerning the government; 2) interest in political affairs; 3) value placed upon affiliation with a political party. With respect to general values about partisanship and the specific choice of a party, it has already been established that this area of attitude is influenced strongly by family membership—one of the few political topics, although an important one, on which families seem to exert considerable influence. Differences in reported interest in public affairs and participation in political discussion are probably genuine differences between adults and children. However, the teachers as a group show relatively high interest when compared with other adults. Perhaps the children of the study are not greatly different from the general adult population of their social class and community. The items dealing with trust in government may represent another true adult-child difference. Teachers express considerable trust in the government, but not at the high level of these children; in addition to reflecting the realistic experience with government which adults have, this may also reflect the extreme wording of some of the questions on this topic. Persons of high education tend to avoid agreeing with extreme statements. This tendency was also apparent in the high status, highly intelligent group of children in this study, who appeared more like the teachers than did other groups.

6

The Effects of Religious Affiliation and Peer Group Participation

Religious Affiliation

Studies of adult voting behavior have documented a strong relationship between church membership and political participation. Catholic voters are particularly likely to be affiliated with the Democratic party even when factors such as social class, ethnicity, education, urban residence, and union membership are controlled in the studies (Glantz, 1959; Gold, 1953; Greer, 1961. These studies reported data from Presidential elections where both candidates were Protestant). Campbell, Converse, Miller, and Stokes (1960) reported that in congressional elections which pair Catholic and non-Catholic candidates, Catholic voters will often cross party lines to vote for a Catholic. The 1960 election which paired a Democratic Catholic Presidential candidate with a Protestant Republican offered an unusual opportunity to examine these tendencies. Scoble and Epstein (1964) reported that in the Wisconsin primary voting for Kennedy was correlated with religion even when social class and education were controlled. Campbell, Miller, and Stokes (1961) reported that in 1956 the national Catholic vote split approximately 50-50, Democratic-Republican. From the general tendency of Catholics to vote Democratic, in the 1960 election one would have expected 63 per cent for Kennedy; he received 80 per cent of the Catholic vote. Apparently many Republican as well as Democratic Catholics voted for him.

If the influence of religious affiliation upon children is restricted to the type reported in adults, the effect upon responses in these data would appear only on questions dealing with the election and political party orientation. The candidacy of Kennedy in 1960, where the religious issue was salient, provides a particularly useful opportunity to determine whether religious membership has this type of impact.

Whatever the influence of religion upon the choice of a candidate, there are theoretical reasons for predicting its moral general effect upon socialization. One striking aspect of young children's comments about the President (whether Eisenhower or Kennedy) was the similarity of their image of the President to images usually associated with religious authority or even the Deity. The President was described as "about the best person in the world," as having absolute power over the nation, as being personally interested in the needs of each individual citizen. Essays about "Uncle Sam," written by children in the pilot studies, described this imaginary figure as the "spirit behind the government." On questionnaire items, children in the younger grades occasionally expressed the view that the pledge of allegiance was "like a prayer." To the young child, the images of political and divine authority have much in common. In line with the Interpersonal Transfer Model one would predict that the teachings of the church which induce respect for religious authority and law would generalize to non-religious authority systems, particularly ones in which the image of supreme authority has certain features common to religious figures.

Denomination of religious affiliation has relatively little effect on basic attachment to the country and government in the elementary school years. Of the 78 indices and items used in this research to define involvement, only two showed consistent and pronounced differences between Catholic and Protestant, compared within social class.

There is a strong relationship in children between religious membership and partisan affiliation and an even stronger relationship to candidate preference. At all class levels, Catholic children selected the Democratic party more often than did Protestant children, the difference in choice being smallest within eighth-graders of high-status level, where the community is most likely to be Republican in partisan sympathies (Fig. 25). The overwhelming preference of Catholic children for President Kennedy was clear (Fig. 26). Even at the high-status level, the difference between Catholics and Protestants was unusually large. This suggests that in the 1960 election the involvement of Catholics with the Catholic candidate went beyond party preference to engage children whose tentative affiliation was with the Republican party.

Religious affiliation and family membership have their most marked effects upon the same aspects of political socialization. It seems likely that the influence of church membership is mediated at least partly through the family. A Catholic child who feels support for a Catholic candidate is influenced both by his family's choice of candidate preference and by his own identification of himself with a candidate of similar faith. There may also be some direct persuasion by representatives of the church, but this is probably less important.

There are few mean differences among children from different religious groups in general political orientations and attitudes; there are few

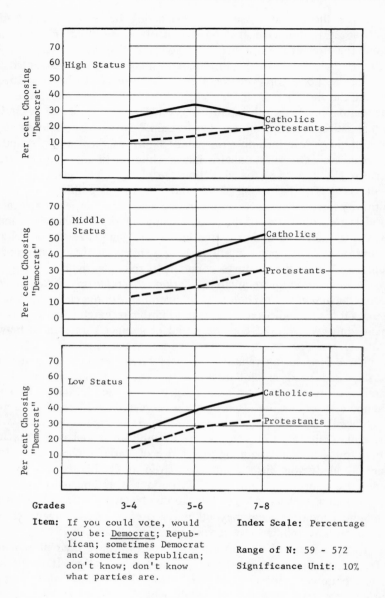

Item: If you could vote, would   Index Scale: Percentage
       you be: Democrat; Repub-
       lican; sometimes Democrat
       and sometimes Republican;   Range of N: 59 - 572
       don't know; don't know   Significance Unit: 10%
       what parties are.

Fig. 25.
Comparison of Catholics and Protestants in reporting Democratic party commitment, within social status and grade.

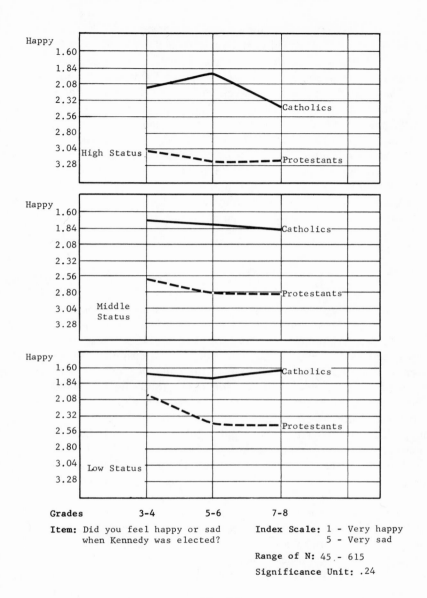

Fig. 26.
Comparison of means of Catholics and Protestants in emotional
response to Kennedy's election, within social status and grade.

differences in participation and active involvement. Many of the apparent differences between Catholics and Protestants disappeared when social status was controlled in the analysis of data. The major influence of membership in the Catholic Church is to increase Democratic party preference and to induce emotional support of Catholic candidates.

The lack of differences between children of different faiths in basic orientations to the political system and the systematic differences in party preference and candidate choice suggest that the effect of religious membership is a special case of the influence of strong group membership and identification. That is, we would expect to find similar patterns of transmission from adults to children within clearly identified ethnic or racial groups. If this is true, it means that the Identification Model is much more useful than the Accumulation Model or the Interpersonal Transfer Model in explaining the influence of religious membership upon political attitudes.

Peer Group Participation

The social systems which may influence a child's socialization are not limited to those composed of adults. The peer group is a powerful force in the development of many social norms. If political socialization were restricted to information and attitudes transmitted by the adult community (Accumulation Model), the influence of the peer group would be limited and indirect. The peer group's effect would be to reinforce the adult norms with group consensus. Children who participate frequently in group activities should then show greater interest in political affairs and more rapid acquisition of attitudes than their non-participating contemporaries.

An alternative possibility is that there is a direct relationship between participation in the community and larger political units and the experience of participation in organized group activities. Such experiences include group decision-making processes, respect for minority opinions, and compliance to rules. Group participation may provide a knowledge of quasi-political behavior that has elements in common with the role of a citizen. This hypothesis analogizes the role of the peer group to that of the family as a source of experience in role relationships which may be transferred to behavior in the political system. This depends upon the Interpersonal Transfer Model.

Another variation of the interpersonal transfer process (suggested by Rose, 1959, to be applicable to adult attitudes) is that persons who are attracted to groups are also attracted to political involvement; that is, the two experiences have a common appeal which is related to socialization or other experience occurring prior to participation in either.

There is considerable evidence that adult political behavior is associated with participation (Buchanan, 1956; Hastings, 1954; Key, 1961; Maccoby, 1958; Rose, 1962; Zimmer and Hawley, 1959).

In his volume *The Joiners*, Hausknecht (1962) discussed in detail the correlates of voluntary group membership. The tendency to join groups may be part of a configuration which Hausknecht labeled "interaction and contact with the environment." Joiners in all social classes read newspapers, listen to the radio, vote, and are interested in politics more than non-joiners. Hausknecht also argues that association membership does not teach participants how a democracy works. Most associations are not democratically run; usually membership is not large enough to accommodate those operations typical of a democratic system. He concluded that members are generally those who are likely to be participants in the political process even without the impetus of group membership, a view supported by the work of Erbe (1964).

The data provide some information about the association between group membership and political attitudes. Three types of activity in which a child may participate were investigated: children's service organizations (YMCA, Scouts, Campfire Girls, etc.); school-sponsored clubs (band, sports, etc.); and positions of leadership (holding office) in these groups.

The most striking examples of the relationship between group membership and political behavior for the research group are presented in Figs. 27 through 29. Of the many comparisons examined, these (and relationships with political interest and with concern about political issues—documented further in Hess and Torney, 1965) were the only ones in which the difference between high- and low-participation groups was sufficiently consistent to indicate that an association exists. These items deal primarily with involvement requiring some active engagement with the political system. That is, social participation influences primarily those attitudes which are closely related to overt political behavior.

Students who join groups express more interest in political affairs, are more actively involved in conversations about politics and current events, and are more likely to defend their opinions on those issues. High social participators were more likely to feel that individual political activity is efficacious (Fig. 28).[1] The differences between high- and low-participation groups was most extreme in their reported political activities (Fig. 29). Differences between high and low social participation

1. Interpretation of these results must take into account the relationship of intelligence to both group participation and efficacy. Brighter children tend to join groups and also tend to feel more effective in relation to the government system. Difference in intelligence is not likely to have influenced the relationship between social participation and political activity, since the relationship between this political index and intelligence was low.

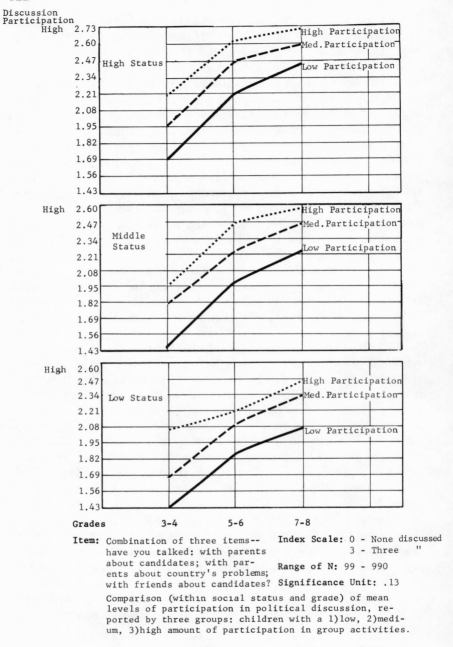

Item: Combination of three items --
have you talked: with parents
about candidates; with parents about country's problems;
with friends about candidates?

Index Scale: 0 - None discussed
            3 - Three   "
Range of N: 99 - 990
Significance Unit: .13

Comparison (within social status and grade) of mean
levels of participation in political discussion, reported by three groups: children with a 1)low, 2)medi-
um, 3)high amount of participation in group activities.

Fig. 27.
Social participation and participation in political discussion.

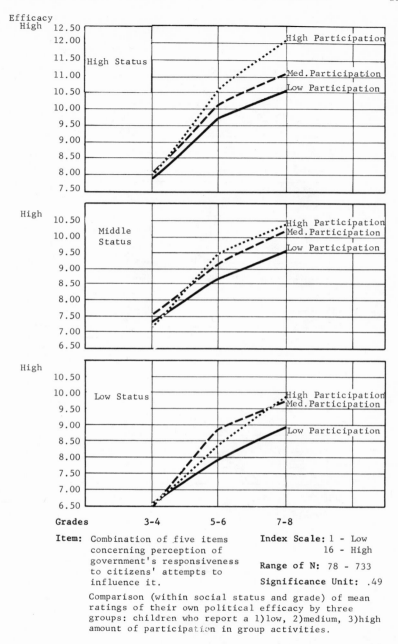

Grades

Item: Combination of five items concerning perception of government's responsiveness to citizens' attempts to influence it.

Index Scale: 1 - Low
            16 - High

Range of N: 78 - 733

Significance Unit: .49

Comparison (within social status and grade) of mean ratings of their own political efficacy by three groups: children who report a 1)low, 2)medium, 3)high amount of participation in group activities.

Fig. 28.
Social participation and sense of political efficacy.

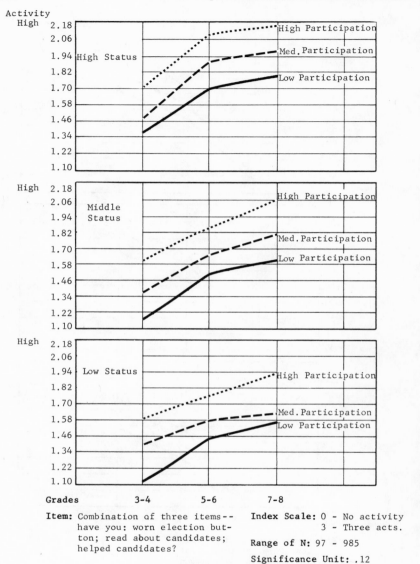

Item: Combination of three items--
have you: worn election but-
ton; read about candidates;
helped candidates?

Index Scale: 0 - No activity
3 - Three acts.

Range of N: 97 - 985

Significance Unit: .12

Comparison (within social status and grade) of mean
levels of political activity of three groups: children
who report a 1)low, 2)medium, 3)high amount of participation in group activities.

Fig. 29.
Social participation and political activity.

appeared in perceptions of the government's responsiveness to citizen influence and reports of active involvement in these political matters.

There is no evidence that social participation has any influence upon basic attachment to the system, acceptance of the norms of citizen behavior, or compliance to political authority. Basic attitudes and orientations toward the political world are not modified by experience in organizations; rather, group membership is associated with a tendency to become actively involved in attempting to influence the political system.

While the data do not permit precise examination of possible causal relationship between membership in organizations and active involvement, they do allow some tentative interpretations. If the peer group reinforces attitudes taught by the adult community, attitudes in all areas should develop at a somewhat earlier age among members. This does not occur.

The Interpersonal Transfer Model is consistent with the findings. Learning to influence political structures in democratically organized childhood activities may lead to greater participation in the larger system. Both Hausknecht (1962) and Erbe (1964) suggest that group membership is one type of active interchange with the social world and that it does not have particularly political implications. This is also the most plausible interpretation for the findings reported here. The tendency to join children's groups is part of a cluster of attitudes, personality characteristics, and preferences, which increases interaction and contact with the environment. The data do not show organization membership to be a distinct factor in the socialization of *political* attitudes. It seems more likely that children who are more politically involved are also more active participants in non-political groups.

7

Social Class and

Intelligence as

Mediating Factors

Introduction

The effects of social class environments within the United States can be observed in many areas of political behavior. Investigators have repeatedly found social class differences both in preference for political party and candidates and in the degree of political involvement manifested in voter registration, voting in elections, participation in municipal bond issues, etc. It is well established that members of the working class favor the Democratic party, while middle- and upper-class groups favor Republicans (evidence summarized by Lipset, 1959).

Social class is a complex phenomenon. It is not a variable in the usual sense but a subtle and complex matrix of influences and experiences that combine to make certain types of personality and response patterns more likely. Social class may be usefully regarded as a statement of probability that an individual has had or will have certain kinds of experience that shape his behavior and orientations toward the society and toward new ideas, information, and concepts. Interaction between children and adults has a different quality in different social class groups in this country, and the effects of social class experience upon children have been described in many studies and reviews of literature (Bronfenbrenner, 1958; Davis, 1948; Havighurst and Davis, 1947; Whyte, 1943).

Although social class differences in intelligence test scores and academic achievement are the most frequently documented, there are other features of social class experience that are probably relevant to political socialization. Between social classes the exercise of control and regulatory patterns in the family structure differ considerably (Hess and Shipman, 1965; Kohn, 1959; Maas, 1951). Working-class parents are more likely to be imperative in their control, showing more concern with obedience, external behavior and appearances than with internal states and feelings. They are less likely to give reasons for their commands or to encourage the child to make his own decisions in family

126

matters. They appear to be less concerned with the child's opinion and to give him fewer alternatives for action or for thought. This type of parental behavior produces external compliance (at least in the early years), depressed verbal and conceptual abilities, and lessens the tendency to be reflective in problem-solving situations. These attitudes and orientations are clearly relevant to the acquisition of political behavior and attitudes. The influence of these family experiences which differ by social class may be generalized to other institutions of the society. For example, children from the lower class might be expected to see fewer opportunities for efficacious action by the citizen.

In the search for explanations of social class differences in adult political behavior, the aspects of political socialization that differ by social class were examined by Greenstein (1965a) in his study of New Haven school children, grades 4-8. He found that upper-class children made more references to political issues. In the seventh and eighth grades, upper-status children (more than lower-status children) tended to volunteer the classification "independent" when asked the party with which they identified. Lower-class children, in general, tended to rate leaders more favorably. Greenstein argued that idealization of leaders in this fashion is an immature response. Lower-class children tended to say that they would go to the teacher for advice about whom to vote for rather than making up their own minds. Greenstein interpreted this to mean that lower-class children do not feel that political choices are theirs to make.

Education has been used infrequently as a variable to explain *direction* of involvement (Democratic, Republican) in adults. Key (1961) asserted that education is unrelated to the direction of opinion unless information activates some particular outlook. For example, knowledge of foreign countries might produce more liberal attitudes toward foreign policy. As discussion turns to the *degree* of involvement in political matters, however, education and social class appear together as variables. Interest in political events is the only area of political involvement which is more strongly related to occupation than to education. Businessmen, even those with elementary-school educations, have high interest in elections (Key, 1961).

Within every occupational group, political participation, feelings of citizen duty, and efficacy increase as education increases (Campbell, Gurin, and Miller, 1954; Key, 1961; Lazarsfeld, 1948). Campbell, Converse, Miller, and Stokes (1960) presented evidence that education is the single strongest predictor of voting and non-voting. Key (1961) suggested furthermore that the influence of education is not limited to the indoctrinating values of the culture; the more highly educated person is also subject to different influences, such as different social groups, and has greater familiarity with the intricacies of public policy throughout his life. In other words, the social reinforcements for political activity are much stronger for the more highly educated individual.

In children, intelligence is the variable which most closely approximates education. Intelligence is most important as it mediates school learning. The curriculum is likely to be absorbed more completely by children of higher intelligence. The greater ability of the bright child allows him to learn more rapidly, giving him tools for synthesizing what he has learned and for relating information and attitudes to action. The reinforcements for political interest and behavior are probably also greater for more intelligent children, whose friends are more likely to be interested in discussing current events and whose abilities allow them to feel competent in dealing with material on an adult level. The influence of this type of mediating variable is best understood within the Cognitive-developmental Model, which stresses the type of concepts a child is capable of understanding.

This study has unusual data for examining and understanding differences in political socialization. Both IQ scores and social class may be examined to understand the interaction between social class and intelligence. There is also information about attachment, compliance, and participation which goes beyond the issue of overt participation in political activities.

Some analysis of data in this study controlled for social class so that it was possible to compare children of high intelligence with those of low intelligence within each social class group. In other analysis intelligence was controlled, so that it was possible to compare children from high-, middle-, and low-status backgrounds within each of three levels of intelligence.

The data presented in this section will follow the outline of the socialization of political involvement used in Chapters Two through Four, including a child's attachment to the country and the system, his definition of it, his perception of and attachment to figures and institutions, and his view of how the system is related to him. A second section deals with a similar outline of his perception of law and his relationship to legal institutions. The third area treats the types of active participation in which adults engage, particularly citizens' attempts to influence government. The fourth deals with the citizen's influence in changing incumbents within the political structure through elections.

Acquisition of Attitudes

The acquisition of attitudes toward political objects is influenced by both social class and intelligence, but in different ways. We may expect a child of high intelligence to be accelerated in his acquisition of attitudes and in the range and level of social concepts which he can understand. He will also learn more rapidly those attitudes which are taught by the school. The effect of social class is less direct but would follow from differences in family and community support for political interest.

High intelligence accelerates the acquisition of political attitudes. Intelligence apparently does influence the *amount* of information and the number of attitudes children express (within each of the social class levels—Fig. 30), though at the younger age levels there was less difference than at higher levels. Younger children of high intelligence were as willing to admit that they did not have attitudes as those in lower IQ groups. This suggests that in the pre-school and early elementary school years, children of high intelligence do not absorb more political information from their families than children of low intelligence. The "Don't know" response of all high-IQ groups decreased sharply, until the mean number of "Don't know" responses for all social class levels at grade eight was less than three out of a total of 32 items. The tendency to respond "Don't know" did not decline so quickly for the other groups.

Social class differences within IQ groups in "Don't know" responses were somewhat less striking. The differences which were observed were most apparent within the high IQ group. The combination of high intelligence and membership in the top social strata work together to produce the most accelerated attitude growth curve.

It appears that bright children are more completely socialized in political attitudes and behavior by grade eight than are children of lower intelligence. If it is true that political concepts and attitudes are more easily acquired by intelligent children, the possession of some basic orientations toward governmental processes and the citizen's role may not be part of the background of the less gifted citizen. For low IQ groups, the ability to understand political concepts may be retarded in a way that limits comprehension of political issues.

Attachment to Nation

Basic attachment to the nation is not influenced by intelligence level or social class. There were some differences by social class in belief that America is best, but these were not large and were less pronounced at grade eight than earlier. It should be noted that for the items "America is the best country in the world" and "The American flag is the best flag in the world," the responses of all groups at all age levels were highly positive and variance was very small. That is, all children by the second grade seemed to feel strongly that America is the best country in the world. By grade eight, high-IQ children were somewhat

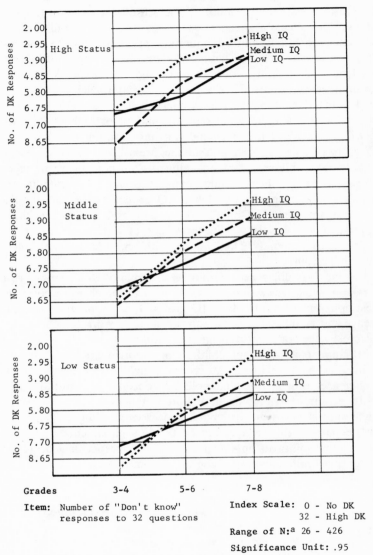

Grades   3-4   5-6   7-8

Item: Number of "Don't know"   Index Scale: 0 - No DK
      responses to 32 questions   32 - High DK

                                        Range of N:[a] 26 - 426

                                        Significance Unit: .95

[a]The lower limit of the Range of N in certain figures results from two factors: some questions were not administered at grade 3; and the low correlation
between some independent variables meant that some group sizes were reduced.
For all graphs, group sizes cluster at top not bottom of reported Range of N.

Fig. 30.
**Comparison of means of IQ groups in acquisition of political
attitudes, within social status and grade.**

less emphatic in agreeing with these statements, reflecting perhaps greater understanding of the flag as a symbol rather than as an object of independent worth. There were virtually no responses that indicated any hesitation about loyalty or patriotism stated in this form.

Attachment to Figures and Institutions of Government

CONCEPTION OF THE SYSTEM

The conception of the governmental system varied markedly among IQ groups. In Chapter Three it was argued that older children have begun to shift attention from individual authority figures to include governmental institutions. It was proposed that the major route to engagement with a social system is through involvement with a representative of the system (for example, the President). This shift from individual to institutional authority is related to the development of certain cognitive processes. Greater cognitive maturity is needed for a conception of government based on institutions than for one based on persons. The more intelligent child is able to develop abstract concepts of a system which are not dependent upon his perception of personal objects but which imply intangible relationships to groups of persons, laws, and processes. Cognitive development as well as the acquisition of information are basic to the development of this system concept.

Differences between IQ groups in choosing Congress as the law-making branch of government are very large. This item is more closely related than others to information taught in the school. Figure 31 indicates that children of high intelligence learn this information about the formal structure of government earlier than medium- or low-IQ children.

The greater the child's ability to abstract, the earlier he is likely to perceive government in institutional rather than personal terms (Fig. 32). IQ differences appeared at all social class and grade levels. Children of high intelligence personalized the government less, conceptualizing it instead in more institutional terms. At all IQ levels, older children were less likely to personalize the government, suggesting that this is a less mature symbolization of the system. The ability to deal with an abstract rather than personalized system is apparently related to cognitive maturity (Cognitive-developmental Model). Social class differences were significant but less marked than the effects of intelligence (Fig. 33). Working-class children also personalized their view of the government. The social class difference may follow from the tendency of working-class parents to emphasize rules and the enforcement of rules rather than offering rationale which are more impersonal and abstract guides for behavior.

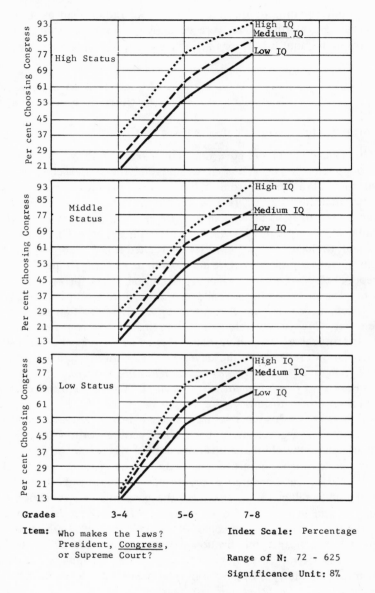

Grades   3-4   5-6   7-8

Item: Who makes the laws?   Index Scale: Percentage
       President, Congress,
       or Supreme Court?   Range of N: 72 - 625

                                   Significance Unit: 8%

Fig. 31

Comparison of IQ groups in choice of Congress as source of laws, within social status and grade.

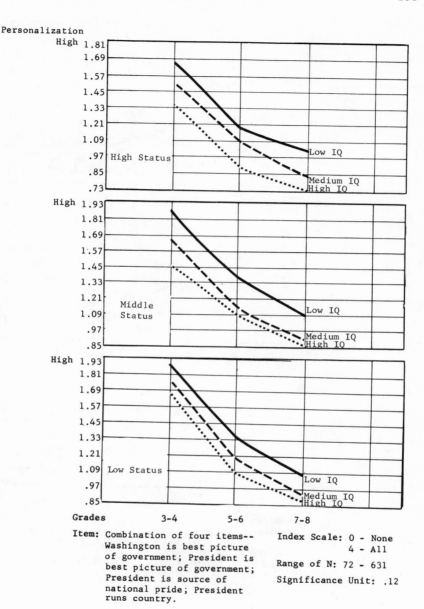

Fig. 32.

Comparison of means of IQ groups in tendency to personify the government, within social status and grade.

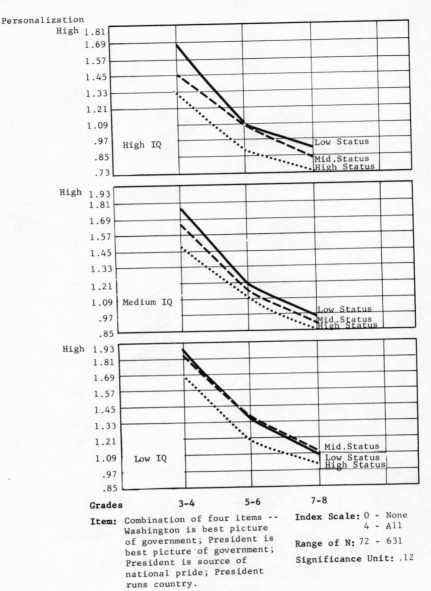

Personalization

Grades   3-4   5-6   7-8

Item: Combination of four items --
Washington is best picture
of government; President is
best picture of government;
President is source of
national pride; President
runs country.

Index Scale: 0 - None
                   4 - All

Range of N: 72 - 631

Significance Unit: .12

Fig. 33.
Comparison of means of social-status groups in tendency to
personify the government, within IQ and grade.

RELATIONSHIP TO THE SYSTEM

It was argued previously that children's initial attachment to the political system is motivated by a need to see authority, particularly distant political authority, as benign and protective. These early attachments are primarily emotional and are not acquired in the same way as attitudes taught by formal instruction. If this is true, early attachment should not be highly related to intelligence or social class.

The child's attachment to governmental figures varies by social status, but the perception of their responsiveness does not. In the items which deal with the child's expectation of protection and help from the government and its representatives (such as, "would want to help me"), some differences appear to be significant at particular ages and in particular IQ and social class groups. However, these differences were not systematic or large. The child's expectation of assistance, help, and protection from government and the President is apparently not strongly influenced by social class membership or level of intelligence.

Another aspect of the child's affiliation to the system concerns his feeling of attachment for its representatives. The feelings children express toward the President showed considerable difference by social class. Differences between IQ groups on the item, "The President is my favorite," were minimal; social class differences were extreme and existed at all grade levels (Fig. 34). Children coming from high-status homes tended to be less attracted to the President of the United States as a personal favorite. This may reflect some partisan feeling. However, similar trends appear in "The policeman is my favorite," which is an item unlikely to be influenced by partisan feeling. These tendencies are consistent with data on personifying the government. Children from working-class homes see the system in more personal terms and are attached to figures that represent it; children from homes of higher status have less investment in individual authority figures, although their attachment to the country is at least as strong as that of children from other social class backgrounds.

We have argued elsewhere (Hess and Easton, 1960; Torney, Hess, and Easton, 1962) that the young child's highly positive image of the President exists because of feelings of powerlessness and vulnerability in the presence of powerful authority. The tendency for the child to compensate by seeing the President as benign and nurturant, by this argument, should also be related to the child's feeling of protection within a group with which he interacts—the family. It would follow from this that children who have less positive images of their fathers would have a greater need to project the qualities of an ideal father onto the President and to become attached to him. This view is compatible with the

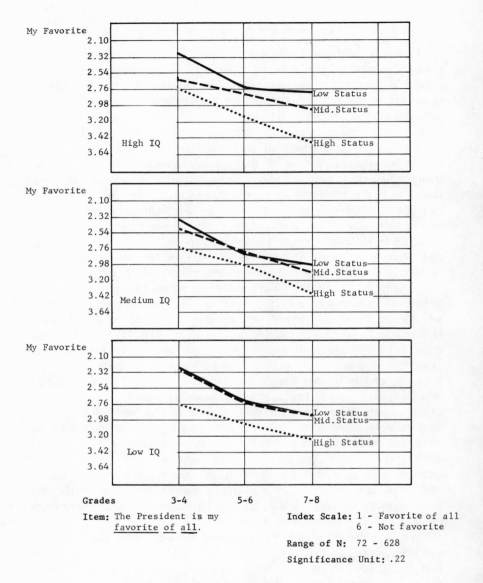

Fig. 34.
Comparison of means of social-status groups in attachment to
President, within IQ and grade.

social class data of this study. Children from working-class backgrounds express *less positive* attitudes toward their fathers than do children from middle- and upper-status homes and more positive attachment to the President.

Children's highly positive image of the President's performance of his role and the persistence of this image through the age span have been discussed in Chapter Three. No notable differences by social class or IQ appeared in judgments of the President's knowledge or decision-making power. These are among the most clearly defined and widely accepted characteristics of his role.

Children of high intelligence see the Supreme Court as more powerful in the decision making process than do children of low intelligence. (Fig. 35). Attitudes toward the Supreme Court appear to be socialized by teachers. Apparently, although all children defined the President's decision-making power as part of his role, information about the particular power of the Supreme Court in making decisions is learned in school and is acquired more rapidly by brighter children. Class differences in image of the Supreme Court were less pronounced and not consistent across grades.

SUMMARY

In the development of attitudes toward political figures, there is an interplay between information, needs, school, and home. The young child sees government as represented by personal figures; he is unfamiliar with institutional structures such as Congress or the Supreme Court. The school is the agent that teaches about these structures, instruction which is effective at an earlier age for children of high intelligence.

Not only does the working-class child see government in personal terms, but he also expresses more emotional attachment to the President. It is interesting, however, that social class and IQ differences are minimal in the child's patriotic attachment to his country and in his expectation of protection from personal figures of government.

Compliance to Law

An individual's experience with law and its representatives varies considerably by social class. Lower-class persons have less access to legal aid than those in the middle class (Ribman and Ribman, 1964). In urban areas, such as those in which this study was conducted, children and adults in different socioeconomic areas of the city receive differential protection from the political system and police. In lower-

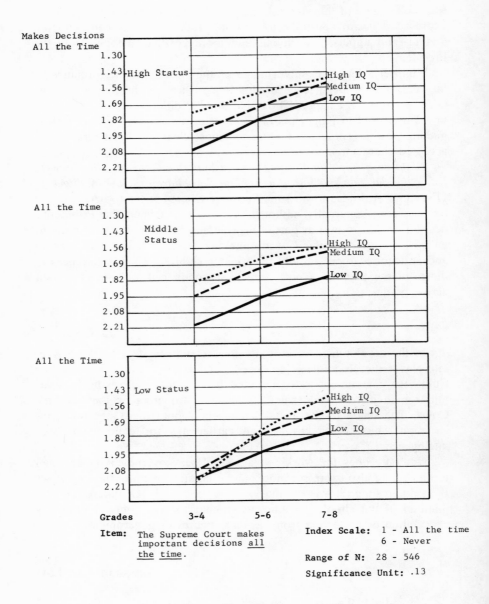

Fig. 35.

Comparison of means of IQ groups in rating role performance of Supreme Court decision-making, within social status and grade.

class neighborhoods, children are more likely to see policemen making arrests or performing punitive roles; middle-class children are less likely to witness this particular exercise of the law, except for the vigilance of traffic policemen.[1]

In the process of socialization into any system of rules—those of family or social group—the child begins with a perception of the system as absolute and unquestionable (Dubin and Dubin, 1963; Kohlberg, 1963; Tuttle, 1943). It is apparent from data reported here, as well as from the work of others, that as the child gets older he sees rules as more flexible and less absolute. This ability to differentiate situations in which obedience to laws and rules must be unquestioning from those in which more flexible choices are available is, to some extent, a matter of experience. It is also a function of the individual's ability to discriminate among highly similar situations. This requires a high level of cognitive ability. These factors lead to the expectation of differences between IQ groups in perception of laws and the need for compliance.

Several theories have been offered to explain the differences between social classes in their manner of indoctrinating children into rules and regulations of the family and society. The working-class parent emphasizes obedience and is more rigid and authoritarian in administering family rules and regulations (Kohn, 1959; Maas, 1951). A perceptive analysis of social class differences and their effects comes from the work of Bernstein (1960, 1962, 1964), who discusses social differences in cognition and IQ by focusing on the techniques parents employ in transmitting standards and regulations. A family may enforce rules on the basis of status, insisting upon obedience based upon arbitrary rules or role definitions (for example, "Do this because I say so," or "Little girls don't act that way"), or rule enforcement may be based on orientation to persons, with parents explaining the effect actions will have upon the child and others. These findings lead us to expect children from working-class families to be less flexible than children from the middle class in dealing with the compliance system.

CONCEPTION OF THE SYSTEM

A young child sees laws as absolute and unchanging, this being a major feature of his conception of the compliance system. The item most closely approximating this concept asked whether "all laws are

---

1. Television may represent a large part of the child's experience with policemen and other law-enforcement officers. Schramm, Lyle, and Parker (1961) report that in 100 hours of programming at a peak viewing time for children, sixteen different detectives, sixteen sheriffs, nine policemen, and various other law-enforcement officers appeared on television. There is some evidence that the effect of television on ideas of law enforcement (in the direction of less positive images) is more pronounced in children of lower socioeconomic status (Scott, 1954).

fair." Presumably, children answering "yes" to this item perceive that the system has an appropriate claim to unquestioning compliance from the individual.

High-status and high-IQ children perceive laws as less rigid than do low-status children. The child's view of the justice of laws varied with IQ, a differentiation which increased with age (Fig. 36). There was also some tendency for those from high-status homes to agree less often that all laws are fair (see Hess and Torney, 1965, Fig. 52). High-IQ and high-status chidren saw the compliance system in less absolute terms, recognizing the possibility that laws may be defective even though they must be obeyed.

This flexibility in interpretation of laws does not imply a belief that laws are made in a haphazard fashion or that they are frequently modified. Intelligent children saw more permanence in the system of law (Appendix D, Fig. D.02). "The law" is like certain institutions in its dependability, although it may not always be fair.

PERCEPTIONS OF THE ROLE OF CITIZEN

Neither social class nor IQ affects children's perception of the importance of compliance as a mark of good citizenship. The tendency of upper-status children to see laws as less absolute did not lead to a disregard of established law. Consensus in the belief that all citizens should obey the law may reflect the school's effectiveness in teaching obedience as a vital characteristic of citizenship.

RELATIONSHIP TO THE SYSTEM

In the same sense that personal role relationships with the President orient the child to the governmental system, the policeman is, to the child, a personal representative of the system of laws (see Chapter Three). A child's interaction with the policeman is therefore important in determining his expectations concerning a more abstract system of laws.

There were only minimal differences by level of intelligence in perception of the policeman's intent—children of low intelligence rated the policeman as slightly "less willing to help" them—but these differences disappeared by the seventh and eighth grades. Social class differences also were minimal. This suggests that virtually all children learn that the system of laws and its major personal representatives are organized to protect the individual. Judgments about the policeman's responsiveness did not decline with age, suggesting that this quality helps to define the role of the policeman; that is, his job is to help those who need assistance. The policeman is among the first figures studied in social

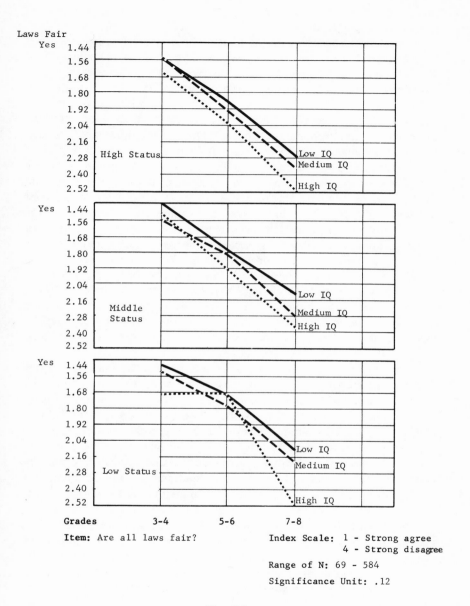

Fig. 36.
Comparison of means of IQ groups in belief that laws are fair, within social status and grade.

studies curricula, and the aim is to teach the child to look upon the policeman as a friend.

Social class differences on the item, "The policeman is my favorite," were marked. Lower-class children expressed more positive feelings about the policeman (Fig. 37). When compared with middle-class children, lower-class children seem more emotionally involved with extra-familial authority. Perhaps this is related to their less positive perception of family authority (see the discussion of similar findings concerning attachment to the President in Chapter Three). IQ differences, though present, were much less striking (see Hess and Torney, 1965, Fig. 54).

There was no difference by intelligence or social class in children's assessment of the policeman's power to punish or to "make people do what he wants." Again, the responses to these items were stable over the seven grades. These are probably defining characteristics of the policeman which show a high level of consensus. However, children of lower social status and intelligence saw the policeman's major role as "catching people who have broken the law," rather than as "helping people" or "making people obey the law" (Appendix D, Fig. D.03; see also Hess and Torney, 1965, Fig. 57). Lower-class children and those who absorb the school curriculum less effectively place greater emphasis upon the "cops and robbers" aspect of the policeman, which suggests that their image of policemen may be formed from experience with mass media rather than by the schools.

The only role quality item in which social class and intelligence differences appeared consistently was in assessment of how much the policeman knows. Children of high intelligence and high status were less convinced of his wide knowledge than others (Appendix D, Fig. D.04; see also Hess and Torney, 1965, Fig. 58). Children in the upper-middle classes have had experience with men who possess a great deal of knowledge. Policemen are seen as educational inferiors by people in professional and executive occupations, but the occupation of policeman is of relatively high status to individuals in the lower class. If children use "most men" they know as the criterion for comparison, it is reasonable that children of unskilled workers will judge the policeman as more knowledgeable than men they know, and that children of professionals and executives will find him less knowledgeable. To the degree that children of high intelligence are also more familiar with knowledgeable men with whom they compare the policeman, the same process may operate.

The child's view of the system's power to enforce compliance was assessed by a number of items: ratings of power to "punish" and "make people obey" which the Supreme Court, government, and senator possess. These items represent the compelling, coercive power of various levels and components of government, apart from the policeman, and

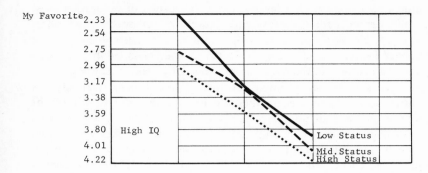

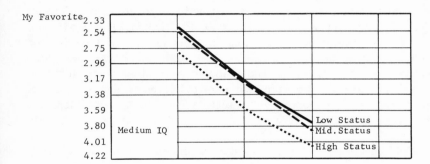

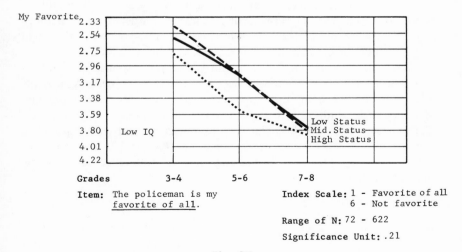

Fig. 37.

Comparison of means of social-status groups in attachment to policeman, within IQ and grade.

are independent of the children's view of the justice of established law. The child's respect for the President's power showed social class differences at certain ages, but these do not indicate consistent social class variations. Perception of the President as powerful is established at a fairly early age and is relatively uninfluenced by school learning.

Except as previously pointed out, these items showed relatively few age differences. There was an increase in assessing the power of the Supreme Court and of the government (as an institutional whole) with age; this increase was consistent with the general tendency for older children to see government in institutional rather than personal terms. As suggested earlier, the relatively bright child learns about the institutional aspects of government from formal classroom instruction at an early age. When compared with the low-IQ groups, the high-IQ groups perceived that both the Supreme Court and the government had more power to punish (Fig. 38; Appendix D, Fig. D.05). This attribution of power to institutions rather than to persons occurred earlier for children of high intelligence. Social class differences were less pronounced on this item. Home and school may combine to reinforce an institutionalized view of government among children of high intelligence. This hypothesis is supported by observing that intelligence differences for both of these items were *least* marked in the lower classes at early grade-levels.

Children's views of the response of the citizen to the system's demands for compliance was measured by two items. In the first, which dealt with the consequences of disregarding the law, children in high-IQ groups were less convinced that all those who disobey the law will be punished (Appendix D, Fig. D.06). This is consistent with findings reported earlier about the low tolerance for ambiguities in the legal system which seems characteristic of less intelligent children.[2]

The second item, which deals with a citizen's response to a policeman who is in error, showed no social class or IQ differences. Age trends appeared on this item, but apparently they represent developmental tendencies for children to feel less awe for authority as they grow older. This absence of social class and IQ differences in children's response to a policeman who asks them to do something they feel is wrong is congruent with the absence of social class and IQ differences in assessing the policeman's power.

---

2. Dolger and Ginandes (1946) reported that children from lower classes prescribe harsher punishments for crimes, but their study did not control for intelligence.

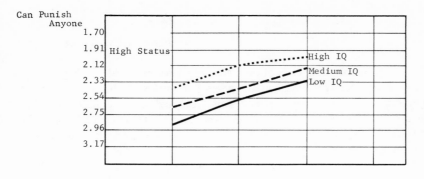

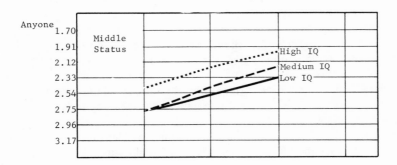

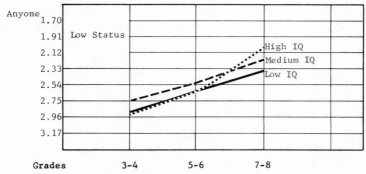

Grades   3-4   5-6   7-8

Item: The Supreme Court can punish   **Index Scale:** 1 - Anyone
          anyone.   6 - No one

                                                Range of N: 28 - 543

                                                Significance Unit: .21

Fig. 38.

Comparison of means of IQ groups in rating punitive power of Supreme Court, within social status and grade.

Influencing Government Policy

Perhaps the most critical element in the complex interaction between the citizen and the government is his perception of his own ability to influence the governing process. This view includes a conception of the government's responsiveness to persons and to groups and an image of his own role—the effective action he can take and the methods by which he can make his opinions known.

Family influence is focused on developing a sense of respect and attachment to the system and may also encourage the child's interest in current affairs and his participation as a member of community groups. Although the child's attachment to the system and his orientation toward compliance with the rules and regulations required by group membership may transfer directly from the family to other groups and organizations, it is more difficult to argue that a feeling of participation in the decision-making processes of the national government can be generalized from experience within the family. The influence of the family may be more directly relevant in the development of affiliation and compliance than for the sense of personal efficacy and ability to influence the system. The family's impact in this area is more likely to come from the child's observation of his parents' behavior and from identification with their pattern of participation and expressions of efficacy, than from the child's experience of effectiveness in influencing family decisions. The Identification Model is probably more important than the Interpersonal Transfer Model for explaining the acquisition of attitudes such as efficacy. The child's perception of familial models for political activity differs by social class, high-status individuals expressing more interest in politics than lower-status persons.

This feeling of effectiveness vis-à-vis the political system is related to earlier stages of attachment and compliance. Evidence already presented demonstrates the faith of young children in the benevolence and omniscience of the President and the government. So long as this unquestioning trust persists, the child sees little need for a citizen to control or influence governmental activities. If it is not necessary to influence the government—if it is sufficiently protective, strong, and perfect that the citizen's needs are automatically served—participation by the citizen is unnecessary. The child who is strongly attached in this fashion would not be likely to develop attitudes which lead to political involvement. The development of a more complex and cautious view of the government and its operation is presumably related to information obtained at school; that is, teaching in the classroom should give the child a more realistic perception of government, redirecting his earlier attachment and compliance.

CONCEPTION OF THE SYSTEM AND ROLE OF CITIZEN

High-IQ children have more reservations about the competence of the government than do low-IQ children. The child's image of government and governmental processes changes dramatically during the elementary-school years. Unlike young children who perceive the government as an undifferentiated object, older children regard the government as more complex and characterize the system more by institutional and formal rules than by personalities and personal interaction. The eighth-grader is much less idealistic, has much less trust in the beneficence of government and its officials. These changes are illustrated by the item "What goes on in the government is all for the best." Although the entire group maintains a basic trust in government, the older subjects express greater reservation.

The relationship of intelligence to the child's image of government is summarized in Fig. 39. There were also some social class divergencies but the pattern was not consistent. The differences between intelligence groups were much greater at higher grade levels. In their absolute trust in the government, children of low intelligence at grade eight were approximately equivalent to children of high intelligence at grades five and six. The impact of cognitive ability as a mediating variable is considerably greater than the effect of social class. There was also a difference between IQ groups in rating the President's infallibility (Appendix D, Fig. D.07). Brighter children were less likely to say that the President makes no mistakes in performing his administrative duties. This is congruent with the greater tendency for brighter children to be skeptical about "what goes on in the government." The decline in the absolute benevolence and infallibility of governmental figures makes vigilance and involvement on the part of the citizen more crucial.

It is apparently not social class or family milieu, but information and teaching provided by the school that encourage the child to view government within certain limiting conditions. This decline in unquestioned faith is part of the process of political socialization and is essential to the emergence of assertive political involvement. This changing image and the effect of cognitive processes in bringing it about seem to be a focal point in the emergence of a politically involved citizen.

The child's knowledge of the process by which influence may be brought to bear on legislation was indicated by ratings of how much influence a variety of figures and groups can exert on legislative deci-

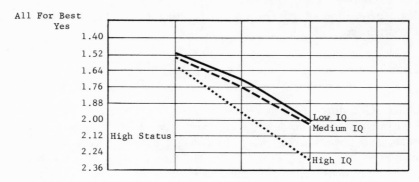

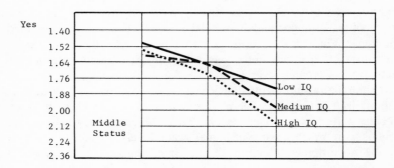

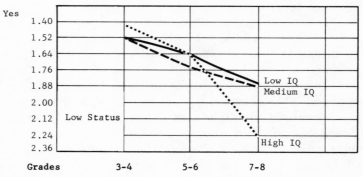

Grades   3-4   5-6   7-8

Item: Is what goes on in the gov-   Index Scale: 1 - Strong agree
      ernment all for the best?   4 -

                                          Range of N: 61 - 527

                                          Significance Unit: .12

Fig. 39.
Comparison of means of IQ groups in belief that the government is "all for the best," within social status and grade.

sions. Social class differences in perception of the legislative influence of groups and individuals were minimal; in general, lower-class students viewed all groups as somewhat more influential.

RELATIONSHIP TO THE SYSTEM

The child's sense of efficacy expresses one aspect of his own relationship to the government. These feelings are indexed in these data by a child's perception of the influence which his family is capable of exercising. We assume that this reflects the child's own feelings as well.

A sense of political efficacy is greater in children of high intelligence and in children of high status (Figs. 40 and 41). Social class differences were large, even at the third and fourth grades, and they increased with age. The differences in responses on the efficacy items are among the most striking social class discrepancies in the data of this study, one of the few variables on which there is a considerable difference between the middle- and the low-status groups. This is particularly important since a number of the familiar social class differences in political attitudes were greatly reduced when the research population was subdivided by intelligence test scores. Differences among the social status groups remain on this index, however, and are very great indeed when social class and IQ groups are compared.

The relatively lower sense of effectiveness on the part of children from the working class is congruent with their judgment about their families' interest in political matters and with their opinions about the decisiveness and power of their fathers. The relationship of the image of the father to the development of a sense of efficacy was discussed in Chapter Five.

In addition to the child's perception of the effectiveness of his family in the larger community, there is apparently some transmission of a sense of personal efficacy as a result of family experiences. There are differences among families from working and middle classes in their child rearing, particularly in the organization and exercise of family authority and decision making (Baldwin, 1948; Dubin and Dubin, 1963; Hess and Shipman, 1965; Kohn, 1959). In middle-class families, the children typically participate more in the decisions of the family.

Differences between IQ groups were even more marked than those between social class levels; the low-IQ group was three or four years behind the high-IQ group in the development of a sense of efficacy. The eighth-grade child of low intelligence was scarcely above the highly intelligent third- or fourth-grader. Moreover, differences between IQ groups increased with age.

Both the rate of change and the absolute level of this kind of involvement showed great divergence among groups. The importance of

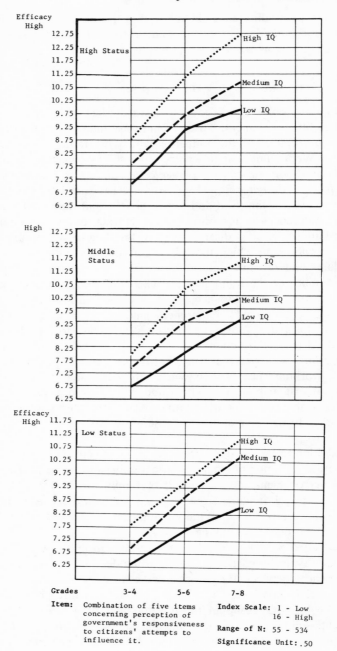

Grades   3-4   5-6   7-8

Item: Combination of five items   Index Scale: 1 - Low
        concerning perception of   16 - High
        government's responsiveness
        to citizens' attempts to   Range of N: 55 - 534
        influence it.   Significance Unit: .50

Fig. 40.
**Comparison of means of IQ groups in sense of political efficacy,
within social status and grade.**

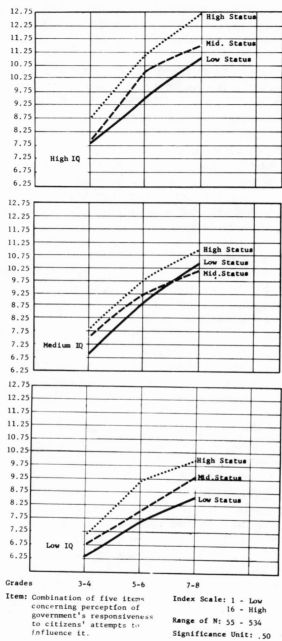

3-4   5-6   7-8

Item: Combination of five items   Index Scale: 1 - Low
concerning perception of   16 - High
government's responsiveness   Range of N: 55 - 534
to citizens' attempts to
influence it.   Significance Unit: .50

Fig. 41.
Comparison of means of social-status groups in sense of
political efficacy, within IQ and grade.

the school as a socializing agent is underlined by the increments that are related to intelligence. This suggests that socialization toward political involvement is retarded in children whose intelligence is below average.

The child's own response to his perception of the citizen's role and the responsiveness of the system was reflected in the item "How interested are you in current events?" This item showed no social class differences at any age. The differences that appeared at grades seven and eight were related to the intelligence of the child (Fig. 42). The greater interest reported by the high-intelligence group may reflect a more general interest in events of the external world, possibly reinforced by a belief that the citizen should be interested in government and a greater understanding of current affairs as presented in the mass media. This increased comprehension may, in turn, motivate the child to follow current events regularly.

Although the child's expression of his own interest does not differ by social status, there are status differences in the level of interest he reports that his family displays (Fig. 20). Social status differences in their reported interest increased by age and were significant at all grade levels, paralleling differences in interest that appear in studies of adults. While many of the questions asked of adults deal with specific events around election time or their interest in particular issues, the greater level of interest found among citizens of higher socioeconomic levels is reflected in this study in children's reports of the general interest of their family. Although not so great as the social class divergencies, IQ differences on this item were also significant.

The contrast between the child's own interest and that of his family raises an interesting point about socialization of political involvement. The child is encouraged by the school to recognize the need for interest and participation in governmental affairs and democratic processes. Sharp variation among social classes in family interest indicates, however, that some of these children have much greater family support (and possibly community support) to carry out and implement involvement norms of which they are aware. At a relatively early age the child recognizes the importance of interest and active participation. If he grows up in a family which supports this interest by showing an interest itself and by participating in community affairs and activities, it is likely that this reinforcement will encourage the child to greater participation and involvement as an adult. The child whose interest is initiated by the school and mass media, but who finds himself in a family that is apathetic and non-participating, is less likely to become involved. In short, there is differential reinforcement for the child's political interest from one family and social class to another. These findings on family interest are further supported by data which show that, while there are

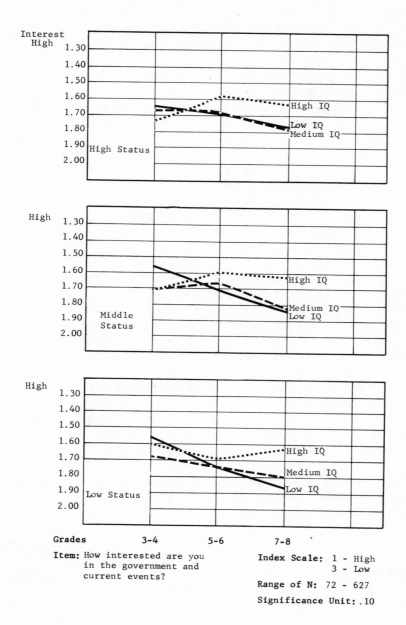

Fig. 42.
*Comparison of means of IQ groups in political interest,
within social status and grade.*

no differences by intelligence, wide divergences appear between social classes in rating the relative importance of the teacher and one's father in teaching citizenship. The teacher is clearly the major source of this training for low-status children (see Fig. 21).

Participation in political discussion and concern with political issues are more frequent among children of high intelligence and social status. Both indices dealing with verbal involvement followed the pattern of the efficacy data discussed earlier. In participation in political discussion, which includes talking with friends, peers, and family, social class differences were large and stable across the age levels; the IQ differences increased with age (Figs. 43 and 44). Consistent with the social class differences in family interest, a child who perceives his parents as uninterested in political news is not likely to discuss this topic with them. This substantiates the importance of the school in socializing specific concern with and discussion of political issues—perhaps through activities such as the analysis of current events.

The involvement of the child with political and ideological issues, reflected in questions dealing with his interest and defense of personal opinions, draws in part from the child's feeling that the good citizen ought to be aware of what is going on in the country. This is a norm that defines behavior and cuts across social classes. There was relatively little social class difference in reporting this type of involvement in political issues, but IQ differences were significant and increased with age (Fig. 45).[3]

In summary, the data presented in this section have shown that lower-status children more frequently accept authority figures as correct and rely on their trustworthiness and benign intent. There is, therefore, more acquiescence to the formal structure and less tendency to question the motivations behind the behavior of the government and governmental officials. The interest that children in all social classes and of all IQ levels display in contemporary political events is differentially supported by the adult models in different social class levels. Some families clearly support participation; other families are apparently contributing to apathy by failing to respond to the child's awareness of the active and responsible citizen's behavior. The school seems to be particularly effective in transmitting information about the structure of the system, but the schools are not doing an equally effective job in socializing children toward active participation. This is particularly crucial because

3. Litt (1963) reported results from several attitude scales administered to high-school students before and after the use of a civics curriculum designed to increase citizen participation. The working-class students, although equivalent to students from higher status levels in their acceptance of democratic principles, perceived politics as being conducted by formal institutions working in harmony for the benefit of all and needing little control from citizens. They had correspondingly lower efficacy and political activity scores.

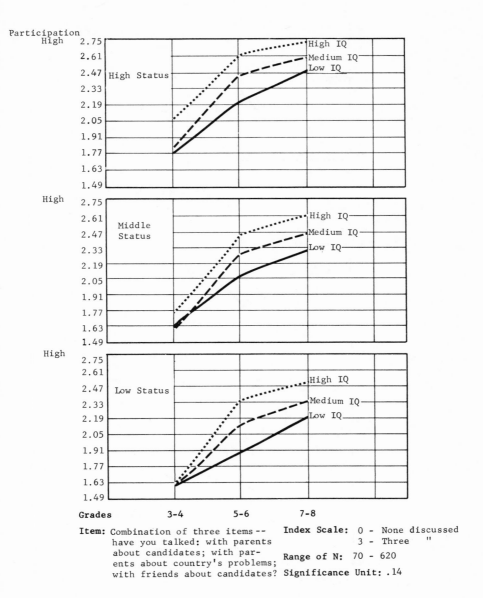

Participation

Item: Combination of three items --
have you talked: with parents
about candidates; with parents about country's problems;
with friends about candidates?

Index Scale: 0 - None discussed
              3 - Three   "

Range of N: 70 - 620

Significance Unit: .14

Fig. 43.
**Comparison of means of IQ groups in participation in political
discussion, within social status and grade.**

Participation

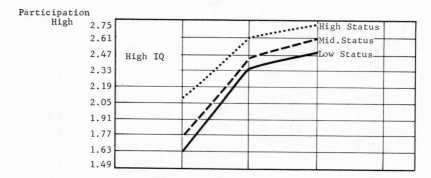

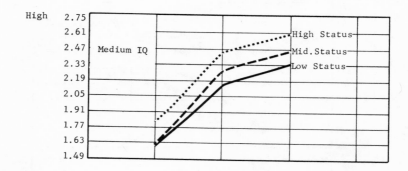

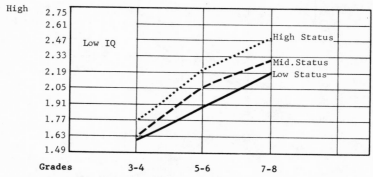

Item: Combination of three items --
have you talked: with par-
ents about candidates; with
parents about country's
problems; with friends about
candidates?

Index Scale: 0 - None discussed
              3 - Three   "

Range of N: 70 - 620

Significance Unit: .14

Fig. 44.

**Comparison of means of social-status groups in participation in
political discussion, within IQ and grade.**

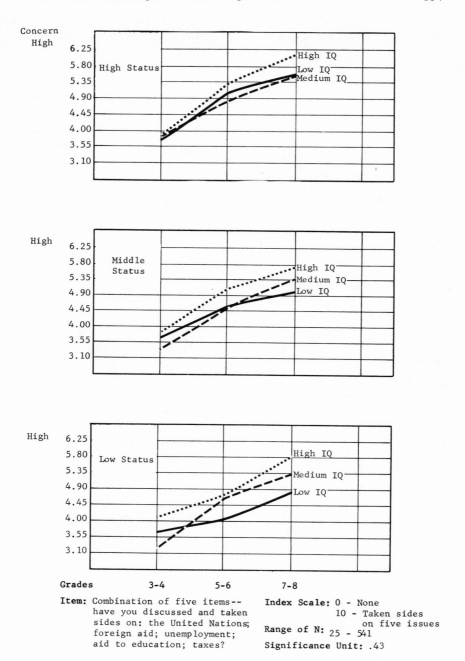

Grades   3-4   5-6   7-8

Item: Combination of five items--   Index Scale: 0 - None
      have you discussed and taken   10 - Taken sides
      sides on: the United Nations;   on five issues
      foreign aid; unemployment;   Range of N: 25 - 541
      aid to education; taxes?   Significance Unit: .43

Fig. 45.

**Comparison of means of IQ groups in concern about political issues,
within social status and grade.**

lower-status children have few institutional or community supports for political participation and involvement in the years following eighth-grade graduation.

Participation in the Election Process

The involvement of citizens in elections is, of course, a critical aspect of political participation and involvement. Although the child's age necessarily limits his participation in election activities, his attitudes in this area are important because they are relevant to his future participation in the party system—one of the mediating organizations through which the citizen may express his views and influence the operation of the governmental structure.

CONCEPTION OF THE SYSTEM

Voting is more salient as a symbol of government to children with high IQ. It was noted earlier that the child's view of government and the objects he selects to represent it focus increasingly upon activities (especially voting) as he grows older (Fig. 46). The influence of intelligence was apparent at all grade levels. This shift in response is part of a general trend toward abstract conceptualization of the system and its operations in relation to the individual. Formal teaching in the school encourages perception of the system in terms of a process and, specifically, in terms of voting.

High-IQ children are more willing to accept the possibility of change in the governmental system. The importance of elections in the child's view of the system and the motivations which lead individuals to run for office are indicated in responses to an item which asked whether people run for elective office to "keep things as good as they are in the country," to "be important and make money for themselves," or to "change things that are not good about the country." The images children of our group had of election candidates were influenced by social class and intelligence (Appendix D, Fig. D.08). Children of high intelligence saw candidates as desiring to change imperfection in the system; this is congruent with the attitudes of these children toward the system. In previous items, it was noted that the child of high intelligence is less likely to be convinced that what happens in government is all for the best and is more likely to show reservations about the government and its representatives. The perception that the system needs to be changed (by citizens and elected officials) indicates an orientation toward change and a concept of the ideal government as one in which reform is always valuable. These children are willing to accept the idea that a system as important as that of government has elements which can be improved. Perhaps their basic confidence in the processes is such that they do not see change as threatening. In contrast, children in the low-intelligence group are more inclined to be oriented toward the status quo; they think of government as representing benign and competent operations needing no change. Social class differences that appeared in this item were in the same direction—high-status groups were inclined to see a candidate's motivation as desire for change, while the low-status groups tended to perceive candidates as wanting to maintain the status quo (see also Hess and Torney, 1965, Fig. 76).

A distinct part of children's ideas about how role occupants are changed is their conception of political parties, the relationships between them, and their value to the total political system. An important element is the perception of "How much difference is there between the Democrats and the Republicans?" The choices on the item presented ranged on a five-point scale from "a *very* big difference" to "no difference." There were no distinctions by social class or intelligence in children's image of differences between the two parties.

Socialization into affiliation with party begins to be differentiated by social class at the fifth and sixth grades and is quite apparent by the seventh and eighth grades. Although at grades seven and eight children begin to choose party affiliation along social class lines (Democrats predominating among the working class), at this age they do not regard their party as essentially different from the other major party.

Although there were minimal social class variations in perception of the amount of difference between parties, children's perception of the Republicans' and Democrats' stands on specific issues and events was somewhat different for the social status groups. An index drawn from the series of items including "Who does most to help people who are out of work?" and "Who does most to keep us out of war?" showed some social class differences (Fig. 47) appearing most clearly in the tendency of the low-status group to attribute more positive activities to Democrats at grades seven and eight—the time when socialization into party affiliation has become most salient for the child. These findings parallel the social class differences in evaluation of Democrats and Republicans found in studies of adults, although they are not as great.

Partisan conflict is a prominent factor in the conceptualization of political parties and their relationship to the system. Children's view of the importance of partisan conflict was assessed in answers to the question: "If the Democrats and Republicans disagreed on important things, would it be good or bad for the country?" Social class and IQ differences were not consistent on this item. There was an increasing tendency with age for children to feel that disagreement has positive functions. This tendency, however, was far less than that in adults (as

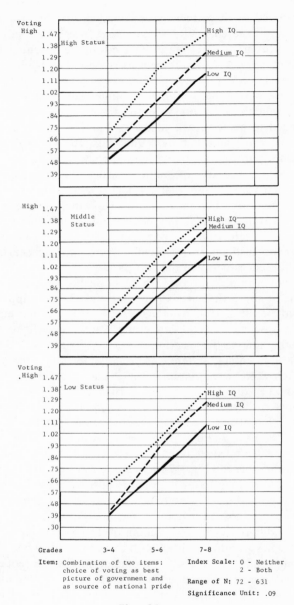

Grades   3-4   5-6   7-8

Item: Combination of two items: Index Scale: 0 - Neither
      choice of voting as best   2 - Both
      picture of government and   Range of N: 72 - 631
      as source of national pride
                                         Significance Unit: .09

Fig. 46.

**Comparison of means of IQ groups in choice of voting as symbol of
our form of government, within social status and grade.**

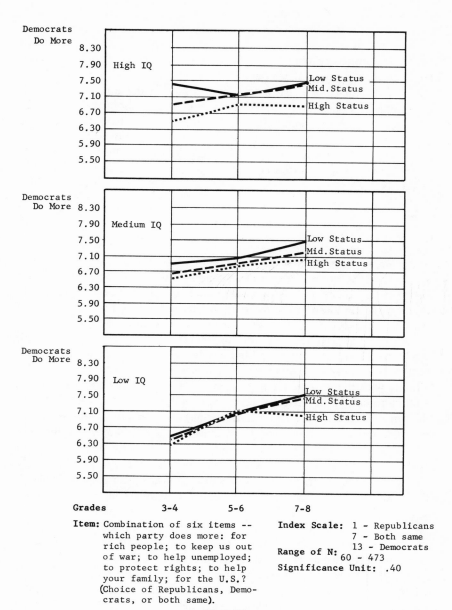

Grades   3-4   5-6   7-8

Item: Combination of six items --   Index Scale: 1 - Republicans
which party does more: for   7 - Both same
rich people; to keep us out   13 - Democrats
of war; to help unemployed;   Range of N: 60 - 473
to protect rights; to help   Significance Unit: .40
your family; for the U.S.?
(Choice of Republicans, Democrats, or both same).

Fig. 47.
**Comparison of means of social-status groups in appraisal of
relative contribution of Democrats and Republicans to
national welfare, within IQ and grade.**

evidenced by teacher responses), which indicates that on this point socialization within the school is relatively ineffective. Although teachers believe that disagreement can result in positive changes, this belief is not being transmitted to children. Data on curricula suggest that very little stress is placed on political parties until late in the elementary school One conclusion from these data is that although the amount of difference perceived between political parties and beliefs about their disagreement do *not* vary by social class or intelligence, the attribution of more beneficial actions and policies to the party of one's choice *does* vary by social class (beginning late in elementary school). These divergencies correspond to known social class differences in political party allegiance in adults.

PERCEPTION OF THE ROLE OF CITIZEN

Perception of the citizen's duty to vote is not related to social class, but a larger proportion of children of high intelligence believe that the good citizen is one who votes. The child's view of the ideal relationship between the citizen and the political system is relatively uninfluenced by social class. Children of the three social status levels in the study showed no difference in their responses to the item dealing with voting as a mark of the good citizen, nor did any social class differences appear in their attitudes concerning whether adults should belong to a political party, should vote with their party, or whether children should eventually affiliate with the same party as their parents. The norms of party voting, affiliation, and party loyalty seem not to be socialized differently in the various social class groups. If socialization of norms about citizen participation in elections and the values of political party membership were accomplished primarily through experiences in the home and community, significant social class differences would emerge. It is likely that the school is primarily responsible for transmitting to the child a definition of the norms of citizen behavior within political parties but not for his particular choice of the Democratic or Republican party.

Children of higher intelligence, more often than those in lower groups, defined the good citizen as one who votes; this was especially true of seventh- and eighth-graders (see Hess and Torney, 1965, Fig. 78). Also, these more gifted youngsters defined the relationship of a citizen to his political party differently since they more frequently rejected the idea that "one should vote along party lines" (Fig. 48), a tendency particularly evident at the seventh and eighth grades. Similarly, children of high intelligence placed less importance upon adult membership in political parties (Fig. 49).

The lack of social class influence and the greater relevance of intelligence in this part of the socializing process indicate that the school is the principal force in teaching that a spirit of independence from party affiliation is part of good citizenship. This is consistent with the responses of the teacher group, which showed a marked tendency to prefer independence from party affiliation.

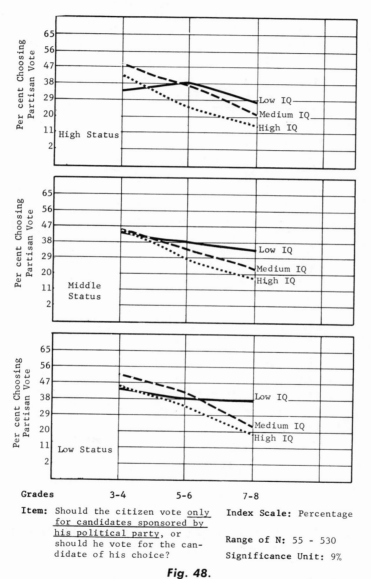

Grades   3-4   5-6   7-8

Item: Should the citizen vote <u>only for candidates sponsored by his political party</u>, or should he vote for the candidate of his choice?

Index Scale: Percentage

Range of N: 55 - 530

Significance Unit: 9%

Fig. 48.

Comparison of IQ groups in choice of partisanship as basis for candidate preference, within social status and grade.

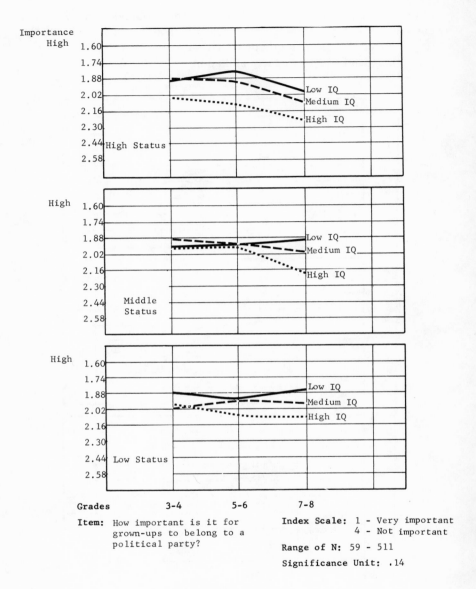

Item: How important is it for
grown-ups to belong to a
political party?

Index Scale: 1 - Very important
4 - Not important

Range of N: 59 - 511

Significance Unit: .14

Fig. 49.

**Comparison of means of IQ groups in rating importance of
party membership, within social status and grade.**

RELATIONSHIP TO THE SYSTEM

The data presented show that it is the school, mediated through the child's cognitive processes, that has the greatest influence upon his image of elections, the voting process, and the citizen's relation to this process through political parties. This topic was explored more intensively with items that deal more specifically with para-adult participation. These questions concern those adult activities which are directly political— inquiries about party affiliation and active interest in elections and candidates.

Political activity is higher in children of high intelligence and social status. While the data in the previous section showed little differentiation by social class in the internalization of norms, political activities quite clearly show differential socialization by social status groups (Fig. 50). Differences between social class levels were considerably greater than those by intelligence (which existed only at the higher grade levels). Family and community apparently support and encourage active participation in the election process. This is consistent with the social class distinctions in family interest previously noted. Participation in the election process is probably also reinforced by the school. Although the social classes do not differ in their acceptance of the norms of affiliation and voting with a party, high-status groups are more active politically.

In partisanship behavior, defined as commitment to a political party and a sense of obligation to vote with it, eighth-graders' views differed significantly from those of teachers. There is a relationship between intelligence and the report that one does not know what the parties are or does not know which party he would choose (Appendix D, Fig. D.09). Parties are not meaningful organizations for expressions of political involvement for children of low intelligence.

Both intelligence and social status are important mediating variables in socializing attitudes of partisan independence. The propensity of children to report that they would vote as Independents rather than as Democrats or Republicans is reported in Figs. 51 and 52. Declaring oneself independent of affiliation with a single party increased with age and was more characteristic of high-status children than of those in working-class levels. Children of high intelligence, particularly seventh- and eighth-graders, also preferred not to commit themselves to a party. Differences between the two extreme groups (high-IQ/high status, low-IQ/low-status) were dramatic. The proportion of low-IQ, low-status children who exhibited political independence by the seventh or eighth grade was not as high as the proportion of high-IQ, high-status third- and fourth-graders with the same orientations. Moreover, in this low-status group, gravitation toward independence from political affiliation

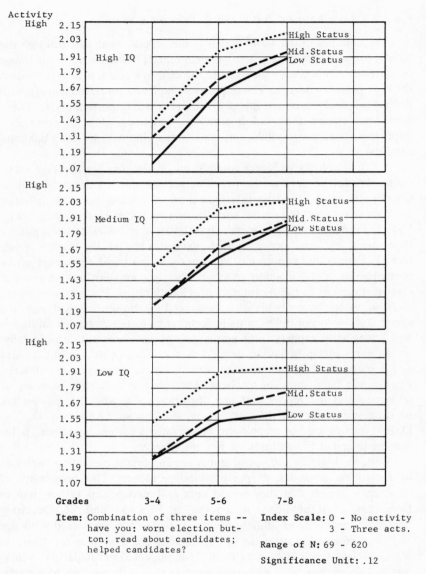

Fig. 50.
Comparison of means of social-status groups in political
activity, within IQ and grade.

did not increase with age, indicating that socialization by the school toward independence is achieved only among the higher-IQ children. Thus, intelligence mediates school experiences, cutting across social class levels to accelerate acquisition of attitudes devaluing partisan activity.

Choice of a party is not related to social status until after grade five. The particular choice of party (Democrat or Republican) in older children shows a pattern that has been found consistently with adults— working class association with the Democratic party. It is interesting to note (Fig. 53) that at grades three and four there was no social class difference in the proportion of children who declared themselves as Democrats. The differentiation began at grades five and six and was well established by the seventh and eighth grades. The period between the ages of 10 and 12 seems to be the point at which partisan commitment begins to be meaningful. However, the difference between social status groups in choice of party was evident at an earlier grade level than difference between assessment of the parties' stands on issues.

Reactions following an election are very strongly related to social status. Social class differences in this item appeared to a striking degree at grade three, the youngest children tested (Fig. 54). The association with social class is probably influenced by the differential distribution of Republicans and Democrats by social class, and in the election of 1960 these differences were augmented by the influence of religious affiliation which is also unevenly distributed by class (see Chapter Six). This pattern in the data does not necessarily indicate commitment to a party; it is a response which concentrates on the figures with whom a child identifies in the election contest. The differences are considerably more striking than social status differences in reporting Democratic or Republican affiliation.

The relation of intelligence to the differences in emotional response is not so easily interpreted (see Hess and Torney, 1965, Fig. 88). Although the less-intelligent children showed more positive responses than the more-intelligent children, these differences were not as marked as those between social status levels. Perhaps more-intelligent children's tendency toward political independence was a factor here.

Political campaigns provide a sense of the dramatic intensity surrounding political life; observing other citizens participating in a national event may orient children toward this aspect of the political process. There were few differences by social class in the intensity of affect toward an election. Data in Appendix D, Fig. D.10 indicate both social class and IQ differences in the children's opinion of what they learn from elections. These were in the expected direction, with high-IQ children more frequently saying that they learned much from having observed the election. This difference increased with age, being most obvious at the seventh- and eighth-grade levels.

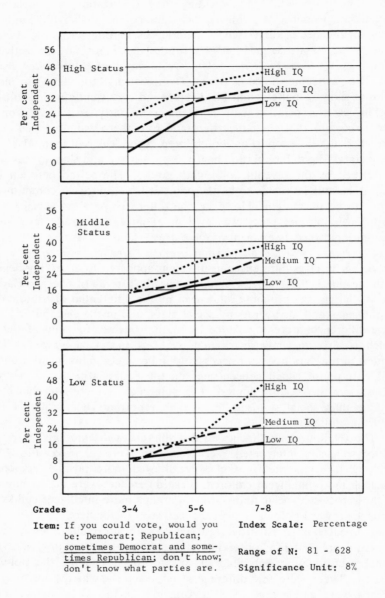

Grades   3-4   5-6   7-8

Item: If you could vote, would you   **Index Scale:** Percentage
be: Democrat; Republican;
sometimes Democrat and some-   **Range of N:** 81 - 628
times Republican; don't know;
don't know what parties are.   **Significance Unit:** 8%

Fig. 51.
*Comparison of IQ groups in reporting independence from
party commitment, within social status and grade.*

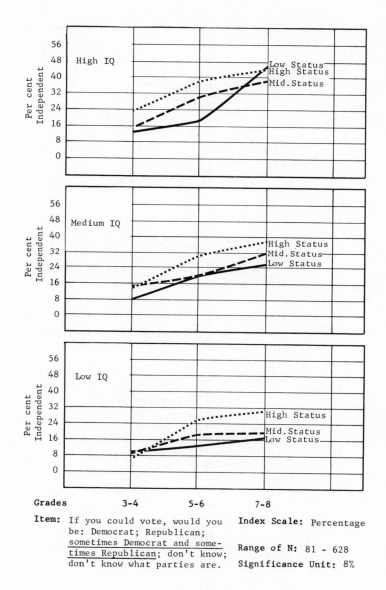

Grades   3-4   5-6   7-8

Item: If you could vote, would you   Index Scale: Percentage
be: Democrat; Republican;
sometimes Democrat and some-   Range of N: 81 - 628
times Republican; don't know;
don't know what parties are.   Significance Unit: 8%

Fig. 52.
Comparison of social-status groups in reporting independence from
party commitment, within IQ and grade.

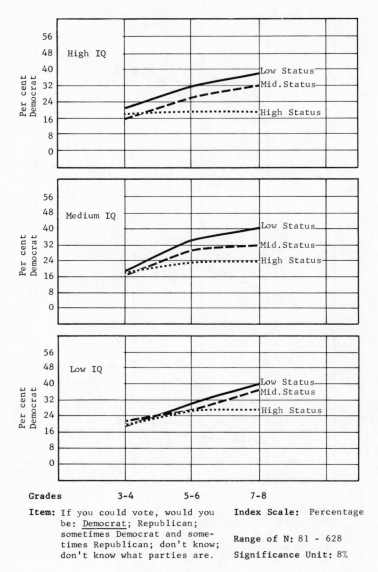

Fig. 53.

Comparison of social-status groups in reporting Democratic party commitment, within IQ and grade.

SUMMARY

Basic attachment to the nation and the government, and the acceptance of compliance to law and authority are relatively unaffected by social class and by the mediation of intelligence in the learning process. These are also areas in which the family and community play strong supporting and socializing roles. Since social class effects would be transmitted in the context of the family, these areas apparently represent consensus in the total community.

The acquisition of more active and initiatory aspects of political involvement (activities, efficacy, participation in discussion, interest) is strongly affected by IQ and by social status. The school apparently plays an important role in teaching these attitudes and skills of participation, and children of high intelligence grasp them more quickly. Also, the family and community in high-status areas tend to provide models for and to support high political interest and active involvement thus accentuating the divergence.

In general, these differences by social status parallel the differences between social status levels in the adult society. Party preference, for example, shows the usual relationship with social class, beginning at about grade five. Candidate preference shows a particularly strong relationship to social class beginning at a very early grade-level. In this feature of involvement, as in most where IQ and social status differences appear, the discrepancy between groups increases with age, reaching its greatest divergence in grades seven and eight. This suggests that the socialization of consensus is completed at an early grade, leaving less agreed-upon aspects to later elementary-school years.

The tendency for children from low-status homes, and for children of relatively low intelligence at all status levels, to be retarded in their socialization into active involvement presents a serious problem for the society and confronts the schools with a difficult task in civic education. These children are graduating from grammar school incompletely socialized into the political community. Since high-school data indicate that there is little change in attitudes during high-school years, it is likely that this gap in socialization is not made up at later education levels. Also, since these children are those who are most likely to drop out of school or have difficulty in high-school courses, they may have limited opportunity to acquire the orientations of more active involvement later. These may be the children who will become apathetic as adults; there is no evidence that this is so, but the parallel between adult attitudes and the attitudes of children at the eighth grade is striking.

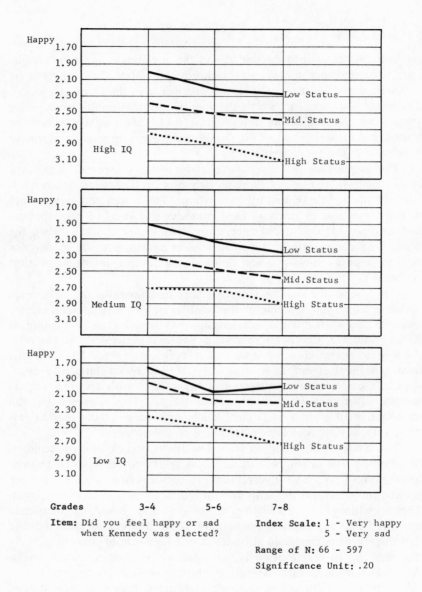

Grades   3-4   5-6   7-8

Item: Did you feel happy or sad   Index Scale: 1 - Very happy
      when Kennedy was elected?   5 - Very sad

                                     Range of N: 66 - 597

                                     Significance Unit: .20

Fig. 54.

Comparison of means of social-status groups in emotional response
to Kennedy's election, within IQ and grade.

8

The Influence of

Sex Role Orientation

Introduction

The focus of studies of adult and adolescent sex differences in political behavior has been on adult modes of activity such as voting, interest in political news, and feelings of efficacy. These studies have not dealt with variations in attachment, compliance, or conceptions of law and relationships to authority. The sex differences reported in research on adult political participation show that women express fewer opinions in public opinion surveys (Cantril and Strunk, 1951), are more interested in candidates than in issues (Campbell, Gurin, and Miller, 1954), and evaluate political objects on a lower level of conceptualization than do men (Campbell, Converse, Miller, and Stokes, 1960). Women also feel less competent and efficacious in their political activity than men (Campbell, Converse, Miller, and Stokes, 1960) and are less interested in political matters and elections (Berelson, Lazarsfeld, and McPhee, 1954); they vote less frequently than men (a difference which is more pronounced at lower educational levels).

The age at which sex differences in political participation and involvement arise has been reviewed by Hyman (1959) and studied by Greenstein (1965a). Hyman reports that adolescent girls show less interest in political matters than boys; boys are better informed about current news and more often choose their ego ideals from among political leaders than do girls. Greenstein (1965a), studying fourth- through eighth-grade children, found that boys scored higher on a test of political information, were more interested in national than regional news, and when asked to name a news story were more likely than girls to cite a political item. Awareness that males are more knowledgeable about politics develops during childhood; Greenstein reported that both boys and girls said they would ask father rather than mother for advice about voting.

There are several possible sources of sex-typing in political behavior.

173

Political socialization, like other learning, is influenced by the sex role and other basic personality characteristics of the individual. Sex role differences lead to different role expectations in other social systems, illustrating the Interpersonal Transfer Model of the acquisition of political behavior. Role expectations are quite different for the two sexes, even at the pre-school level. Among 2- to 4-year-olds, for example, the boys are expected to be more aggressive and dominant than girls. Children of this age are aware of role differences between males and females (Kagan, Hosken, and Watson, 1961). The sex-role learning which occurs at this period mediates much of the child's later interaction with other social systems.

Lynn (1962), attempting to clarify the sources of these sex differences, suggested that they arise both from the nature of the sex role to which the child is directly socialized and from the process of socialization. In his formulation, girls learn the feminine sex role primarily by directly imitating their mothers; boys, however, must model many men, since fathers work away from home and are less available for imitation. Since women also direct the development of masculine sex role, the boy learns a stereotyped rather than specific male role. To learn the masculine sex role requires the ability to abstract principles of masculinity from several different models. Lynn (1962) derived predictions about sex difference which concur with the findings of other investigators; girls have a greater need for affiliation or social response from others, they are more influenced by the standards of others, and are less dependent upon internalized moral standards; girls are less concerned with problem-solving and with forming abstract principles.

In his evaluation of theory and research on sex differences in moral development, Kohlberg found no evidence of differences in the degree of adherence to internalized moral standards. He attributed these results to "naturally-sociologically" determined perceptions of sex role:

> Girls are expected to be, and expect themselves to be, more obedient, more fearful, more affectionate, and more dependent. . . . These differences are similar to the differences in children's perceptions of mother and father already mentioned. These differences in self-perceptions of role would be expected to lead to great compliance to authority by girls, regardless of general degree of internalization of moral rules (1963, p. 312).

Kohlberg did find, however, that boys are oriented more toward impersonal justice in their development of conscience than are girls. This, he believes, is related to the fact that adult male roles involve legitimate rule-enforcing behavior while the housewife-mother role primarily involves person-oriented norms; these are roles with which the child identifies. Johnson (1963) conceptualizes sex-role learning as an incorporation of social roles learned from interaction with parents, not as identification with traits or qualities of the parents. The child's sex may also influence the expectations others have for his political activities. To the degree that parents and teachers subscribe to the cultural stereotype that political activity is more appropriate for men, different norms and expectations will be presented to boys and girls.

In summary, sex differences in political involvement result from a complex set of influences. There may be a tendency for parents and teachers to induct boys into more active political roles because they subscribe to the norm that politics is a man's world. Boys may perceive that their fathers are more politically active than their mothers and incorporate this as part of the male image with which they identify. Another aspect of pre-adult socialization is that role expectations, patterns of needs, and behavior differ for boys and girls and mediate political socialization.

Acquisition of Attitudes

Girls acquire attitudes less rapidly than boys. Boys are about a year ahead in attitude growth, but sex difference diminishes with age (Fig. 55). Girls earn higher school grades and score higher on reading achievement tests than boys (Anderson, 1957; Hughes, 1953), but apparently girls' greater interest and achievement in school does not extend to the acquisition of political attitudes. Greenstein (1965a) asserted that boys have greater interest in political affairs; this would explain the sex difference but would not predict the lack of differentiation between boys and girls evident at the seventh- and eighth-grade levels. This implies that the school socializes both boys and girls to equal levels of attitude. As adults, however, group and institutional supports for female political participation may no longer be sufficient to maintain this attitude level.

Attachment to Nation

Boys and girls do not differ in their basic attachment to the country. There are no differences between girls and boys in symbolization of the country (determined by asking which picture best represents America) and no sex differences in attachment to America as the best country in the world. These attitudes are so widely held in the population that sub-groups are not differentiated.

Boys have a somewhat different view of international morality than do girls (Fig. 56), answering that it is acceptable for the government

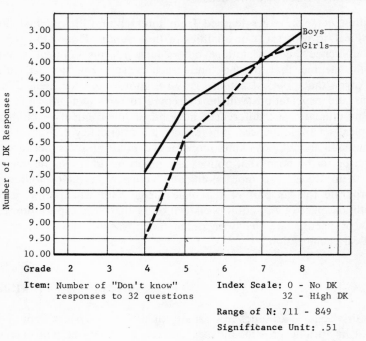

Fig. 55.

**Comparison of means of boys and girls in acquisition
of political attitudes, within grade.**

to lie in order to protect the American people. Girls are more likely to apply personal morality to political actions, feeling that all lies are wrong, while boys judge governmental actions in terms of political expediency.

Attachment to Figures and Institutions of Government

CONCEPTION OF THE SYSTEM

Girls symbolize government as a personal figure rather than as an institution. The discussion of previous research on sex role suggests that girls are more involved with persons and less able to handle abstractions than boys. This is supported by these data (Fig. 57). Significant sex differences in the personalization of government appeared in every grade except the second; this differentiation between the sexes increased with age. This conceptualization is important because it indicates that girls approach the government with a different set of expectations, expectations similar to those they have learned in personal relationships within the family.

RELATIONSHIP TO THE SYSTEM

Girls are more attached to personal figures of the system than are boys. Girls conceptualize the government in personal terms, and their relationship reflects this perception. The item "the President is my favorite," shows the greater attachment of girls clearly at the later grades (Fig. 58), a tendency also apparent in the item measuring the child's "liking" for the President. These findings are similar to those of Beloff and Beloff (1961), that female college students attributed higher positive valence to Eisenhower than did males. In the study reported here, girls also perceived these figures as more personally con-

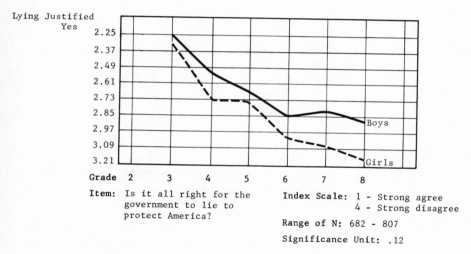

Fig. 56.
Comparison of means of boys and girls in justifying expediency to protect national interest, within grade.

cerned with them. The President was seen as more nurturant by girls, more likely to want to help them and more responsive if they wrote to him, a sex difference which increased with age (Fig. 59).

Girls emphasize the protective quality of personal figures and are attached to them, while boys stress protection by more impersonal and institutionalized structures. There are dissimilarities in the quality of boys' and girls' attachment to the system. In spite of a relatively low

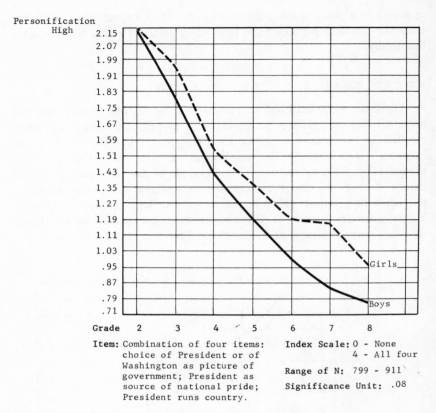

Personification

Fig. 57.

**Comparison of means of boys and girls in tendency to personify
the government, within grade.**

level of interest in political matters and issues, the girls are more
attached to figures of government and see them in more favorable terms
than do boys. The picture is quite different in the impersonal institutionalized aspects of government. Through the middle grades, boys
rated the Supreme Court higher in willingness to help (Fig. 60). When
compared with boys, girls rated the President and policeman higher
on a number of specific aspects of role performance (Table 27). These
differences were more pronounced at the later grade levels. In most
items, favorable judgments decreased for boys, while they remained
constant for girls. There was some tendency for boys to assess the
Supreme Court as more infallible; this is consistent with the differential
value of personal and impersonal authority.

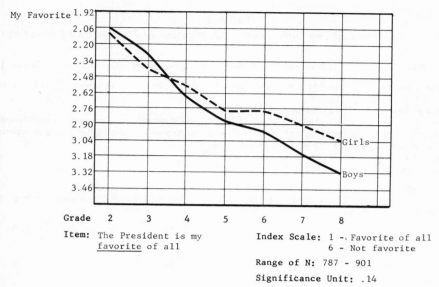

Item: The President is my
      favorite of all

Index Scale: 1 - Favorite of all
             6 - Not favorite

Range of N: 787 - 901

Significance Unit: .14

Fig. 58.

Comparison of means of boys and girls in attachment to President, within grade.

Compliance and Response to Law

CONCEPTION OF THE SYSTEM AND ROLE OF THE CITIZEN

Girls were more likely to feel that "all laws are fair." This difference began at the sixth grade and remained at the same magnitude through the rest of the grades (Appendix D, Fig. D.11). Girls more frequently than boys reported that the most important duty of the adult citizen is to obey laws (Fig. 61). This is consistent with studies showing that girls are more obedient in early childhood at home and in school. The stress that teachers place on obedience and conformity to school rules and laws is more effective for girls, and they may also learn the norms of citizenship behavior more quickly than boys. This is an exception to the general pattern of more rapid acquisition of attitudes by boys.

Table 27
Summary of Sex Differences in Perception of Figures and Institutions [a]

Item	President	Policeman	Supreme Court	Government	Senator
Never makes mistakes	no difference	girls higher [b]	boys higher	no difference	no difference
Keeps promises	no difference	girls higher			
Knows a lot	girls higher	girls higher [b]	no difference	no difference	no difference
Makes decisions	girls higher [b]	girls higher [b]	no difference	girls higher	girls higher
Never gives up	girls higher	no difference			
Is a leader	no difference	girls higher [b]			
Works hard	girls higher [b]	girls higher [b]			

a. Differences include items 1 unit apart at 2 grade-levels out of grades 4-8.

b. A particularly large difference: 2 units apart at 2 grade-levels, or 1 unit apart at 4 grade-levels, or equivalent.

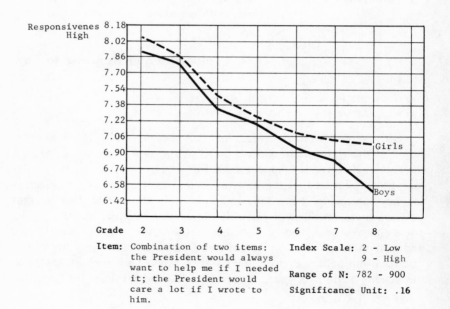

Fig. 59.
Comparison of means of boys and girls in rating President's responsiveness to individuals, within grade.

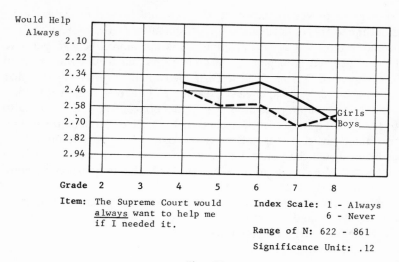

Item: The Supreme Court would
always want to help me
if I needed it.

Index Scale: 1 - Always
6 - Never

Range of N: 622 - 861

Significance Unit: .12

Fig. 60.
Comparison of means of boys and girls in rating Supreme Court's responsiveness to individuals, within grade.

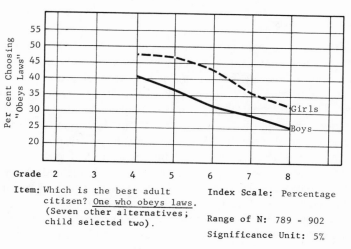

Item: Which is the best adult
citizen? One who obeys laws.
(Seven other alternatives;
child selected two).

Index Scale: Percentage

Range of N: 789 - 902

Significance Unit: 5%

Fig. 61.
Comparison of boys and girls in choice of "obey laws" as citizen's most important obligation, within grade.

RELATIONSHIP TO THE SYSTEM

Girls see legal authorities as more responsive than do boys. A major part of the child's compliance is based upon his perception that the system has power to enforce laws. From this perspective, the child's relationship to the policeman as a representative of the system of laws is an important point of socialization. Girls are more likely to perceive that the policeman is responsive to their needs and would want to help them (Appendix D, Fig. D.12). Girls also rated the policeman higher in role-performing competence (Table 27). Consistent with their perception of greater protection from the policeman, girls were also more likely to be personally attached to the policeman and to say that he was their favorite (Fig. 62). At the older grade levels, boys were more likely to tell the policeman he is wrong if they felt they had been unjustly treated. This is also consistent with the unquestioning compliance that is part of the feminine sex role.

Sex differences in perception of the power of individuals and institutions are large and consistent. Girls saw all personal figures (President, policeman, senator, and father) as more powerful and as more able to punish others and to make other people do what they want (Figs. 63; and Appendix D, D.13). This differentiation was more pronounced at the later grade levels. Boys, in line with their conception of the government in institutional terms, saw the Supreme Court as more powerful (Fig. 64).

DISCUSSION

Girls see the government in more personalized terms: they perceive the personal figures in the government as more nurturant, feel more attached to them, attribute more power to them, and see them as fulfilling their roles more adequately. Boys, however, see the Supreme Court and impersonal objects as more powerful and helpful. These differences were particularly evident at the later grades. This seems congruent with Parsons' (1955) discussion of polarization of masculine and feminine roles; he suggested that women and girls are oriented toward expressive roles while men and boys are oriented to the impersonal occupational roles within the social system. This may be analogous to the orientation of girls to the personal-expressive aspects of the political system, and that of boys to the impersonal-instrumental facets.

Sex differences were particularly pronounced in ratings of the policeman, with girls rating him consistently higher, particularly on performance of his role. This suggests that girls compensate for feelings of powerlessness in response to the policeman by seeing him as a benevolent, helpful, competent figure. Young children tend to feel vulnerable and powerless when they consider their own power in relation to authority, and girls feel particularly anxious, helpless, powerless, and insecure. Bronfenbrenner (1961), for example, maintained that girls are particularly sensitive to punitive influence. Previous data (Torney, Hess,

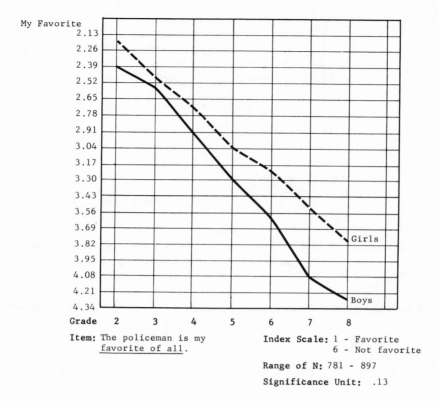

Item: The policeman is my   Index Scale: 1 - Favorite
      favorite of all.   6 - Not favorite

                                  Range of N: 781 - 897

                                  Significance Unit: .13

Fig. 62.
**Comparison of means of boys and girls in attachment to
policeman, within grade.**

and Easton, 1962) indicated that children's idealized image of the
President, particularly among lower-class girls, may be a response to
these feelings of vulnerability. The idealized perception of the President
and the policeman may be motivated by need to see benevolence in a
powerful figure.

In these data, most of the sex differences increased with age. Frequently, boys showed pronounced age trends, while girls changed
substantially less from grade two to eight. Older girls resemble younger
children in their responses to these figures. Dependency is characteristic
of young children and of girls at all ages. Need structures, particularly
those involving dependency, may be important in the differential orientations of boys and girls to the political system.

These sex differences are also remarkably consistent when viewed

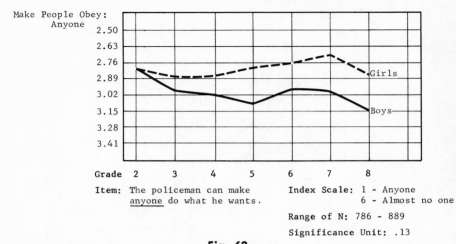

Item: The policeman can make   Index Scale: 1 - Anyone
      anyone do what he wants.   6 - Almost no one

                                     Range of N: 786 - 889
                                     Significance Unit: .13

Fig. 63.
Comparison of means of boys and girls in rating coercive power of
policeman, within grade.

within the framework of role relationships. Girls define the system as one
in which all the laws are just. Reciprocally, they define the citizen's role
as obedience to these laws. Girls see personal figures in the government
as particularly powerful; in return, they are more reluctant to challenge
a personal authority (the policeman).

Influencing Government Policy

    This section considers political activities in which the child cannot
yet engage but for which he can prepare himself. These include attempts
to influence the governmental system other than voting (writing to Con-
gressmen, participating in political activity other than that during elections, supporting groups which lobby for certain laws). Although less
research has been directed toward this area than toward behavior surrounding elections, discrepancies between men and women have been
reported in both interest and efficacy.

    In interpreting sex differences in attempts to influence governmental
policy, it is important to consider two prerequisites for effective political
activity. The first is knowledge of the procedures by which influence
may reasonably be attempted—particularly knowledge of the responsiveness of elected representatives and the most effective channels of
influence. The second prerequisite is competence in presenting one's
opinion to governmental figures, an action which demands an assertive

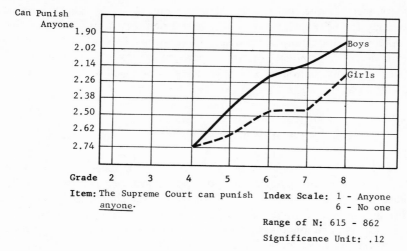

Item: The Supreme Court can punish   Index Scale: 1 - Anyone
anyone.   6 - No one

Range of N: 615 - 862

Significance Unit: .12

Fig. 64.

Comparison of means of boys and girls in rating punitive power of Supreme Court, within grade.

approach to the political system. In this area the socialization of passive compliance in females may have an effect on political activity.

CONCEPTION OF THE SYSTEM AND ROLE OF THE CITIZEN

A conceptualization of the system as one in which the citizen's right and duty is to make his opinion felt is shared by boys and girls in this group. The definition of democracy as a system in which "the people rule" and "if most of the people agree, the rest should go along," showed no sex differences. Assertive participation in government assumes an implicit acknowledgment of the need for change. It involves perception of the system as one in which things do not automatically serve the best interests of the citizen. There are no variations between the percentages of girls and boys who agreed that "what goes on in the government is all for the best," and, although girls attributed more ideal qualities to personal figures, they did not see government and its actions more positively.

Differences between males and females in beliefs about the influence which the average citizen and pressure groups have on legislation were measured by ratings of eight persons and pressure groups on "how much they help decide what laws are made for the country." The three individuals listed were the President, the policeman, and the average person; all were rated higher by girls—a difference that was much more pronounced at the later grade levels (Fig. 65). There was some tendency for girls to make a higher assessment of the influence of rich people and labor unions in determining laws. This may be another expression of the tendency of girls to personalize governmental processes. There was no variation by sex in ratings of newspapers, big companies, or churches.

RELATIONSHIP TO THE SYSTEM

The individual's interchange with the system, particularly his perception of the effectiveness of political action, is measured by the Index of Efficacy. Although adult surveys show that males feel more efficacious, data showed no sex differences on this index. After men enter the occupational system, the institutional supports for political action may be much greater for them, but in elementary school the sex differentiation is limited.

Boys, however, are more interested in political matters than are girls in grades four through seven (Fig. 66). This is in contrast to girls' greater tendency to see interest in current events and political issues as part of the good citizen's role (Fig. 67). Girls apparently learn this norm of citizen behavior earlier than boys; however, they do not report their own interest to be as great as the interest reported by boys. The discrepancy between girls' perception of norms and their behavior illustrates the importance of inquiring independently about the acquisition of norms, about how one should behave, and about what one actually does. It also illustrates the usefulness of thinking of the process of political socialization in terms of several alternate models. For example, girls' attitudes about the norms of political interest seem to follow from the Accumulation Model—they learn in school that the good citizen is supposed to be informed about current events. Their relatively lower level of actual interest, however, seems more congruent with the female sex role, illustrating the Interpersonal Transfer Model.

Two indices were used to measure the child's tendency to discuss political and governmental issues with other persons and to support one side of an argument. Responses indicated that girls engage in general political discussions with friends and family as frequently as boys do. There was, however, a consistent trend for boys more frequently to report that they had discussed and taken sides on specific issues such as unemployment, foreign aid, etc. (Fig. 68). In other words, girls were not surpassed by boys in the frequency of discussions of general nature with friends and family, but boys were more likely to engage in discussions of a specific or controversial nature. This is a further

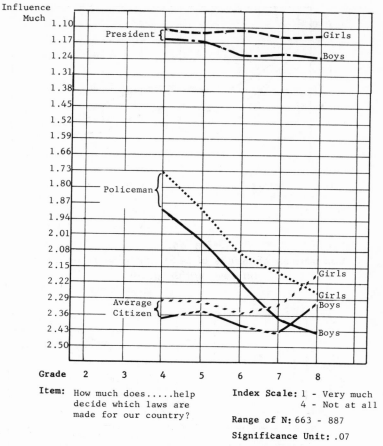

Influence
Much

Grade   2   3   4   5   6   7   8

Item: How much does.....help   Index Scale: 1 - Very much
       decide which laws are   4 - Not at all
       made for our country?   Range of N: 663 - 887
                                      Significance Unit: .07

Fig. 65.
**Comparison of means of boys and girls in rating influence of
policeman, President, and average citizen on legislation,
within grade.**

example of the particularly political nature of boys' involvement, in
contrast to the more social orientation of girls' involvement.

S U M M A R Y

One of the first prerequisites for political activity is to perceive the
system as responsive to individual and group pressures upon it and to
realize the importance of citizen interest. Girls were not different from
boys in their knowledge of the process and norms of the system. Girls

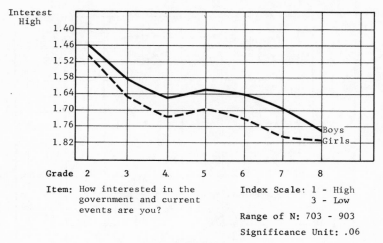

Fig. 66.

Comparison of means of boys and girls in political interest, within grade.

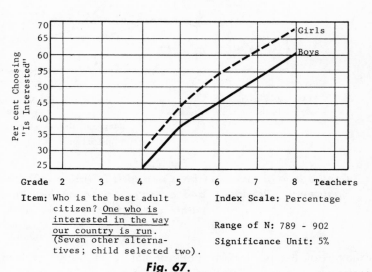

Fig. 67.

Comparison of boys and girls in choice of "interest in way our country is run" as citizen's most important obligation, within grade.

and boys did not differ in perceiving the government to be all for the best or in their feelings of efficacy. Girls accepted somewhat earlier the norm that citizens should be interested in the government.

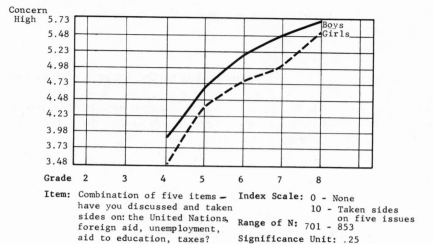

Fig. 68.

Comparison of means of boys and girls in concern about political issues, within grade.

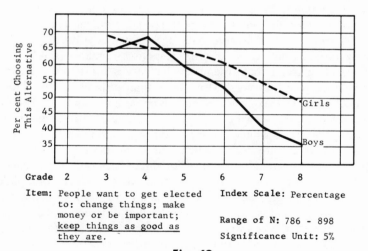

Fig. 69.

Comparison of boys and girls in choice of "keep things as good as they are" as reason candidates seek office, within grade.

The second prerequisite for active political involvement is the possession of appropriate feelings about one's self which encourage active participation. Boys were consistently superior on two indices of active political involvement (Interest in Government and Concern with Political Issues). Boys are more likely to participate in active political roles.

Participation in the Process of Elections

This section deals with the perception of two precursors of participation in the election process—the activities surrounding voting and those involving partisan preference.

CONCEPTION OF THE SYSTEM AND ROLE OF THE CITIZEN

There were no sex differences in identifying voting as a mark of democracy. Likewise, there were no differences in selection of voting as a symbol of government. Apparently, boys and girls become equally sensitive to the role of elections in the political processes of this country.

One characteristic of the perception of the electoral system did show divergencies between males and females. When asked what the motivation of candidates is for seeking election, more females said, "They want to keep things as good as they are in our country" (Fig. 69). This is consistent with their tendency to see government as a protective system. The difference increased with age. Older boys were less likely to choose this alternative, while girls' responses remained stable across the age span, a trend that resembles the curves for items concerning the President's protectiveness. More boys than girls chose the alternative: "They want to make a lot of money or be important." This choice may result from boys' viewing politics as an occupation like others, with motivations like those which are important in choosing any job.

Political parties are more salient for boys than for girls. Boys' perceptions show a greater tolerance for differences between parties on issues and attribute more positive functions to differences of opinion. The awareness that political parties exist is a recognition of conflict and divergence on political issues, a recognition that different groups of people would manage the country and solve its problems in different ways. Boys claimed to know about parties at an earlier age. Boys, to a greater extent than girls, identified parties with issues. This appears on responses to "which party does most for the country?" (Appendix D, Fig. D.14). Girls more frequently said that both parties have the same stand or contribute the same amount, while boys associated the Republican and Democratic parties with different points of view on specific issues. Girls more often saw disagreement between the parties as having negative effects (Fig. 70), stating that it would be bad for the country if the

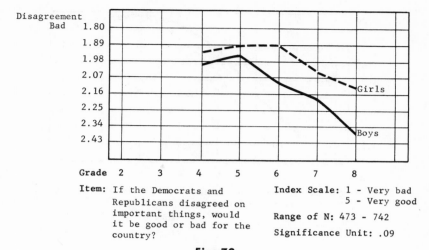

Item: If the Democrats and
Republicans disagreed on
important things, would
it be good or bad for the
country?

Index Scale: 1 - Very bad
                5 - Very good

Range of N: 473 - 742

Significance Unit: .09

Fig. 70.
Comparison of means of boys and girls in attitudes toward
interparty disagreement, within grade.

two political parties disagreed on important issues. Girls defined the
system as one in which consensus between parties is the most important
goal. These results may be interpreted either as a result of girls' greater
orientation to candidates rather than issues, or of their desire to minimize conflict and disagreement.

There were no differences between boys and girls in perceiving that
the good citizen's duty is to vote and in saying that the good citizen
should vote for the best man and not necessarily for a particular party's
candidates. This response must be interpreted in light of the tendency
for children to view political parties with suspicion. There were no differences in acceptance of norms concerning political parties. Boys and
girls did not vary in their tendency to say that children should belong
to the same political party as their parents, in their judgment of how
important it is for adults to belong to a political party, or in their
assessment of the age at which political party choice is most appropriately made.

RELATIONSHIP TO THE SYSTEM

Virtually all children in this study understood that voting is a particularly important mode of adult participation in the system because it
enables them to place men of their choice in office. Elections may act
as socializing events because they bring political activities and figures

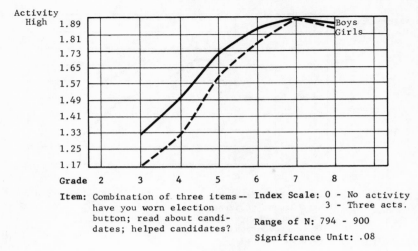

Item: Combination of three items --   Index Scale: 0 - No activity
      have you worn election   3 - Three acts.
      button; read about candi-   Range of N: 794 - 900
      dates; helped candidates?
                                      Significance Unit: .08

Fig. 71.
Comparison of means of boys and girls in political activity,
within grade.

into the spotlight. This function of elections is equally important for
both sexes; there was no difference in girls' and boys' reports of how
much they learned from the last Presidential election.

Boys reported more political activity than girls in the third through
fifth grades (Fig. 71). Although children cannot directly participate
in changing the administration, there are certain appropriate activities
for them. These include commitment to a party, expressing involvement
with election outcomes, and engaging in political activities (such as
wearing a button to show which candidates one supports). Sex differences in these attitudes and activities appeared primarily at the younger
age levels and decreased with age.

Boys were also more likely to identify with a political party, that is,
to report that they were Democrats or Republicans rather than independents or undecided (Fig. 72). This was true through grade six.
There was no sex difference in the amount of emotional reaction or
concern children expressed after hearing the results of the last election.
The finding that males are more politically active and partisan-aligned
is in line with data on adults. Although these differences decrease by
grade eight, they apparently reappear at some time during adolescence
or adulthood, perhaps because of diminished institutional support for
political activity by women after they leave school.

Conceptions of the constitutionally defined election system and
norms of citizen voting behavior show very few divergencies between
boys and girls, the largest differences being evident in the realm of

political parties and candidates. Girls tend to see discord as bad for the country and to see the government as needing little change. Congruent with their concern over party disagreement, girls see Republicans and Democrats as taking similar stands on political issues. Girls avoid taking sides on issues and refuse to recognize discontent. Parties are impersonal structures; it may be for this reason that girls become less involved with them.

The lack of significant differences—particularly in norms of election behavior—contrasts with the more pronounced sex differences previously reported in adult election and voting behavior.

SUMMARY

In developing sex role, children acquire a set of expectations about their own and others' behavior. Boys and girls hold different expectations for themselves in their relationships with peers, parents, and teachers in situations involving emotional response and compliance. These expectations become part of a child's approach to new situations and influence his relationship with the political system.

Girls form a more personal attachment to the political system than boys because experience with their major role model (mother) is a more personal one and because authority figures deal with them in more expressive and personalized ways. For boys, personalization of the system declines with age; this does not occur for girls because they

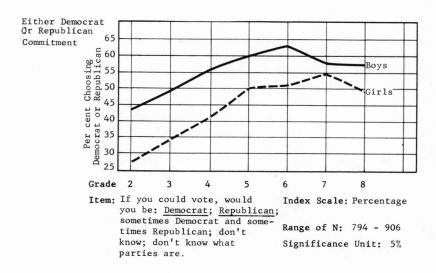

Fig. 72.

Comparison of boys and girls in party commitment, within grade.

are not obligated to renounce dependency ties as boys are. Girls relate to the political system through role expectations acquired in the more familiar home and school environments. Boys are more capable of dealing with abstract entities since their experience encourages an abstract conceptualization of the male sex role.

In absorbing and learning the rules, norms, and sanctions which are peculiar to the political system, girls and boys differ only minimally. These are the areas in which the school's influence seems to be the most pronounced. In teaching citizenship behavior, the school does not distinguish between the sexes, and personal needs and relationship expectations are unimportant. Some divergencies in the political perception of men and women which appear in the years following school graduation may result from declining support for female participation by institutions other than the school.

Boys consistently display more active involvement and politicized concern than girls, especially in partisanship and in polarization on political issues, similar to adult participation. These differences may result from an emphasis upon active rather than passive approaches for males and from their ability to deal with problems in a more instrumental fashion. The less active concern shown by girls may result from overpersonalization and too great a stress on attachment. This proceeds to such an extent that flaws are disregarded and lack of disagreement and conflict is sought as the greatest good.

9

The Impact of
Party Affiliation

The relationship between party allegiance, voting behavior, and alignment on national issues has been a popular research topic for students
of American political behavior. An extensive literature documents the
relationship between party commitment and political involvement in
adults; citizens apparently depend upon party pronouncements for
guidance in forming their own stands on public issues and may also be
pressured by party representatives to vote for the candidates of "their
party."

Josephson (1959) distinguished between "mass parties," those
which maintain the large and active membership they require by inculcating and recruiting youth, and "parties of individual representation,"
which have few disciplined members, make few demands, are generally
inactive between elections, and make few attempts to induct youth
since their major strength comes from alignment with institutions and
influential people of the society. The latter party system prevails in
the United States. To adults and adolescents, the term "political party
member" assumes a meaning different from that associated with certain
other kinds of membership. Eulau (1962) suggested that parties are
role systems. If his party serves as a significant frame of reference in
the voting act for an individual, the political party role system is important to him. In studying children's partisan affiliations, it is useful to
look at this incorporation of party role structure into a child's thinking
about the political system, since it is impossible to examine its direct
influence upon voting.

The independent voter has been a focus of particular concern for
political sociologists. Campbell, Converse, Miller, and Stokes (1960)
reported that, in general, independents are not psychologically involved
in political affairs. Independents in their sample had a poorer knowledge
of issues, less interest in campaigns, and when compared to party
members were less likely to choose their candidate on the basis of an
evaluation of national politics. Agger (1959) distinguished between two

types of independents: poorly educated persons who are disinterested in issues but interested in particular candidates, and persons (usually better educated) who are concerned with both candidates and issues. Banfield (1961) asserted that many suburban voters harbor the notion that political independence is a hallmark of middle-class sophistication, which suggests other motives for reporting that one does not support a political party.

These studies have not altogether clarified the nature of independent voters, but it is clear that they are not a monolithic group. They are represented neither by the well-informed individual, interested but aloof from the blind conformity of party loyalty, who examines candidates and issues carefully in order to support the best candidate, nor are they represented by the apathetic and uninterested citizen. The divergent results reported, however, indicate the importance of this group.

The relationship between party commitment and a voter's behavior is clear. For example, Berelson, Lazarsfeld, and McPhee (1954) reported that respondents perceived their candidate's stand on issues to be similar to their own and the opponent's stand as dissimilar; Democrats and Republicans disagreed on two major issues of the 1948 campaign: the Taft-Hartley Act and price controls. They did not disagree on other topics such as the relative importance of election issues or on criteria for selecting the President.

The significance of party membership and sympathy makes socialization of partisanship a topic of particular importance in this study. It has already been shown that the tendency for children to report alignment with a political party increases with age. From these age trends, it appears that party preference begins to assume some meaning for children during the fifth and sixth grades. Although many children claimed a preference for one of the parties earlier, this preference has little relation to well-known correlates of party membership such as social class and reaction to Kennedy's election. A number of children (14 per cent even at grade eight), however, said they did not know which party they favored. Another 32 per cent indicated a potentially changeable party alignment. In this section, the effects of commitment and non-commitment on the development of political orientations and involvements will be examined along with the role of schools in the emergence of partisanship among pre-adolescent children.

The individual citizen's involvement in American political life is obviously determined, in part, by the structure of the party system and its relation to national political events both during and between elections. Although technically not a part of our governmental system, political parties provide a basic network of communication and influence between citizens and government. It would be both cynical and inaccurate to argue that individual action is completely futile; but it is apparent that parties, as well as other organized groups and special interests, shape and limit the effectiveness of the individual citizen's impact on government. The book, *Political Influence* (Banfield, 1961), presents a case study of the process by which governmental decisions are made and the minimal influence any one person, even a civic leader, can exert on the making of basic political decisions. The role of the party as a vehicle for expression of individual political influence has not been carefully explored.

The party system represents the major cleavage in the political life of this country; it encourages and preserves a beneficial disagreement and conflict, opposing the national tendency toward consensus. This division is evident in children at the elementary school grades, particularly during the national election. Early commitment to a party, in itself, represents a form of political involvement. Other writers on political socialization (particularly Hyman, 1959) have concluded that the most significant effect of socialization in children is partisan affiliation. Hyman maintains that logically coherent ideologies are too complex to be socialized while political party affiliation may be transmitted much more easily, since there is limited choice and the symbols are simpler. Political party identification, then, serves as a frame of reference for approaching any novel issue. It seems plausible that partisan feelings act both as a mediating influence in the acquisition of attitudes toward political objects and as encouragement to become involved in political activities and issues.

The primary data to be discussed in this section come from responses to the following question: "If you could vote what would you be?" (Choose one)—

1. A Republican
2. A Democrat
3. Sometimes a Democrat and sometimes a Republican
4. I don't know which I would be
5. I don't know what the words Democrat and Republican mean

Children who marked "Don't know" are called "Uncommitted"; those who marked "Republican" or "Democrat" are regarded as "Committed"; and those who responded, "Sometimes a Democrat and sometimes a Republican" are called "Independents," although the term as used here does not have precisely the same connotation as in reports of studies of adult voting behavior.

Partisanship in children has no relation to basic attachment and compliance. The effect of partisanship upon attitudes and involvement will be examined by these comparisons among subgroups:

1. "Uncommitted" compared with all others;
2. "Independents" compared with those committed to either national party;
3. Children who are aligned with the Republicans compared with those who identify with the Democrats.

These comparisons clearly indicate that party commitment primarily affects active participation. Apparently the choice of a political party does not influence basic commitment to the nation, attachment to symbols, rituals, authority figures, roles of the system, or compliance to its laws. The areas of political orientation and involvement which showed no difference between the Uncommitted and others are listed in Table 62 of Hess and Torney (1965). These items are primarily concentrated in the initial stages of involvement—*attachment* and *compliance*. In the section dealing with the child's perception of the government's responsiveness and the appropriate behavior of the citizen, the items which are unrelated to partisan commitment are those which deal with norms of adult behavior and conception of the system, not with active involvement of the child. This summary of data indicates that a basic attachment to the nation and political system, compliance to its authority, norms and definitions of the system and the citizen's role are not functions of party preference or commitment.

Children who are uncommitted to a party are less active and less interested in political affairs. Commitment to a party *is* associated with a cluster of responses that indicate relatively greater involvement and active participation in elections and in contemporary political events and issues. An array of attitudes differentiated the Committed (Republicans, Democrats) and Independents from the Uncommitted (those who had no feeling of party loyalty; Figs. 73 and 74; Appendix D, Figs. D.15 and D.16). Those expressing some commitment to a party (even if a changeable one) showed greater interest in political events, more political activity, participated in more discussions, were more concerned with issues, and reported learning more from elections. This group exhibited active political participation appropriate for its age level.

The Uncommitted group is, perhaps, most analogous to the apathetic adult citizen; its lack of party commitment was only part of a more general disinterest. Figure 75 shows the inflated tendency in the Uncommitted group to offer "Don't know" responses to many questions dealing with political topics and attitudes. The percentage of children reporting that they did not identify with a party or that they did not know anything about the parties is larger in the low-IQ and lower social-status groups (see Appendix D, Fig. D.09). Children uncommitted to a political party also reported fewer organizational memberships.

Children who do not identify with a political party share characteristics with those showing low involvement in the outcome of a particular election. This was assessed by comparing those who reported "not caring one way or the other" when they learned of Kennedy's election, with children who had positive or negative reactions. There was a moderate association between non-commitment to a party and "not caring." Like children who reported no party preference, the youngsters who had little concern with the election reported less interest in government, less participation in political discussions, fewer political activities, and said they learned little from the election (Fig. 76; Appendix D, Figs. D.17, D.18, D.19). They also had high "Don't know" scores (Fig. 77).

Underlining the similarities, children who reported no subjective involvement in the election assigned little importance to membership in political parties (Fig. 78). Teachers who reported not caring about the election outcome were remarkably similar to children who held this attitude. These children are apathetic; not only are they unaffiliated with political organizations, they are not even interested in the outcome of the election. Children with no interest in the election form a small group (16 per cent of the total population) which draws equally from all social classes and IQ groups. There were no age trends in reporting lack of interest in the election. Usually, the disinterested children were not Catholics (average percentage of non-concern in Protestants was about 18 per cent; in Catholics, about 6 per cent).

Children who are independent of party show the most active involvement in political affairs. The data show this group to be highly intelligent, and usually from high-status backgrounds (see Figs. 51 and 52). This group most closely approximates the image of the independent, thoughtful voter who is informed on issues and chooses his candidate after careful reflection. The differences in response patterns between Independents and Committed groups are shown in Figs. 79 through 82 and Appendix D, Fig. D.20.

Independents supported their non-partisanship with the acceptance of norms prescribing this behavior. They saw less difference between Democrats and Republicans (Fig. 79), assessed adult partisanship to be less important (Appendix D, Fig. D.20), maintained that the best citizen does not necessarily vote for his party's candidates (Fig. 80), and less frequently said that children should belong to their parents' party (see Hess and Torney, 1965, Fig. 130). Teachers who reported independence from partisan commitment differed in similar ways from teachers who were Democrats or Republicans.

In perceiving relationships between themselves and the political system, this group was overly convinced of the individual's effectiveness —a sort of "personal clout illusion." They overrated the participation of the individual citizen as a technique of political influence. Expression of a greater sense of efficacy (Fig. 81) is congruent with this group's

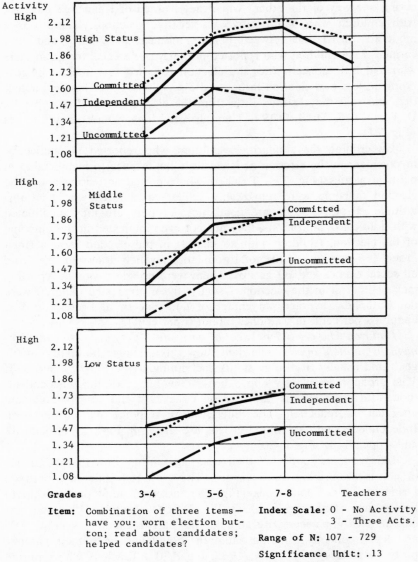

Grades   3-4   5-6   7-8   Teachers

Item: Combination of three items —   **Index Scale:** 0 - No Activity
        have you: worn election but-   3 - Three Acts.
        ton; read about candidates;
        helped candidates?   **Range of N:** 107 - 729

                                        Significance Unit: .13

Comparison (within social status and grade) of mean
levels of political activity of three groups: 1)those
committed to a party; 2)those uncommitted; and 3)inde-
pendents.

Fig. 73.

Party commitment and concern about political issues.

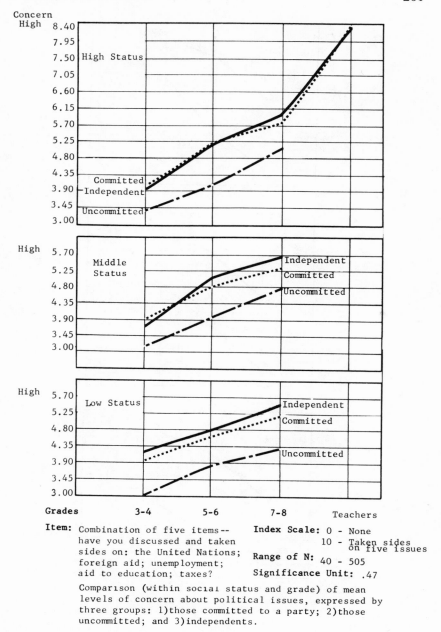

Concern
High

Grades   3-4   5-6   7-8   Teachers

Item: Combination of five items--   Index Scale: 0 - None
      have you discussed and taken   10 - Taken sides
      sides on: the United Nations;   on five issues
      foreign aid; unemployment;   Range of N: 40 - 505
      aid to education; taxes?   Significance Unit: .47

      Comparison (within social status and grade) of mean
      levels of concern about political issues, expressed by
      three groups: 1)those committed to a party; 2)those
      uncommitted; and 3)independents.

Fig. 74.
Party commitment and political activity.

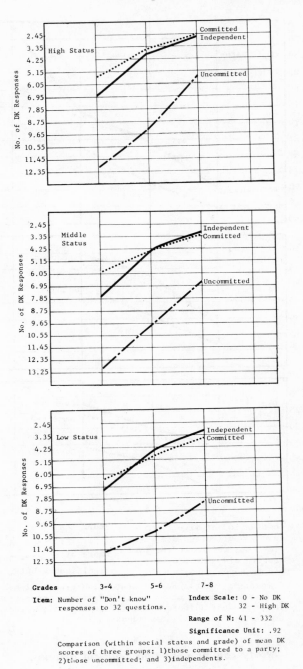

Grades   3-4   5-6   7-8

Item: Number of "Don't know"   Index Scale: 0 - No DK
      responses to 32 questions.   32 - High DK

                                       Range of N: 41 - 332

                                       Significance Unit: .92

Comparison (within social status and grade) of mean DK
scores of three groups: 1)those committed to a party;
2)those uncommitted; and 3)independents.

Fig. 75.
Party commitment and acquisition of political attitudes.

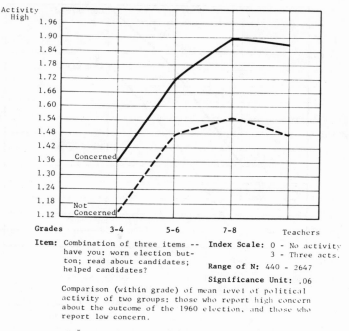

Fig. 76.

Concern with election outcome and political activity.

high evaluation of voting as a symbol of government (Fig. 82) and as a behavioral norm for the good citizen (see Hess and Torney, 1965, Fig. 135). This attitude reflects a preoccupation with the election process—especially voting (as opposed to the events leading to nomination) as the central arena of political decision making and power, and ignores the powerful network of lobbies, influential individuals, and pressure groups.

This pattern is remarkably congruent with teachers' attitudes concerning the importance of individual action as an ideal mode of involvement and with the tendency for schools to undervalue party membership. Children's attitudes toward partisan commitment appear to be socialized by the school—a conclusion supported by the high intelligence level of this group as compared with that of others (Fig. 51).

Although teachers cannot require children to be independent, they can inculcate the concepts that parties do not really differ, that good citizens do not vote only for party candidates, and that children should not affiliate with the political party of their parents. These are the values that teachers hold. After learning these norms, the resulting student role behavior is partisan independence. Teachers, because of

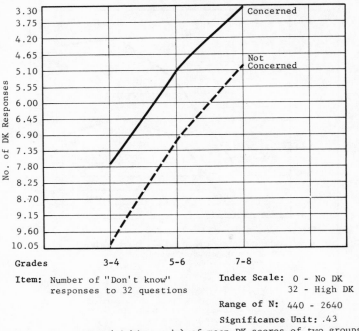

Item: Number of "Don't know"   Index Scale: 0 - No DK
      responses to 32 questions   32 - High DK

                                       Range of N: 440 - 2640

                                       Significance Unit: .43

        Comparison (within grade) of mean DK scores of two groups:
        those who report high concern about the outcome of the
        1960 election, and those who report low concern.

Fig. 77.
Concern with election outcome and acquisition of political attitudes.

strong community constraints, cannot express partisan preferences
openly; but they can and do teach norms which orient students toward
political independence.

*While independents are characterized by the importance they place
upon voting for candidates rather than parties, the two partisan groups
divide on a more personal and subjectively competitive basis.* Items
showing differences between Democrats and Republicans are presented
in Fig. 83 and in Appendix E, Fig. E.21. These differences appear in
emotional reactions to the outcome of the election and to the candidate,
who is known to be Democratic or Republican. Differences were also
observed in evaluation of the parties' contributions to the national
welfare.

Views of the President's competence in performing his role and
respect for his power did not differ between Democrats and Republicans.
Emotional reactions following the 1960 election showed strong association with political party preferences (Fig. 83), as did the rating of
the President as a personal favorite (Appendix D, Fig. D.21). There
is evidence that ratings such as these are highly predictive of voting

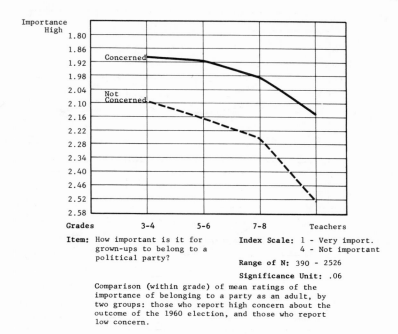

Item: How important is it for
grown-ups to belong to a
political party?

Index Scale: 1 - Very import.
4 - Not important

Range of N: 390 - 2526

Significance Unit: .06

Comparison (within grade) of mean ratings of the
importance of belonging to a party as an adult, by
two groups: those who report high concern about the
outcome of the 1960 election, and those who report
low concern.

Fig. 78
Concern with election outcome and rating importance of party membership.

preferences of adults.[1] Similar differences between Democrats and
Republicans appeared on evaluations of which party does the most for
the country (see Hess and Torney, 1965, Fig. 138), suggesting that
party preference, at this level of development, evokes response differences only on items which the child can relate directly to a partisan
frame of reference—specific evaluations of the parties and of candidates
who are labeled Democrat or Republican.[2]

The school's efforts to stimulate interest in elections may assist
socialization into party loyalty by family and community. Our evidence
showed similarity between child's report of parents' and of his own
political preference. This is reflected both in the similarity between
siblings' partisan leanings and in the tendency for party preference to

1. Strickler (1963) had voters rate Nixon, Kennedy, and the ideal President;
difference scores between each candidate and the ideal and the mean evaluative
ratings assigned to each candidate would predict voting for 90 per cent of a
group of 218.
2. Campbell, Converse, Miller, and Stokes (1960) explored the relationship
of their multidimensional measure of partisan attitude to voting choice and evaluation of political parties, with results highly similar to those reported here.

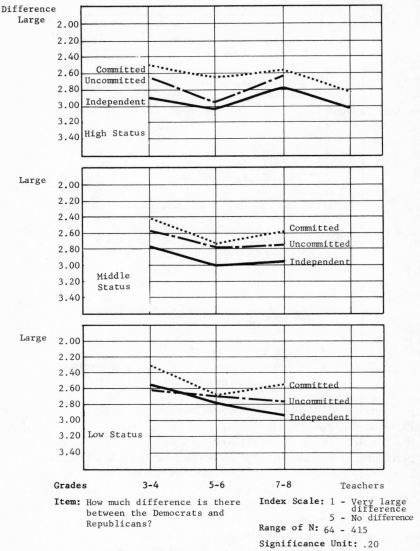

Item: How much difference is there between the Democrats and Republicans?

Index Scale: 1 - Very large difference
             5 - No difference

Range of N: 64 - 415

Significance Unit: .20

Comparison (within social status and grade) of mean amounts of difference between Democrats and Republicans, as perceived by three groups: 1)those committed to a party; 2)those uncommitted; and 3)independents.

Fig. 79.
Party commitment and perception of differences between political parties.

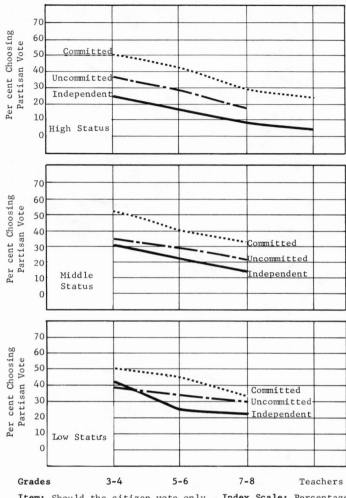

Grades   3-4   5-6   7-8   Teachers

Item: Should the citizen vote only   Index Scale: Percentage
      for candidates sponsored by
      his political party, or
      should he vote for the candi-   Range of N: 60 - 503
      dates of his choice?   Significance Unit: 10%

Comparison (within social status and grade) of choice
of partisan voting over individual candidate selection,
by three groups: 1)those committed to a party; 2)those
uncommitted; and 3)independents.

Fig. 80.
***Party commitment and view of importance of voting along
party lines.***

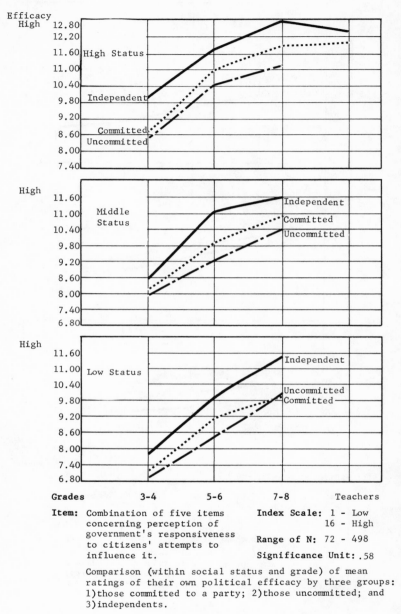

Item: Combination of five items   Index Scale: 1 - Low
       concerning perception of   16 - High
       government's responsiveness
       to citizens' attempts to   Range of N: 72 - 498
       influence it.   Significance Unit: .58

       Comparison (within social status and grade) of mean
       ratings of their own political efficacy by three groups:
       1)those committed to a party; 2)those uncommitted; and
       3)independents.

Fig. 81.
Party commitment and sense of political efficacy.

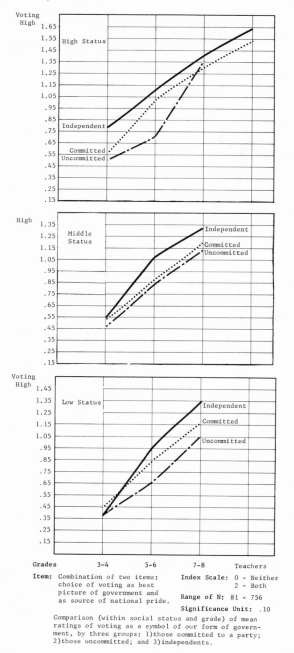

Grades   3-4   5-6   7-8   Teachers

Item: Combination of two items: Index Scale: 0 - Neither
      choice of voting as best   2 - Both
      picture of government and
      as source of national pride.   Range of N: 81 - 756

                                       Significance Unit: .10

Comparison (within social status and grade) of mean
ratings of voting as a symbol of our form of government, by three groups: 1)those committed to a party;
2)those uncommitted; and 3)independents.

Fig. 82.
Party commitment and choice of voting as a symbol of
our government.

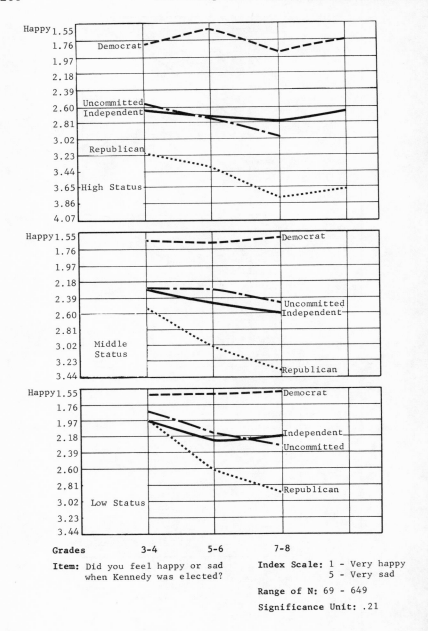

Fig. 83.

Comparison of means of party preference groups in emotional response to Kennedy's election, within social status and grade.

follow social class patterns. It is possible that teachers have some influence upon the child's party choice, but this is probably not extensive since they seem to press for independence and non-partisan active involvement.

In summary, major partisan divisions characterizing America's political field do not significantly influence the child's orientations toward the system and its values and rules; consensus on basic attachment and compliance is fixed quite independently from party affiliation. Differences between children who are not committed to a single party (either totally uncommitted or independent) and those who express a party preference were more widespread in this questionnaire than differences between Democrats and Republicans. The school attempts to teach the value of involvement and interest and that individual action is the most effective means of political influence. The further overlay of party preference for children seems to be relatively superficial and limited to areas which are clearly labeled as partisan.

10

Summary and
Conclusions

The purpose of this study was to examine the socialization of children into the political system of the United States. The initial thrust of the study was descriptive—an attempt to chart and document the growth of political behavior. This is one of a growing number of studies of the development of citizenship and political behavior in children and adolescents, representing a relatively recent interest of political scientists, sociologists, and child psychologists. As a result of this and other similar studies, future investigations will be more focused and more precise. It will be important to examine from different perspectives some of the issues raised in this volume.

Political socialization has been studied in this project as a special case of socialization into institutions, examining the ways that individuals learn to interact with these large segments of the social system. The assumption is that social learning in the political area bears certain similarities to socialization into other institutions. This process is viewed not as one which involves the acquisition of traits or opinions, but rather the development of relationships between the individual and the institutions. In this complex process, the individual acquires images of institutions and persons and complementary attitudes about himself and how he should behave (what the institutions and their representatives expect of him).

For the purposes of analysis and presentation of data, we have distinguished among several types of behavior: relationships to the nation, to authority figures and institutions representing the national government, to laws and authority figures who enforce them, to processes of influence on public policy, and to elections and political parties.

The focus of the study is not limited to children's beliefs but attempts also to delineate the procedures through which they acquire political behavior. These processes of acquisition include the accumulation of specific knowledge and attitudes taught by other individuals— teachers, parents, and other authority figures; the acquisition of beliefs, attitudes, and orientations by transfer of feelings held toward other authority figures in the perceptual environment; accepting ideas, beliefs, and behavior by imitation or identification; and modification by the mediating effects of level of conceptual development and ability that the child possesses.

The data summarized here are taken from hour-long questionnaires administered to approximately 12,000 children in elementary grades two through eight. The data were collected in one large city and one small city of each major region of the United States (West, South, North Central, Northeast) during the period from December 1961 through May 1962. In each city, two schools from working-class areas and two schools from middle-class areas were tested.

In this summary, the findings are grouped to respond to three questions: First, what is the content of attitudes which children develop during the elementary-school years—what are their beliefs about political figures and organizations and their ideas about how citizens should behave? Second, from which sources or agents are political attitudes and behavior acquired and what experiences influence this process? Third, what is the pattern (rate and sequence) of change and growth in attitudes, and through what processes are they acquired?

Political Attitudes Acquired
during Elementary School

The young child's involvement with the political system begins with a strong positive attachment to the country; the United States is seen as ideal and as superior to other countries. This attachment to the country is stable and shows almost no change through elementary-school years. This bond is possibly the most basic and essential aspect of socialization into involvement with the political life of the nation. Essentially an emotional tie, it apparently grows from complex psychological and social needs and is exceedingly resistant to change or argument. It is a powerful emotional bond that is particularly important in time of national emergency.

The young child perceives figures and institutions of government as powerful, competent, benign, and infallible and trusts them to offer him protection and help. This early faith in political authority figures seems to be general among young children in this country. There is also reason to believe that it is characteristic of other countries (Hess, 1963). The age trends in the data give little support to the notion that all these attitudes are learned as primarily political orientations. The child also draws from previous experience with family figures and may endow figures whom he sees as powerful and authoritative with benign and helpful qualities. This response appears to be *compensatory;* it develops as a result of the child's inferior and vulnerable place in the system and serves to reassure the child that powerful authority is not dangerous (Hess and Easton, 1960; Torney, Hess, and Easton, 1962).

The child's initial relationship with governmental authority is with the President, whom he sees in highly positive terms, indicating his basic trust in the benevolence of government. Indeed, interviews of first- and second-grade children indicated that the President is the major figure in the child's emerging political world. The small child often believes the President is available to the individual citizen, either by visits to the White House or by telephone. The President's concern is personal and nurturant. He is the tie to the governmental system through which other objects—institutions, processes—become familiar and understood. The Vice President, for example, is described in interviews as the President's helper, and the Congress frequently is seen as working for the President. The President is the critical point of contact for the child in the political socialization process.

The early image of the President centers around personal qualities. With increasing age of a child, the President's qualities directly related to his office become more prominent than his personal attractiveness, and the child develops a concept of the *Presidency* as separate from the President. This distinction appears when one compares children's attitudes toward President Eisenhower with those toward President Kennedy. Despite his narrow victory, and lacking the popular image that was characteristic of Eisenhower, Kennedy within weeks of his inauguration was rated as positively as Eisenhower had been in his second term (Hess, 1963). Emerging along with attitudes toward the President are attitudes toward other positions in the system which endow their incumbents with status and prestige in the eyes of the child. The expectations that are developed with regard to these roles (judge, senator) will later allow the child to criticize the occupant of a role without expressing disloyalty to the system.

The policeman is also among the political figures which are salient to the young child. Children believe that the policeman is nurturant and that his job is to help persons in trouble and to prevent crime, rather than to exercise the more punitive functions of catching and punishing criminals. Despite his importance as an authority figure, however, children do not see him as a representative of national government. They express a strong personal liking for the policeman; this attraction declines steadily throughout the elementary-school years to a level which is positive but considerably lower than their regard for the President.

On most attributes, policemen were rated at approximately the same level as senators and consistently lower than the President. They were somewhat lower than "father" on personal items ("I like him") but superior to "father" on role performance items ("Knows more," "Is a leader," "Makes important decisions"). The child holds the policeman in awe. Most young children have high regard for law and for law-enforcement authorities. The elementary-school child, especially at early grade-levels, sees laws as just and unchangeable and believes that punishment is an inevitable consequence of wrongdoing. The young child believes that laws are made by persons in administrative positions, especially by the President; this view is later modified to recognize the legislative process. There are some changes with age in this general picture, as will be noted later, but norms about the justice of law and necessity for conformity are established firmly at an early age. Deviations from these norms do not result from ignorance or from a failure to accept the norms themselves. The reasons for noncompliance must be sought in other areas of personality and socialization. As with orientations toward authority figures, the attitudes toward law appear to be transferred from attitudes toward rules in other systems, especially the school and the family. If this transfer model is valid in these basic areas of orientation toward authority and law, the child's experiences with rules in other groups (family and school) are very influential in the political socialization process.

The young child's trust in the political system is expressed not only by a view of figures and institutions as benign, but through a view of the obligation of the citizen primarily to be a good person. This image of the citizen persists, but the obligations to vote and express interest in governmental affairs become more dominant elements of the norms of adult citizenship as the child grows older. The belief that the citizen should be interested in political matters is apparent in the behavior reported by elementary-school children; by the end of the eighth grade most children have acquired some interest in governmental activities and have participated in discussions about political issues and problems.

Children begin engaging in political activities (such as wearing campaign buttons) at an early age, occasionally as early as the third grade; there is a gradual increase through the eighth grade in the number of children who report such activities. The elementary-school child's view of the election process and of the mechanisms of influence on governmental action is dominated by an image of the citizen as powerful and the individual vote as the most effective force in the political process. The sense of efficacy in influencing political processes increases with age. Children in elementary school, even in the eighth grade, have a very limited knowledge of the techniques and effectiveness of pressure groups in elections and in determining governmental policy.

The child's image of political parties develops late, and the nature of the differences between the two major parties is not clearly defined. Parties are apparently first associated with candidates who are identified as Republican or Democrat; interest in an election and a candidate may be the most instrumental mechanism for developing party affiliation. Although taking sides in an election is a prominent aspect of children's political behavior, a meaningful party commitment is usually not acquired until the upper grades of elementary school. Even at this age, a large proportion of children report that, if they could vote, they would vote independently of party affiliation; in general they believe that partisan commitment may be desirable for adults, but that it should be deferred until adulthood.

In viewing politics, particularly the relationship between the two parties and the conduct of elections, children wish to minimize conflict. They see disagreement as undesirable and prefer to believe that politicians never say unkind things about one another during an election campaign. They also have a firm conviction that following an election campaign the conflict that may have arisen should be forgotten; the loser should join in support of the winning candidate and he, in return, should be gracious and forgiving. Thus by the end of the eighth grade, children have developed a sense of the need for consensus and majority rule in democratic processes. Typically, they have not recognized the role of debate, disagreement, and conflict in the operation of a democratic political system.

These are the dominant themes in the responses obtained to our questions. There is a great deal of agreement about certain basic points, especially loyalty to the country and respect for the office of the President. Regard for law and recognition of the need for law enforcement and obedience on the part of the citizen are equally important. The obligation of the citizen to vote is also prominent. Of particular note is the strong emphasis children place upon independence from party affiliation and upon voting for the most qualified candidate rather than supporting the party of one's choice. This may be an idealistic but temporary view of the operation of the political system which is supported by belief in the power of the individual vote and ignorance about the importance of pressure groups.

Children are socialized toward an ideal norm; this norm provides a standard against which the behavior of candidates and of individual citizens, as well as of persons who occupy positions in government, may be judged. The importance of early faith in government, attachment to the system, and belief in the power of the individual citizen as necessary bases for further political socialization should be considered in discussing possible curricular changes in civic education. It seems likely that before the child is informed about conflict and disagreement he should have sufficient time to internalize and become attached to the ideal norms of the system. Building on this firm attachment and acceptance of the basic worth of the country and the individual citizen, it may then be possible to explain the usefulness of disagreement and debate and to show the function of consensus in uniting a nation after the conflict of a political campaign. Recognition of the need for disagreement, its resolution, and subsequent consensus can probably be introduced at a relatively early age, perhaps as early as the fourth or fifth grade. The unpleasant aspects of political life (corruption) should perhaps be left until a later time, when they can be viewed as deviations, rather than being mistaken for normal or usual behavior.

Agents for Political Socialization

What are the agents (institutions, persons) from which political attitudes and behavior are acquired? What experiences are related to the acquisition of political attitudes?

From the viewpoint of the totality of socialization into the political system, these results indicate that the effectiveness of the family in transmitting attitudes has been overestimated in previous research. The family transmits preference for a political party, but in most other areas its most effective role is to support other institutions in teaching political information and orientations. Clearcut similarities among children in the same family are confined to partisanship and related attitudes, such as feelings of distress of pleasure over the outcome of an election campaign. Aside from party preference, the influence of the family seems to be primarily indirect and to influence attitudes toward authority, rules, and compliance.

There is some relationship between family structure and the child's interest in the political system. Children who see their fathers as powerful tend to be more informed and interested in political matters; children who see their mothers as the dominant authority in the family tend to be less interested in politics and to acquire attitudes at a later period than do children who see the father as the dominant parent or see both parents as equal in authority.

The school apparently plays the largest part in teaching attitudes, conceptions, and beliefs about the operation of the political system. While it may be argued that the family contributes much to the socialization that goes into basic loyalty to the country, the school gives content, information, and concepts which expand and elaborate these early feelings of attachment.

The young child's attitude toward authority or institutions, however, seems not to correspond directly to the amount of emphasis on these topics reported by the teachers. Compliance to rules and authorities is a major focus of civic education in elementary school. Teachers' ratings of the importance of various topics clearly indicate that the strongest emphasis is placed upon compliance to law, authority, and school regulations. Indeed, it seems likely that much of what is called citizenship training in the public schools does not teach the child about the city, state, or national government, but is an attempt to teach regard for the rules and standards of conduct of the school.

In contrast to its emphasis on compliance, the school curriculum under-emphasizes the rights and obligations of a citizen to participate in government. The school focuses on the obligation and right to vote but does not offer the child sufficient understanding of procedures open to individuals for legitimately influencing the government. Nor does it adequately explain and emphasize the importance of group action to achieve desirable ends.

Teachers tend not to deal with partisanship or to discuss the role and importance of conflict in the operation of the system, perhaps because of the position of the school in the community. They apparently stress the virtue of independent political action oriented toward assessment of candidates' worth rather than an alignment with a group or political party. This preference may follow from explicit or implicit prohibitions against teaching controversial topics; or perhaps it reflects the desire of the school to present political life and information without bias. In either case, it leaves the elementary school child with inadequate information at a time when he is becoming oriented toward the importance of political participation.

The school stresses ideal norms and ignores the tougher, less pleasant facts of political life in the United States. While it would probably be unwise to discuss political corruption in early grades, the process of socialization should include a somewhat more realistic view of the operation of the political system. For example, achieving political goals and influencing elected officials are facilitated by participation in organized groups, particularly political parties. Yet the school appears to spend relatively little time dealing with the functions of political parties, community action, and pressure groups in achieving community goals. It may be argued that by teaching a myth of governmental responsiveness to the average voter, the school produces an unjustified sense of confidence. The "average" voter may be ineffective because he has been socialized to believe that the citizen has more power than is actually the case.

The school is particularly important for children who come from working-class or low socioeconomic areas. Much of what working-class children learn at school is not reinforced by home and community. It may be for these reasons that the school seems to have somewhat less effect upon children from these areas of the city than it does on the children from more prosperous sections.

Participation in peer group organizations within the school or outside it does not have a significant effect upon the political socialization process. Group membership and activity seem to be related to political activity, but apparently only because the child who is active tends to be active in several areas of endeavor. Our data give no evidence that participation in group activities or membership in any one of several youth organizations leads to a greater or earlier acceptance of the basic elements of citizenship and democratic process.

Religious affiliation has a strong but limited effect on political socialization in the elementary-school years. The most marked relationship between religious affiliation and involvement is the socialization of party affiliation and candidate preference. The data were gathered in the year and a half following the election of President Kennedy, and the relationship between religious affiliation and reaction to the selection of a President who was of the Catholic faith was particularly strong. This preference cut across the influence of social class and outweighed, in many cases, the importance of party affiliation.

It is our conclusion from these data that the school stands out as the central, salient, and dominant force in the political socialization of the young child. Since this study began at the second-grade level, where a firm attachment to the country had already been established, it is difficult to specify the effectiveness of the school in transmitting this early loyalty to the nation. The recital of the pledge of allegiance and singing "The Star Spangled Banner" are rituals supporting this attachment.

The influence of the family is, of course, considerable, but in our opinion, much less than has been assumed by many other researchers. The influence of the family upon party choice is well-known and important; this aspect of the process of political socialization seems to be similar to the selection of a particular church denomination as a result of family loyalty and identification. Choices of this type obviously are influential in adult life, but they are independent of the much larger process of socialization into a network of behavior that relates a citizen to the government, and citizens to one another.

The role played by the school in this process suggests a need for greater attention and more systematic evaluation of the methods, curriculum, and timing of political socialization. In the school curriculum, the topics that deal with civic education and the concepts that are part of our democratic heritage are usually taught unsystematically. There has been relatively little attempt to state which concepts are basic to the operation of the democratic system and to teach these at an early age in an effective manner. It seems likely that many children who can recite the articles of the Bill of Rights would not be able to explain why these sections are important or what the consequences would be if they were not upheld. Underlying the political behavior and attitudes which can be observed are basic concepts which provide the logic for a democratic system—such as a view of conflicts as a dimension of behavior, a regard for the rights of minorities, and compliance to majority rule. These elements can be taught and should result in more informed and rational political attitudes and action. In our opinion, there has been little attempt to seek out and define the basic concepts on which our system is based and to construct a curriculum in the early grades to transmit these concepts and an understanding of their importance. Perhaps what is needed is a revising of the curriculum in ways comparable to the new advances in the teaching of mathematics and the sciences. Such an effort would examine the conceptual bases of civic education and teaching, then order them in a sequence that would lead the child to an emerging sense of how the system should operate, the principles on which it depends, and his own effectiveness and role within it.

Processes and Mediations of Political Socialization

The process of political socialization can be considered within two major categories. The first has to do with the rate and sequence with which attitudes are acquired by children; it is concerned with developmental changes and patterns of acquisition related to chronological age or grade in school. The second has to do with the factors which influence the transmission of political orientations; it deals with the circumstances which retard or facilitate children's acquisition of attitudes.

DEVELOPMENTAL PATTERNS: THE RATE AND SEQUENCE OF POLITICAL SOCIALIZATION

The most striking feature of political socialization in the elementary school is the extent to which basic orientations have been acquired by children by the end of the eighth grade.[1] Many attitudes, concepts, and types of involvement approximate toward the end of the eighth grade the attitudes and orientations of the teachers. Although there are exceptions (noted below), political socialization is well advanced by the end of elementary school.

This conclusion seems not to apply in the areas of partisanship and in the understanding of the role of pressure groups in forming governmental policy. The tendency of many children to see themselves as independent of party affiliation appears to reflect the socialization within the school. It seems likely that some subsequent re-socialization will

1. Our data underestimate the true extent of socialization since testing was spread over a period of time beginning in the fall and ending in late winter, not toward the end of the school term.

stimulate greater affiliation with one of the major parties and a loyalty to the candidates of that party.

The acquisition of political orientations and information proceeds rapidly but not evenly during the elementary-school years. In some areas, such as attachment to the nation, attitudes are acquired early. In others, particularly voting and partisan behavior, the emphasis seems to occur relatively late in the elementary-school years. The period between grades three and five seems to be especially important in the acquisition of political information. Before this time, concepts such as government and political party may evoke some recognition in the child, but few children understand more than their most elementary aspects.

The child's early conception of the nation is vague, and national symbols such as the flag are crucial points of focus. Evaluative judgments of political objects in all areas are acquired first. These are supplemented later by acquisition of more complex information and attitudes which are usually consistent with these evaluations.

The process of induction into the governmental system seems to occur initially through a feeling of high regard for political authority figures. The point of contact and initial affiliation is *persons;* the governmental image later includes institutions and less personal aspects of the system. The early attachment of the child to political authority figures seems not to derive from teaching in the home or the school but to reflect the child's need to see authority figures as benign because they are powerful. The tendency to attribute benevolence to authority appears to be a way of dealing with feelings of vulnerability in the face of superior power.

Despite the decline in the personal respect for authority figures, a basic regard for the roles of authority in the system and for the competence necessary to perform these roles seems not to diminish. Apparently the feelings of liking for political authority figures are transformed into feelings of confidence in and esteem for the roles which these figures occupy and for institutions.

The young child's conceptions of law and the rules of the school and home are not greatly differentiated. His early regard for law is an extension of his feeling that it is important to obey adults. Thus the induction into compliance with authority and law appears to be mediated through visible authority figures, initially through the parents, possibly through the classroom teacher, and in the political arena through the policeman and the President.

INDIVIDUAL CHARACTERISTICS
WHICH AFFECT THE ACQUISITION OF
POLITICAL ATTITUDES AND BEHAVIOR

In this study, the major mediating influences investigated were sex, social class, and intelligence (estimated by IQ scores). Though many of the sex differences in political attitudes and activities were not large, they were consistent across grades. There was also considerable consistency among the items on which sex differences appeared. Among the most prominent differences is that the boys acquire attitudes more rapidly than girls and they are more interested in political matters. In addition, boys report more political activity than do girls.

Compared with boys, girls tend to be more attached to personal figures of the system. They relate to the political system more through trust and reliance on figures and the inherent goodness of the system than do their male peers. There are no differences between males and females in basic attachment, loyalty, and support of the country. In general, the differences between males and females are consistent with sex differences reported by other investigators. Girls tend to be more oriented toward persons, more expressive and trustful in their attitudes toward the system, its representatives, and institutions. Boys tend to be more task-oriented and are more willing to accept and see benefit in conflict and disagreement.

Party affiliation in itself has relatively little effect upon the acquisition of basic attitudes and political orientation. For example, it has no relationship to attachment to the nation or compliance to the system of law. Children who favor the Republican party show no difference whatsoever in basic loyalty to the country when compared with the children who express preference for the Democratic party. Although there are no differences between children who identify with the two major parties, children who do not identify with any political party—that is, who are uncommitted—are less active and less interested in political affairs. It may be that the first sign of political apathy in the socialization process is a lack of concern about elections, campaigns, and party affiliation. At the elementary-school level, children who see themselves as politically independent are the most active of all in political affairs, exceeding the involvement of children who identify themselves as Democrats or Republicans. This tendency toward independence seems to reflect the ideal independent voter as he is sometimes portrayed in adult political situations—intelligent, evaluating the merits of the campaign or issue, interested in political affairs and election outcomes, active in political matters, and deeply involved in the operation of the political system.

The intelligence of the child is one of the most important mediating influences in the acquisition of political behavior. In general, the effect of high IQ is to accelerate the process of political socialization for children of all social status levels. For example, children of high intelligence at a given age are more likely to see the government represented by institutions rather than by a powerful leader. Although the acquisition of political attitudes and of the concept of institutional aspects of government is accelerated in children of higher IQ, there is no difference between children of high and of low intelligence in their basic attachment to the nation. These fundamental allegiances are apparently taught so thoroughly that virtually all children within normal IQ range have been socialized in these critical areas.

Children of high intelligence tend to regard the system in less absolute terms. They are less likely to see laws as unquestionably fair, or to view punishment as an inevitable consequence of lawbreaking. This is not to suggest that they are casual about the importance of law; the obligation of the citizen to comply is accepted equally by children of high and low intelligence. However, brighter children seem to be more critically aware of the possibility that lawbreakers may not always be apprehended by the police and brought to justice in the courts, and more aware of the possibility that some laws may be unjust.

Children of high IQ also have more reservations about the competence and intentions of governmental figures and institutions. They are less idealistic about the system and expect less from it. Brighter children are somewhat more realistic about the operation of the system, without sacrificing the ideal norms which they have been taught. This interpretation is supported by the finding that these children are more interested in governmental matters and tend to emphasize the importance of interest in political affairs more than do other children. They are also more likely to participate in political discussions and to express concern about questions that are of contemporary interest to adults.

Feelings of efficacy in relation to government are very strongly related to level of intelligence. Some of the largest differences among the IQ groups appear in the sense of efficacy. Voting is also more salient as an aspect of government to children of high intelligence. They are more inclined to see voting as an obligation of the good citizen than are children who are less gifted. Children of high intelligence seem less bound to the status quo and more willing to accept change in government. They are particularly likely to be independent of party affiliation and to accept the idea that the citizen should vote for the candidate rather than conform with party allegiance.

In summary, children of high intelligence are more active, more likely to discuss political matters, more interested in current events; they have a greater sense of efficacy and a greater sense of the importance of voting and citizen participation. Intelligence is associated with greater involvement in political affairs.

The influence of social status seems to be less marked than the impact of IQ. When intelligence is held constant, social status differences are greatly reduced in most political orientations and attitudes studied in this research. Basic affiliation and loyalty to the nation do not vary by social status. It seems to be a consistent finding that socialization into national loyalty occurs early within all social groups. Differences in political involvement and behavior which are observed within the population are apparently built upon this basic feeling of loyalty to the country.

Differences by IQ increase with age; this is less true of differences by social status. Some very distinctive social class differences remain, however. There is a difference between social status groups in their attachment to certain governmental figures. Children from working-class homes tend to have a higher regard for policemen and for the President than do children from higher-status homes. However, the perception of responsiveness and willingness to help exhibited by governmental figures shows no social class variation. Like high-IQ children, children from high-status families see laws as less rigid, but they accept on a par with working-class children the citizen's obligation to comply to law.

The expression of interest in political matters is not related to social status. However, the child's report of his parents' or his family's interest in government is strongly related to social class, with children from higher-status homes reporting more parental interest in government and national affairs than other children. Children from high social status also report more frequent participation in political discussions and a greater concern for contemporary national issues. These children are similar to those of high intelligence. However, this relationship with social status is maintained when IQ is held constant. Although there are differences in these types of participation and concern, no social class differences appear in the acceptance of voting as a duty of the citizen. This obligation is accepted equally by children of high and low status.

Perhaps the most marked social class difference in these data is the tendency for low-status children to feel less efficacious in dealing with the political system than do children from high-status homes. The combination of intelligence and social status in their effect upon feelings of efficacy make for dramatic differences between the high-status/high-IQ children and low-status/low-IQ children. Although there are no social status differences in expressed interest in political affairs, there are differences among the status groups in the amount of political activity reported. This may reflect, as indicated earlier, a greater tendency for middle-class communities and families to support and reinforce the teaching of the schools with regard to obligations of political participation and involvement.

Choice of political party is related to social status similarly for children and adults. The tendency for working-class children to favor the Democratic party does not appear until grade five, however, suggesting that party affiliation is not salient to younger children and that the effect of family and social class in this area becomes stronger during the late elementary-school and high-school years.

There are a number of parallels between the effects of social status and the effects of IQ in the socialization of political orientations and involvement. Our data lead to the conclusion that children in working-class areas of the city are less completely socialized (in the sense of being prepared for political participation) than children from middle-class homes. The same general conclusion may be made about children of low intelligence. These effects are compounded by the fact that schools in working-class areas have a disproportionate number of children with relatively low IQ's. An evaluation of the curriculum and of the role of the school in political socialization must take into account this relative disadvantage of children who come from working-class homes and those of every social class level who are not intellectually gifted. For these children, it may be necessary to devise more effective teaching methods or to spend a greater amount of time in teaching the basic concepts of government and political behavior. Low-status children perceive their teacher as relatively much more effective than their own parents in teaching citizenship. This is probably an indication of a general lack of community and family support in working-class areas for the attitudes and concepts taught by the school. Perhaps the school should exert particular effort to transmit to these children an understanding of the operation of the political system and the importance of the democratic principles on which our system operates.

APPENDIX A

Method

of the Study

Selection of Subjects and Characteristics
of the Research Population

AGE AND GRADE

Since previous work had demonstrated the importance of the elementary-school years in growth and development of attitudes and opinions about political objects and affairs, this project included only elementary-school children. The project plan required that participating children be able to deal with printed materials. In pilot testing, it was found that children in grade two were able to deal with a simple multiple-choice questionnaire format, while most children in the first grade were not. The lower limit of the research population was set at grade two. It was desirable to have representatives at every grade level for this cross-sectional study in order to chart the development of attitudes from grade to grade.

The most important characteristic of the research group was its range of age and grade, and one of the first decisions involved in the analysis of the data was the choice of grade rather than age as the major independent variable. Grade in school is highly correlated with age ($r = .96$). Because we tested in classroom groups, obtaining equal numbers of children at each grade level, there was a definite advantage in analysis by grade.[1] In using grade as a basis for differentiating the research groups, it was assumed that grade in school and chronological

1. The use of grade did introduce a slight bias between socioeconomic groups: high-status groups tended to be slightly younger on the average than did the other groups, while the older children in each grade were disproportionately from working-class backgrounds. However, as indicated by the social-class data presented later, the difference between status groups—where it exists—shows somewhat more rapid development on the part of the middle-class child. Thus the slight error introduced by using grade rather than age attenuates the social class differences.

226

age relate to the same function; that is, each year the child gains additional experience and is subjected to formal and informal socializing influences from various agents in the community.

Once the study had been limited to children in grades two through eight, consideration was given to the selection of other independent variables. The second major decision was to select the research population in a way that would facilitate analysis of particular variables rather than to take a random sample of elementary-school children in the United States. The time and expense involved in interviewing a random sample and in obtaining supplementary school data and information from teachers did not seem justified at this stage of research in this field. Our aim was to examine the process of political socialization rather than to obtain precise estimates of the level of already identified attitudes in the elementary school population.

GEOGRAPHIC AREA

The study was conducted in eight cities in different regions of the United States. Since one of the most obvious features of political behavior and attitudes in this country are the differences between various geographic sections, cities were selected from each of four regions. Within each region, one large city (population over 1,000,000) and one medium-sized city (population under 400,000) were chosen.[2] Appendix B reports the classification of states into the four regions and some of the demographic characteristics of the eight participating cities.[3] Within each city four schools were chosen, two from a middle-class area and two from a working-class area. Two classrooms were tested at each grade level in each school. This design gave a research population roughly balanced by grade, size of city, region, and social status. The actual number of subjects tested in each category is shown in Appendix B.

2. Although regional variation is difficult to define and demonstrate in a precise way, regionalism has been of interest to students of political behavior. Some of the authors who present evidence for systematic regional variations and who discuss the meaning of the intranational differences are: Holcombe (1924), Grassmuck (1951), Key (1947), and Truman (1959).

3. It was intended to choose the cities and the schools within each city solely on the census characteristics of the city and the representativeness of the schools. Occasionally, however, such practical considerations as local laws, the availability of schools, and the cooperativeness of Boards of Education intervened. In some states, for example, inquiring about occupation of the father is prohibited by law. Since socioeconomic status was a major variable in the study, we were unable to include cities from states with those prohibitions.

SOCIOECONOMIC STATUS

One of the demonstrated features of adult political behavior in the United States is the difference in attitudes and activity between persons from different socioeconomic levels. These differences are reported in virtually all major studies of political involvement, voting behavior, and interest. Briefly, research shows the middle-class citizen to be more informed, interested, involved, and active in political behavior at city, state, and national levels than is the working-class citizen.

Since it was one of the purposes of the project to inquire into the effects of social class at pre-adult levels, approximately equal numbers of schools were selected from the cities' middle-class and working-class areas, as determined from census records. The grouping of children by school and neighborhood areas not being sufficiently precise for purposes of analysis, the questionnaire included an item about the occupation of the child's father. Although occupational status is not equivalent to Warner's conception of social class (Warner, Meeker and Eells, 1949), it is highly correlated and is suitable as an estimate of social status. For this reason, information about the occupational level of his father was obtained from the child, using a scale incorporated into the questionnaire. Pilot work resulted in a six-point scale, which testers also used to rate father's occupation from school records.

Because occupation of father was rated reliably by the children, this rating was taken as an adequate estimate of social status for our subjects. Testers obtained information about parental occupation from the school files. This was used when information was not available from the child. The correlation between occupation as rated from the school files and occupation as designated by the subjects on the questionnaire was .64. If neither data was available, the student was assigned to the modal category for his school district and grade, on the assumption that students in the same grade at a given school live in the same neighborhood and are likely to come from similar social and occupational backgrounds.

Table A.01 shows the distribution of the occupational status ratings assigned to the subjects, using both ratings based on self-report, on school files, and on the median occupational rank in the child's class. Three social-status levels were designated by grouping these occupational categories: low status—unskilled workers; middle status—skilled workers, clerical workers, sales workers and owners of small businesses; and high status—executives, professionals, and owners of large businesses. Upper-middle class children (professional and managerial fathers) are over-represented in the tested group, and graphs and tables

Table A.01
Number of Subjects and Per Cent of Total in Each
Occupational Status Category

Occupation	N	Per cent	Occupation	N	Per cent
Unskilled worker	2793	23.2	Executive	1432	29.1
Skilled worker	2360	19.6	Professional	1617	13.4
Clerical, sales,					
small business	3503	29.1	Large business	343	2.9

Notes.—Occupation of father was determined from child's report if available; if not, from school files. If neither source had information, occupational status was assigned from the modal category for the child's grade and school.

—Correlation between occupation as rated from school files and as designated by subjects on questionnaire was .64.

showing age trends for the total group are biased for those items where the upper-class group differed from the other social classes.

Appendix B reports the distribution of social status (assessed by child's report of father's occupation) as it varied in the eight cities. Although almost equal numbers of children from a middle-class and a working-class school were tested in each city, middle- and high-status occupations were over-represented in some cities. School districts classified as middle class in one city apparently contained different proportions of persons with skilled and clerical occupations than did schools classified as middle class in other cities. This social-class imbalance, likely to contaminate regional comparisons, was a major factor in the choice of occupation rather than school district as the indicator of social status for the analysis.

ETHNICITY

The purpose of this project was to examine the most characteristic forms of political socialization in the United States. To focus on this objective, it was decided to defer consideration of subcultural groups in which political socialization might differ from the dominant culture. It was hoped that this study would establish a base line of socialization patterns in urban areas, from which future studies could investigate subcultural variations. Groups were selected to include equal numbers of children of each sex, from seven grade levels, from a range of status backgrounds, and from the four major geographical regions of the United States; it was not feasible to investigate systematically the influence of ethnic background or race in this project. Testing was conducted, insofar as possible, in city neighborhoods which were not primarily populated by ethnic groups.[4]

INTELLIGENCE TEST SCORE

Intelligence test scores were available from school files for 84.4 per cent of the subjects. If more than one test score was available, the most recent was taken. Tables compiled by Flanagan and Schwarz (1958) were used to convert IQ's to a common stanine scale.[5] This method provides some confidence in interschool comparisons. For example, a child whose IQ on the Otis Test places him in stanine 5 has ability comparable to a child in another city whose IQ on the Kuhlmann-Anderson Test places him in stanine 5.

The distribution of IQ in the research population departed from the theoretical stanine distribution. There was a disproportionate number of children with high IQ, as Table A.02 shows. Only in the lower

Table A.02
Distribution of IQ Scores [a]
(N = 10,165)

Base	PERCENTAGE SCORING WITHIN EACH STANINE								
	1	2	3	4	5	6	7	8	9
Total research group	1.3	1.8	5.5	9.7	18.0	20.3	19.1	12.7	11.7
Expected distribution of stanine scores	4.0	7.0	12.0	17.0	20.0	17.0	12.0	7.0	4.0

a. Obtained from school records and converted to stanine scores.

social status does the profile of IQ stanine correspond to the expected distribution (see Appendix B). The high average IQ in the total group is due in part to the relatively greater proportion of middle-class chil-

---

4. The policy with respect to readily identifiable groups, where there may be subcultural influences, was to collect the questionnaires but not to analyze them as part of the national study reported here. Data from 269 children who were identified in the field administration as Mexican, Negro, or Oriental will be compared with findings from the national group in a subsequent publication.

5. Flanagan and Schwarz formed a common scale for IQ by determining equivalent scores for 11 different intelligence tests. The resulting scores were graduated in units called stanines, a stanine being a form of standard score in which the scores are transformed into 9 groups as follows: the first stanine represents the lowest 4 per cent of the population; the second, the next 7 per cent; the third, the next 12 per cent; the fourth, the next 17 per cent; the fifth, the middle 20 per cent; the sixth, the next 17 per cent; the seventh, the next 12 per cent; the eighth, the next 7 per cent; and the ninth, the top 4 per cent of the population.

dren in the research group than in the population on which these stanine norms were developed.

The extent to which the IQ distribution was positively skewed varied among the eight cities (Appendix B). For example, in one city, instead of the expected 23 per cent in the top three stanine categories, 61 per cent of the children were classified there. The disparity in IQ level between cities interferes with an accurate analysis of city differences, particularly in view of our findings on the effect of IQ upon political socialization.

SOCIAL PARTICIPATION SCORE

For the subjects tested, clubs and athletic groups were the two principal areas of organized social activity outside the home and classroom.[6] Four questions were used to assess the subject's social participation. A social participation score ranging from 0 to 6 points was derived in the following manner: If the subject answered that he belonged to a school club, 1 point was added to his score; if he belonged to an out of school organization, 1 point was added; 2 points were added if he belonged to two organizations, 3 if he belonged to three or more organizations. One point was added to the score if the subject answered that he had been an officer and another point if he had been a member of an athletic team. Appendix B shows the distribution of specific group and team activities, for all subjects, by social status and grade.

RELIGIOUS AFFILIATION AND CHURCH ATTENDANCE

The children in the research group were asked to indicate the religious preference of their families. Appendix B shows the distribution of membership or preference for all subjects by social status. The association between social status and religious affiliation apparent from these tables is in the expected direction for the cities tested—Catholics are over-represented in lower-status groups; Jews are over-represented in high-status groups.

CHARACTERISTICS OF FAMILY BACKGROUND

In addition to the information about families' occupational activity, the school files yielded data on parents' national origins; 95 per cent of the students' fathers were born in the United States; 94 per cent of

6. Correlations between a summed score based on organizational activities alone and one which also included athletic activities ranged from .81 to .86 for the two sexes at two grade levels.

the mothers. The files also showed that 87 per cent of the children were living with their fathers at the time of testing and 97 per cent were living with their mothers. The child's perception of the relative power of his two parents in family decisions was also assessed.

POLITICAL PARTY PREFERENCE

In Chapter Nine of this book, the relation of party preference to other areas of political involvement and interest is discussed in some detail.

Development of the Questionnaire

The first year of the project was devoted to designing and pretesting the questionnaire. This initial phase of the study was strongly influenced by four considerations. First, the research dealt with young subjects whose reading and comprehension skills were relatively undeveloped, requiring an adaptation of the concepts and techniques devised for measuring the opinions and attitudes of adults. Second, since the instrument was not administered individually, it had to be comprehensible and intrinsically interesting to children with a wide range of ability and motivation. Third, the phenomena to be studied included both cognitive and affective elements—calling for items which dealt, on the one hand, with non-intellective responses and, on the other hand, with abstract concepts. Fourth, since the project was committed to investigate an area relatively uncharted by earlier research, there were few guide-lines to indicate the grade level at which questions of a given type and specificity should be asked. The research procedure at this early stage was to utilize broad, open-ended questions, then progressively to narrow the scope of questions presented until a general picture of the concepts understandable at a given age was apparent in the subjects' responses.

Actual construction of the questionnaire was preceded by individual interviews with children in grades two through eight in lower-middle class and upper-middle class schools. Children were asked to talk about political terms such as "government" and to tell about their experiences with persons such as the policeman. Response to pictures revealed the prominent position that symbols such as the flag have in the child's mind. Some of the respondents were asked to draw pictures about political themes and to write short stories about their pictures. These interviews revealed some of the vocabulary difficulties which questionnaire procedures present for children. A list was compiled of commonly misunderstood words, such as "politician," "government," "union," "Congress," "citizen," and "Supreme Court," gathered from early forms of pilot questionnaires on which students were asked to check the words they thought would be "too hard for boys and girls your age to understand."

After exploratory interviews with students, the project staff began to draft pilot forms of the questionnaire. This pretesting phase covered ten months of experimentation with twelve different pilot questionnaires.[7] During the pretesting phase, many items were revised or abandoned on the basis of group response patterns or information obtained in interviews. More than 5,000 grade-school students participated in this pretesting stage of the project. Some scaling techniques were much more useful than others with children in this age range. For example, it appeared that much information could be obtained by presenting a single stimulus, either an object such as "The President" or a statement such as "All laws are fair," and asking the child to indicate his opinion along some scaled dimension. Following a suggestion made by Baurerfeind (1955), a graphic device was adopted which clarified questions requiring agree-disagree responses by matching the size of box and size of print to alternative intensities of feeling. For example:

All laws are fair:

Don't Know

1. ☐ YES 2. ☐ yes 3. ◯ 4. ☐ no 5. ☐ NO

No Opinion

In questions which required rating a stimulus object on some dimension, each alternative was labeled to reduce ambiguity.
For example:

7. Although the majority of the questions in the final instrument originated in interview material or in the earlier high-school questionnaire, some questions were incorporated which had been used by other investigators. "If you could vote, who would be best to ask for voting advice?" had been used by Greenstein (1965a); "The American flag is the best flag in the world"; "America is the best country in the world"; "People in other countries think their country is best" were adapted from interview questions which had been used by Weinstein (1957) to study children's concepts of the flag and national identity. The Efficacy Scale and the question concerning the relative contributions of political parties were similar to questions used to study adult political attitudes (Campbell, Gurin, and Miller, 1954; Stillman, Guthrie, and Becker, 1960).

Think of the *President* as he really is. . . .

1	2	3	4	5	6
Would always want to help me if I needed it	Would almost always want to to help me if I needed it	Would usually want to help me if I needed it	Would some- times want to help me if I needed it	Would seldom want to help me if I needed it	Would not usually want to help me if I needed it

This type of 6-point scale was used in rating all government figures and institutions. Figures A.01 and A.02 present examples of questions where pictures were used to make the choice more graphic for children.

The final selection of items was done by the research staff on the

(24)   Here are some pictures that show what our government is. Pick the two pictures that show best what our government is.

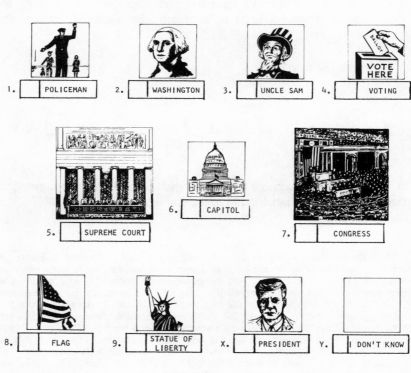

Fig. A.01.
Example of picture question.

basis of a number of considerations: (1) the relevance of the item to political behavior and socialization theory; (2) the similarity of the item to areas of behavior studied in adults, to permit comparisons between adult and pre-adult levels; (3) statistical properties of responses such as shape of distribution, stability of response from one testing to another, similarity of an item to other items already selected, correlation among items, and variance of an item between age and social

(63)   If the President came to your town to give prizes to the two grown-ups who were the best citizens, which grown-ups would he choose? Put an X beside the two he would choose as the best citizens.

1. [   ] Someone who works hard.

2. [   ] Someone everybody likes.

3. [   ] Someone who votes and gets others to vote.

4. [   ] Someone who helps others.

5. [   ] Someone who is interested in the way our country is run.

6. [   ] Someone who always obeys the laws.

7. [   ] Someone who goes to church.

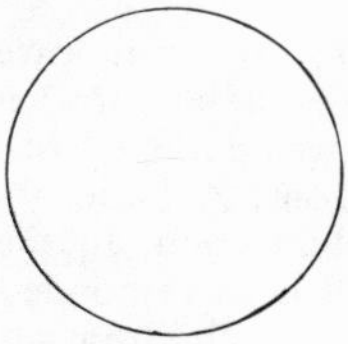

8. [   ] I don't know what citizen means.

Fig. A.02.
Example of picture question.

status groups; [8] (4) the frequency of "Don't know" responses, a consideration used both to evaluate items for inclusion and to decide the age placement of the item in the final instrument; (5) the controversiality of the question's content (that is, the likelihood that it would touch on a point of such community conflict that school authorities would be reluctant to approve the use of the questionnaire). The majority of the items were chosen on the basis of these criteria.

A single form of the questionnaire was used for subjects at all grade-levels. This strategy called for a format based upon a progression of item difficulty. Students in grade two were asked to complete only the first 16 pages of the 40-page instrument; students in grade three were asked to finish 24 pages; students in grades four through eight completed the entire questionnaire.

To preserve the confidentiality of every respondent's answers, each questionnaire was prenumbered with a 7-digit code stamped on the top and the bottom of the first page. The student wrote his name and his teacher's name on the bottom of the first page. On the top of the page testers recorded information from the school files about the child's IQ, birthplace, etc. Then the bottom half of the first page was detached along a perforated line and the principal of each school retained the half that contained the student's name and code number. The principal had no further information about the child's responses,[9] and there was no way for the investigators to connect the responses given with a particular child.

8. The tendency to eliminate an item that had little variance by grade or social status introduced a selection bias. On those items, consensus is apparently almost complete and established at an early age. To leave out such items meant to discard potentially useful information about socialization; to include them used part of the questionnaire merely to establish on a large group a point that seemed evident from pilot data. The piling up of responses on a single alternative in some instances merely indicated an inefficient or badly worded item, and did not provide new information. Therefore those items showing a great deal of consensus in the pilot results were ruled out of the final instrument and are referred to directly in our discussion of relevant topics. Each table which reports data from a pilot sample rather than from the nation-wide group includes as a footnote a reference to the pretest on which the item was included. Appendix B specifies the grade and social status of the group which answered each pilot instrument.

9. On this same lower half of the first page, in some districts, the child wrote the names of all brothers and sisters who attended the same school. This information was gathered to carry out an analysis of intrafamily similarity in political orientations. A basic assumption of any study of socialization is that the family is a potent agent in the process. To test this assumption, 205 pairs of siblings who had both responded to the questionnaire were selected. Approximately equal numbers of children were chosen from each of the grade-levels between grades three and eight. The general hypothesis was that since the family affects attitude development, there would be greater similarity between the attitudes of siblings than between the attitudes of non-related children who were matched by sex, grade, and social status. The results of this substudy are reported in Chapter Five.

A copy of the questionnaire used to assess the children's attitudes has been

Teacher Questionnaires

In addition to the basic instrument devised to obtain information about children's attitudes, questionnaires were constructed to measure both educational practices and attitudes of individual teachers in the schools which participated in the project.

TEACHER ATTITUDE QUESTIONNAIRE

Teachers' attitudes were measured to compare their responses with those of their students and to assess their influence on the attitudes of the younger subjects. Each teacher whose class was being tested was asked to complete a modified version of the children's questionnaire. Personal items, such as those dealing with family attitudes, were deleted; in every other respect the questions were identical. Three hundred and ninety-two teachers completed the teacher questionnaire. They were divided approximately equally between the eight cities where testing was conducted.

CURRICULUM QUESTIONNAIRE

As part of an attempt to examine the role of the school in socializing children into the political system, another instrument was constructed for teachers. The curriculum questionnaire covered 21 major topic areas and asked the teacher to specify (a) how much time she spent on each topic, (b) whether the teaching was planned or incidental, (c) her assessment of the appropriateness of the topic for her grade, and (d) its importance compared to subjects like reading and arithmetic. The curriculum questionnaire asked whether political pictures and symbols such as the flag were displayed in the classroom. Other questions inquired about political rituals—the singing of patriotic songs and the recitation of the pledge of allegiance to the flag. One hundred sixty-nine teachers returned this curriculum questionnaire.

---

deposited as Document number 9365 with the ADI Auxiliary Publications Project, Photoduplication Service, Library of Congress, Washington, D.C. 20540. A copy may be secured by citing the Document number and by remitting $2.50 for photoprints, or $1.75 for 35mm microfilm. Advance payment is required. Make checks or money orders payable to: Chief, Photoduplication Service, Library of Congress.

Field Testing

During the early months of the second year of the project, the final form of the questionnaire was completed. This was pilot-tested with several hundred subjects in two of the eight cities which had been selected. These data were analyzed and minor revisions made before the final 12,000 subjects were tested.

The second six months of the second year were devoted to data collection. During this phase, teams of four test administrators traveled to each of the cities for one to two weeks. In most cases the school administrators arranged to send a letter to both teachers and parents explaining the purposes of the research. When the tester arrived in the classroom, the teacher was given a copy of the teacher attitude questionnaire to complete while the tester administered the instrument to the class. Frequently, the teacher was absent during the administration of the questionnaire. The testers read the entire instrument aloud to the class while they followed in their booklets and indicated their answers. After the testing at a school was complete, testers recorded the pertinent information about each subject from the school files and detached the student's name from the questionnaire.

The importance of interpreting the goals of this research not only to the subjects but also to the faculty and to other interested people in the community was apparent. Generally, the project director discussed the project thoroughly with the superintendent and with members of the board of education. At the time of testing, members of the staff met with the president of the Parent-Teacher Association as well as with representatives of religious, professional, and business organizations who might be interested. Parents who had questions about the study often turned to key people in the community. This preliminary briefing of these people proved to be an effective mode of transmitting the objectives of the project.

Stability of Responses

The stability or instability of an attitude or opinion is one of its most significant characteristics. This is especially relevant in the study of attitudes developing in childhood, where a reasonable level of response stability is necessary to give meaning to responses. To examine the stability of replies to this questionnaire, 1,158 subjects (chosen from those cities where the time schedule was flexible enough to permit retesting) in grades two, four, six, and eight were retested four to fourteen days after they had initially filled out the questionnaire. The second testing situation was as similar as possible to the first.

The product-moment correlation between score on first test and score on second testing has been the most popular statistic for reporting item stability. This is usually referred to as a stability coefficient, test-retest coefficient, or test-retest correlation. Although ordinal scales do not meet all the statistical assumptions of correlation, this method has been widely used with such scales. The percentage of individuals giving identical responses on two occasions has been used to report stability of true-false, agree-disagree items.

It was difficult to compare the data obtained from the test-retest group with results of other studies since adult studies have rarely reported the stability of opinion measures. The problem of assessing stability was complicated by the multiplicity of item types in the questionnaire: on some, the numerical continuum for rating corresponded to an ordinal scale (like the rating scale cited); others gave only a discrete choice (for example, "Is a democracy where the people rule? Yes, No, Don't know"), and attained only the nominal level of measurement. Hess and Torney (1965) report the test-retest correlations (Pearson r) for most of the items which used scalar measurement. Table A.03 presents the median correlation and range of correlation for each grade group for the 109 attitude items which could be analyzed in this way. Items with stability coefficients at the lower end of this range were not used extensively in the analysis.

Table A.03
Stability Coefficients by Grade

Grade	Number of children who repeated test	Number of items correlated [a]	Median stability coefficient [b]	Range of stability coefficients
2	360	30	.38	.27-.60
4	414	109	.42	.20-.80
6	225	109	.51	.25-.86
8	159	109	.54	.27-.83

a. All political attitude items which could be scaled on a numerical continuum were included.

b. Product-moment correlation between response on test and retest.

Most correlations reported in the literature have been computed for scale scores which combine a number of single items and for which the scores are spread across a wide range.[10] The majority of the correlations for the questionnaire were based on *single items,* which frequently had restricted distributions. The reliability of the indices and scales which were composed of several items is also presented by Hess and Torney (1965). In general, these indices had higher stability coefficients than the single items. It is difficult to evaluate the magnitude of these correlations in relation to other studies since few investigators have reported information about item stability. Some comparative figures are available from a study of high-school students made by Litt (1963). For instance, the stability coefficient obtained in our study on the Efficacy Scale for eighth graders was .71; Litt reported a stability coefficient of .85 for a very similar efficacy scale used with high-school students.

For those multiple-choice items which had no numerical continuum, the percentage of students who gave identical responses on the two administrations was computed. These percentage-agreement figures must be interpreted with reference both to the number of alternatives offered by the item and the distribution of responses. Fiske (1957) and Cohen (1960) have noted that the percentage of agreement one would expect by chance is dependent on the number of response alternatives and on the distribution of responses on test and retest. The extensive analysis required to compute indices such as that suggested by Cohen did not offer sufficient additional yield of information to justify the time and expense required.

For some items, the percentage-agreement and correlation coefficients give quite different impressions of the stability of response. Several bivariate distributions of items were computed which compared Test 1 and Test 2. These distributions revealed that a combination of high percentage of agreement and low correlation usually occurred when a small number of points of the scale had been chosen by a high percentage of the subjects. This restriction of range artificially reduced the correlation.

Data Analysis and Presentation

ANALYSIS AND STRATEGY OF PRESENTATION

A series of analyses was conducted with the data from the national respondents: first, basic tabulations of each question on the question-

10. Harris (1957), for example, reported correlations of .60–.70 for an 89-item Social Responsibility Scale given at a four-month interval to grade 8–10 students. Cronbach (1960) reported that for the *Allport-Vernon Study of Values* stability correlations over a three-month period for summed scale scores ranged from .39 to .84.

naire—by grade, by sex, and by social status; second, correlational
analysis and factor analysis of the dependent variables to determine the
structure of political attitudes and to guide the combination of items into
indices (the item combinations which have been used in this final report
are specified in Appendix C); third, regression and chi-square analysis
to determine the significance of relationships between independent variables (such as grade, IQ, social class) and political attitudes; fourth,
tabulation of political attitude items by grade, or by IQ (holding grade
and social status constant), or by sex (holding grade constant), and so
on. The majority of the data included in this report comes from the
fourth type of analysis.

It was decided to present most of these comparisons in graphic
form. Following the orientation of the project, the child's grade in school
was the most important independent variable in designing formats for
graphic presentation. The use of grade as the abscissa (horizontal co-
ordinate) and the attitude variables as the ordinate (vertical coordi-
nate) makes the changes with grade more apparent than would tabular
presentation.

Graphs appear in Chapters Two, Three, and Four (which consider
age changes) for items in which the mean is an appropriate measure of
group tendency. Tabular presentation is used for items where format
is multiple choice and for which percentages must be reported.[11] In such
items, graphing each alternative would have presented too many lines on
a single graph. All data which appear in Chapters Five, Six, Seven,
Eight, and Nine (where group differences are considered) are presented
in graphic form. Thirty-six groups were compared in some graphs (three
grade groups by three social classes by four political party alignments)
and while tabular presentation would have been difficult to scan, graphic
presentation makes findings obvious at a glance.

CONSTRUCTING ORDINATE UNIT FOR GRAPHS

Our purpose was to chart descriptive information about the process
of political socialization, to assess the impact of the school and family,
and to determine the variations in this process for boys and girls and
for children of different social class and intelligence levels. The study
began with questions rather than definitive hypotheses. This required
techniques for ordering the data and for examining the consistency of
group differences. A yardstick was needed to estimate the likelihood that
observed differences were non-random, even though there was no attempt to verify or disprove specific hypotheses. A study such as this,

11. N for all tables and graphs is the number who gave a response to the
question. Those who omitted a question could not be included in computations of
means or percentages.

which included a large number of discrete items with differing formats and alternatives and widely differing range,[12] and which was conducted with a large number of potential group comparisons, presented further problems in the analysis and descriptive presentation of data.

In order to obtain an estimate of the probability of chance occurrence and simultaneously to form a unit for graphing, the *Significance Unit* was developed for judging group differences and as a unit for graphic presentation which would be equivalent for different items.[13] This unit is a type of standard error of the mean which may be applied to any group comparison presented in one graph or table.[14]

The average standard error of the mean was used to derive an ordinate unit (on the vertical axis) for graphs; the abscissa unit (on the horizontal axis) in every case was grade in school. In these graphs political-attitude scores were plotted as functions of grade of the group. Each graph represents one index or item and compares the responses of a number of groups. The number of groups being compared varies according to the placement of the item in the questionnaire (whether it was in the section which grade two children answered) and according to the comparison being made. Assessment of age trends compares five, six, or seven grade-levels with each other, while assessment of sex differences holding grade constant compares twice as many groups.

For most graphs, groups were large and of fairly uniform size. The assumption was made that the variance within every comparison group was equivalent. Group size was in most cases at least 250. The mean group size (not including teachers) was used as the N for the computations. This information was already available at the time the decision about data presentation was made. The average within-group variance (not including the variance of the teacher group) was divided by the average group size and its square root taken to obtain the average standard error of the mean for each graph. Because the purpose was to

12. Some items had a range of 3 points, others of 18 points. In some items all scale points had been used with equal frequency; in others, only a portion of the range had been used.

13. Standard scores would have been an alternate solution for this problem but would have destroyed the item metric.

14. What were the alternatives to this method of analysis and presentation? We could have taken the total sample, regardless of grade, and tested social class differences for significance. The sample is so large, however, that very small differences would have been highly significant. A complex analysis of variance could have been used to test for main effects of age, social class, intelligence, etc., and for interactions. However, we were interested in observing directly the shape of the age trends, the grade at which group differences appeared, and the consistency of differences across the age span. Also the number of items, the number of subjects, the necessity for eliminating subjects who had omitted responses or given "Don't Know" responses, the skew of some distributions, and the nonparametric nature of some items made complex statistical analysis impossible even using the 7094 computer. This led to the adoption of graphical presentation.

compare group means, the unit for the ordinate of a graph was derived from this average standard error:

$$s_{D_M} = \sqrt{s_{M_1}^2 + s_{M_2}^2}$$

Assuming $\quad s_{M_1}^2 = s_{M_2}^2 = s_M^2$

$$s_{D_M} = \sqrt{2s_M^2}$$

$$s_{D_M} = 1.41\, s_M$$

From a table of normal deviates, the 5 per cent level (2-tailed) was chosen, corresponding to a Critical Ratio (z) of 1.94. The amount of difference between means required to produce a Critical Ratio of this magnitude was computed:

$$\frac{M_1 - M_2}{1.41\ s_M} = 1.94$$

$$M_1 - M_2 = 2.74\ s_M$$

If a single difference between group means is to be significant, the two means must differ by 2.74 times their average standard error. The ordinate unit for a graph is therefore 2.74 times the average standard error of the mean for the item or index being graphed, and each line on the ordinate is separated from the next by this unit. This unit is referred to as the Significance Unit.

Because it is difficult to be accurate to 2 decimals in graphing, these calculations have been computed and rounded off as follows: for each item tabulation, the average standard error of the means was computed and multiplied by 2.74. This figure has been reported as the *Significance Unit* at the bottom of every graph or table. If the result was between .01 and .30, it was rounded off to two places beyond the decimal. If it was greater than .30, it was rounded to the nearest .05 (for example, .326 would be rounded to .35). This rounded figure was used as the ordinate unit, providing a rough indication of the significance of differences.

In approaching these graphs, the reader should recall that the Significance Unit is used as a gross measure. Any pair of means (each mean represented by the intersection of a vertical line and the plotted line) which are separated by one ordinate unit differ at approximately the .05 level. In almost all the items reported, age trends are progressive and linear, and differences appear between several pairs of groups without reversals. Replications in independent samples of such consistent differences decrease the probability that these are chance findings. Keeping in mind that with 7 age groups there are 42 pair-wise comparisons (of which two might be significant at the .05 level by chance) no importance has been attached to isolated differences. In the independent variable analysis, groups have been compared within a given grade, and—when a variable has been controlled—within a block. In most of these analyses there have been 27 possible pair-wise comparisons. Items which showed more than one significant reversal have not been cited.

Items where parametric scaling was not appropriate were analyzed by using proportions or percentages. These items were also scaled using the Significance Unit. The standard error of the difference between two proportions depends on both the size of the proportion and the group size. Standard errors of proportions near .50 are larger than those near .10. In order to give the most conservative estimate, the standard error for the proportion .50 was computed using the average group size. The result was multiplied by 2.74. The resulting proportion, converted into a percentage, was used as the Significance Unit.

The preceding method has been used to scale the ordinate whenever one item or index appeared in a single graph. When more than one item was to be graphed on the same page (as in comparing the rated helpfulness of father, President, and policeman), the largest Significance Unit for the items appearing on that page was used as the ordinate unit. Because the same population rated father, policeman, and President, the means at any one grade level are not independent. Estimates of the significance of differences *between lines* on these graphs are less exact.

INTERPRETING GRAPHS IN CHAPTERS TWO, THREE, AND FOUR

The purpose of graphs in Chapters Two, Three, and Four is to illustrate differences between groups of children who are in different school grades. Figure A.03, based on fictitious data, is given as an illustration. The following types of information appear on each graph:

(1) *Title.*—The title describes in general or abstract terms the political-attitude variable which is being graphed.

(2) *Item.*—This citation appears below the graph on the left-hand side of the page and describes the political-attitude variable in more explicit terms, often quoting the item or listing items which have been combined to form an index. If the item is a scalar rating, "Item" quotes the most extreme positive rating on the scale with the word or words which vary to form less positive positions underlined. In the example Fig. A.03, the most positive rating is "would *always* want to help me if I needed it." The underlining of "always" indicates that this term is varied to indicate less positive evaluations of helpfulness.

(3) *Index scale.*—This citation appears below the graph on the

right-hand side of the page. It indicates the range of scores on the item and whether high numbers represent more or less positive attitudes than low numbers. In the example, "1.—always" corresponds exactly to the item citation because it is the most positive rating; "6.—never" indicates the least favorable scale position. Thus, in this example, the ratings may range from 1 to 6, with the lower numerical values standing for more positive evaluations.

(4) *Range of N.*—This citation presents the size of the smallest and largest group used in computing the Significance Unit and the means.

(5) *Significance Unit.*—The Significance Unit as reported in Fig. A.03 has been rounded off to the nearest tenth (since it is less than .30). Any two adjacent horizontal lines on the graph are separated by one Significance Unit.

(6) *Scale label.*—The label at the top left-hand side of the graph indicates whether the top of the graph represents more positive or more negative attitude, higher or lower interest, agreement or disagreement with an item. This label indicates the *direction* of the graphing. It is not attached to any particular value on the scale. In the example Fig. A.03, although the *always* corresponds to scale position 1 in the questionnaire, "Would help always" appears next to scale value 1.12, indicating that higher positions on the ordinate approach the positive end-point of the scale. The ordinate scale may be interpreted in absolute terms by referring to the Index Scale which indicates the labeling of its end points. The bottom of the graph scale does not stand for the lowest possible score but rather for the score necessary to allow graphing of the lowest mean score of any grade group. The word "percentages" appears next to the graph itself when this unit is graphed.

To determine from Fig. 1 the mean rating given to the mayor by second-grade children, read up the vertical line which represents grade two until the plotted line is reached; then read the ordinate label on the left margin of the graph opposite this point. (In example Fig. A.03, the mean rating given by second graders is 1.24.) To assess changes in means with age, follow the plotted line from left to right on the page. Any two grades which are separated by one or more Significance Units differ at approximately the .05 level. In example Fig. A.03, grades two and three are not significantly different from each other; grades four and five are significantly different, etc. The distance between grade eight and teachers cannot be evaluated for significance because the size of the teacher group has not been included in the computation of the Significance Unit. To indicate this, the mean rating given by teachers is connected to the grade-eight mean by a broken line.

The purpose of the graphs in Chapters Five through Nine is to illustrate the *differences* between groups of children divided by variables other than grade (for example, intelligence, or social class). Graphs such as those in the section on attitude differences between boys and girls are easy to interpret (see Fig. 62). There are two age-trend lines on this graph; one connects the means of each grade group of girls, the other represents the means of boys. In this example, the sex differences at grade three are not significant, while sex differences at all other grade levels are significant. "Item," "Index Scale," "Range of N," and "Significance Unit" are to be interpreted as in the graphs for Chapters Two, Three, and Four.

The majority of graphs in Chapters Five through Nine are of the type illustrated in Figure 34. Grades have been grouped for this graph; grade-two subjects are not included; grades three and four, grades five and six, and grades seven and eight have been combined. Three graphs or blocks appear on each page. Each block represents children who have in common the variable which is being controlled or held constant. Each block is labeled with the variable which is controlled. In the example Fig. 34, the top block represents the means of groups of children who are high in intelligence, the second block represents those of medium intelligence, etc. The lines within each block are labeled with the variable on which the groups are compared, in this case social status. By comparing the points on a single vertical line within a block, the reader may hold IQ and grade constant and compare the means of the three social status groups. In this example, at grade three-four, holding IQ constant, children from low-status homes are significantly more attached to the President than those from high-status homes. This difference is not significant in the medium IQ groups at grades five-six, but it is significant in every other grade and IQ group. Children from middle-status homes are more like children from low-status homes than they are like those of high-status homes, and differences between middle- and high-status children in some IQ-grade groups are significant.

Only one comparison (between social classes in Fig. 34) can be made from any one graph. Because of the crudeness of this Significance Unit, we have stressed only main effects which are replicated in several groups, like those shown in Fig. 34. This analysis can point out the most clear-cut groups differences, leaving the examination of interactions among independent variables for more complex statistical analysis.

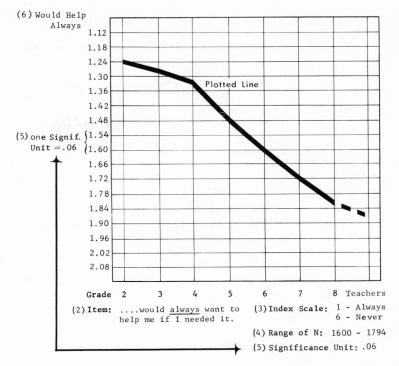

(6) Would Help
Always

(5) one Signif.
Unit = .06

Plotted Line

Grade   2   3   4   5   6   7   8 Teachers

(2) Item: ....would <u>always</u> want to   (3) Index Scale: 1 - Always
           help me if <u>I</u> needed it.   6 - Never

                                         (4) Range of N: 1600 - 1794

                                         (5) Significance Unit: .06

THIS IS A SAMPLE AND REPRESENTS HYPOTHETICAL DATA

Fig. A.03.
Example of graphing.
(1) Comparison of means of grades 2 through 8 in rating
responsiveness of mayor to individuals.

Demographic

Information

Table B.01
Characteristics of Participating Cities
(1960 census data for standard metropolitan areas)

	Large North-eastern	Large Southern	Large North Central	Large Western	Small North-eastern	Small Southern	Small North Central	Small Western
Population [a]	2,589,301	1,017,188	6,220,913	2,783,359	120,655	187,045	107,849	321,590
Percent increase 1950-60 [a]	7.4	39.9	20.1	24.2	.6	31.6	3.8	16.6
Percent foreign born [b]	12.4	9.9	9.7	10.8	6.8	.4	3.0	7.1
Percent of persons 14-17 in school [b]	88.5	86.3	87.6	92.0	90.4	90.5	88.3	89.5
Median school years completed by 25+ [b]	12.1	11.1	10.9	12.1	11.9	11.9	11.3	11.6
Median family income [c]	$6,687	5,758	7,342	7,092	5,668	4,783	5,539	5,950
Percent white collar workers [c]	49.7	48.2	45.5	51.0	48.0	47.0	44.0	44.3
Manuf. ration percent in manuf. industries [c]	28.8	22.1	34.2	21.0	21.1	14.2	20.2	22.7
Percent non-white [a]	3.4	22.8	14.8	12.5	.4	40.0	1.8	5.1

a. *General Population Characteristics*, U.S. Census of Population: 1960.
b. *General Soc. & Econ. Characteristics* (1960), Final Report Table 22.
c. *General Soc. & Econ. Characteristics* (1960), Final Report, Table 33.
d. In selecting cities for the project, states were divided into the classifications used by the United States Bureau of the Census: Northeast, North Central, South, and West. States on the borders between regions were eliminated so schools were chosen from cities in the following states:

1) Northeast: Maine, Vermont, New Hampshire, New York, Pennsylvania, New Jersey, Massachusetts, Connecticut, and Rhode Island.
2) North Central: Ohio, Michigan, Indiana, Illinois, Wisconsin, Iowa, and Minnesota.
3) South: Virginia, North Carolina, South Carolina, Georgia, Florida, Alabama, Mississippi, and Louisiana.
4) West: California, Oregon, and Washington.

Table B.02
Number of Subjects by Region, City Size, Socioeconomic Status of Neighborhood, and Grade in School

Region	City size	Socioeconomic status of school area	GRADE-LEVEL						
			2	3	4	5	6	7	8
North-east	Large	Middle class	114	113	107	97	85	104	83
		Working class	102	87	106	120	98	125	106
	Small	Middle class	105	119	109	119	119	103	117
		Working class	89	113	120	132	97	119	124
North Central	Large	Middle class	92	105	110	112	128	107	110
		Working class	122	121	120	142	115	125	109
	Small	Middle class	91	90	105	98	114	107	115
		Working class	96	107	104	111	106	50	44
South	Large	Middle class	111	122	120	127	130	112	78
		Working class	109	112	108	92	100	102	101
	Small	Middle class	128	129	134	128	112	121	114
		Working class	129	81	111	117	121	101	121
West	Large	Middle class	97	91	109	116	120	100	119
		Working class	115	116	121	109	121	116	123
	Small	Middle class	81	116	110	101	108	94	105
		Working class	125	91	100	103	102	122	132

Table B.03
Distribution of Social Status (Child's Report of Father's Occupation) by City

Cities	N	Unskilled worker	Skilled worker	Clerical, sales, small business	Executive	Professional	Large business
Large North Central	972	31.1%	19.1%	20.4%	14.2%	12.2%	3.0%
Large Southern	887	18.5	17.6	28.2	14.9	14.0	6.9
Small North Central	1000	31.0	18.7	23.6	12.2	11.1	3.4
Large Western	1034	23.0	24.0	25.2	12.3	11.6	3.9
Small Western	973	25.2	25.8	30.8	6.0	9.5	2.8
Small Southern	1142	14.1	15.3	32.4	16.4	16.6	5.2
Small Northeastern	1105	29.1	20.3	25.3	11.9	10.7	2.7
Large Northeastern	991	13.7	17.0	24.9	18.3	21.3	4.7

Table B.04
Distribution of IQ Scores by City
(In stanines)

Cities	1	2	3	4	5	6	7	8	9
Large North									
Central	1.8%	1.7%	4.6%	8.8%	17.0%	26.0%	17.3%	12.0%	10.8%
Large Southern	2.6	3.6	8.3	12.7	20.2	18.9	16.9	11.2	5.6
Small North									
Central	1.2	2.3	7.5	12.7	23.7	22.6	16.9	8.8	4.1
Large Western	2.4	3.4	6.8	11.0	21.1	18.9	16.7	12.0	7.8
Small Western	.4	1.2	5.0	8.8	14.1	19.5	21.0	14.5	15.5
Small Southern	.6	.6	2.3	4.7	11.2	18.7	26.0	19.1	16.9
Small									
Northeastern	.6	1.9	6.0	11.5	19.8	19.2	17.4	10.8	12.8
Large									
Northeastern	1.0	.8	4.3	8.7	17.8	18.4	19.6	12.5	17.0

Table B.05
Distribution of IQ Scores [a] by Grade and Social Status

	N without IQ data	N with IQ data	PERCENTAGE SCORING WITHIN EACH STANINE								
			1	2	3	4	5	6	7	8	9
Grade 2:											
Low status	141	198	2.5	1.0	8.0	17.6	15.1	18.1	21.6	10.1	6.0
Middle status	287	635	.5	.6	2.1	6.8	19.7	28.8	23.6	11.3	6.6
High status	205	189	.5	1.1	.5	6.3	14.2	18.4	31.6	15.3	12.1
Grade 3:											
Low status	83	315	2.9	3.2	10.2	14.9	21.0	23.5	12.4	6.7	5.4
Middle status	206	709	.4	1.6	2.7	8.7	21.0	23.7	22.1	13.7	5.9
High status	95	270	.4	1.1	1.9	7.8	11.9	16.7	25.9	18.9	15.6
Grade 4:											
Low status	52	344	1.7	3.2	10.8	11.6	27.6	20.6	14.5	6.1	3.8
Middle status	96	742	.3	1.5	5.5	9.8	19.4	19.7	21.6	12.1	10.1
High status	54	461	.4	1.1	3.0	5.6	14.1	20.2	20.4	19.1	16.1
Grade 5:											
Low status	47	384	3.1	3.7	8.3	13.8	21.6	18.0	13.5	8.9	9.1
Middle status	94	740	1.0	1.9	5.0	9.3	16.6	22.0	18.2	13.2	12.7
High status	68	470	.0	.6	1.9	7.0	12.8	17.5	21.3	15.5	23.4
Grade 6:											
Low status	41	364	2.6	2.8	9.3	16.5	21.4	20.9	13.5	9.3	3.6
Middle status	69	733	2.1	2.2	7.0	10.9	18.1	21.4	15.3	11.6	11.5
High status	44	498	.8	.8	2.2	3.8	12.7	16.9	20.3	17.7	24.9
Grade 7:											
Low status	29	396	4.6	3.0	11.4	14.7	22.7	20.0	12.9	6.1	4.8
Middle status	73	699	1.7	1.9	6.6	11.2	17.9	20.5	20.2	10.0	10.2
High status	42	484	.6	.4	1.5	3.5	12.0	20.3	22.5	18.4	20.9
Grade 8:											
Low status	36	365	1.4	4.1	11.8	14.5	22.7	19.5	15.6	6.6	3.8
Middle status	80	701	1.0	2.6	6.1	11.3	20.1	18.4	17.8	12.7	10.0
High status	45	468	.4	1.5	3.4	6.6	12.2	14.1	18.4	19.9	23.5

a. Obtained from school records and converted to stanine scores.

Table B.06
Distribution of Group Membership (Child's Report) by Grade and Social Status

	N	Boy Scout	Girl Scout	Camp-fire G.	Y-Clubs	CYO	Boys' club	4-H	Belong to no club	School club [a]	Sport team [b]	Club officer [c]
Grade 3:												
Low status	378	19.1%	16.4%	8.5%	5.0%	.8%	13.2%	.5%	40.5%	18.4%	22.2%	20.4%
Middle status	897	22.3	21.2	11.2	3.1	.9	6.0	1.3	34.7	16.5	21.6	22.9
High status	360	31.4	29.4	10.3	1.7	.6	5.0	.6	21.7	15.4	25.1	35.1
Grade 4:												
Low status	374	18.5	21.1	5.6	7.0	1.1	10.7	2.9	41.4	17.4	28.8	23.3
Middle status	808	26.5	23.6	6.3	3.6	.5	7.6	1.0	31.6	23.2	29.7	30.5
High status	495	29.9	35.2	6.9	1.8	.0	5.1	1.4	19.8	30.2	37.0	38.7
Grade 5:												
Low status	413	22.3	18.9	4.4	7.5	1.4	13.8	4.4	36.3	33.0	33.2	41.0
Middle status	810	27.9	28.0	6.5	6.1	.5	12.1	3.1	25.9	38.3	37.5	46.0
High status	518	36.1	36.1	7.1	3.5	1.4	7.5	1.9	13.5	43.1	46.7	62.6
Grade 6:												
Low status	390	21.3	19.2	4.4	8.5	1.5	16.2	3.6	34.6	43.2	37.4	48.5
Middle status	768	27.3	22.9	7.7	4.4	2.0	9.9	3.0	29.7	37.3	41.1	49.9
High status	522	31.6	34.9	3.1	5.9	1.2	5.6	2.7	17.2	40.5	53.6	61.0
Grade 7:												
Low status	414	26.3	20.3	4.8	6.5	1.2	12.8	3.6	33.1	42.6	45.8	42.2
Middle status	739	28.3	26.0	5.7	7.9	1.6	11.1	4.3	24.1	49.7	46.6	51.2
High status	510	33.7	35.9	4.3	7.1	1.2	6.7	4.3	13.3	60.6	48.8	64.2
Grade 8:												
Low status	367	18.5	15.0	2.2	7.4	2.7	12.8	6.0	46.1	45.6	43.8	46.3
Middle status	727	22.7	21.5	4.3	6.5	2.3	9.4	3.4	35.2	53.8	46.0	50.0
High status	477	26.8	31.9	2.9	5.9	2.3	7.3	2.9	21.2	64.8	56.3	67.6

a. The range of N for this item is 355 to 901.
b. The range of N for this item is 359 to 899.
c. The range of N for this item is 360 to 897.

Table B.07
Religious Preference of Family by Social Status

RELIGIOUS PREFERENCE OF FAMILY

Social status	N	Catholic	Jewish	Protes-tant	Other	None
Lower	1860	25.2%	1.3%	62.3%	5.3%	5.9%
Middle	3539	15.6	4.2	71.1	5.7	3.4
Upper	2182	9.9	12.2	72.0	4.3	1.6

Table B.08
Number of Pilot-test Respondents by Grade and Social Status of School District

Pilot test	Grade	Middle status	Low status
High school			
Pilot study 1—1958			
	Freshman	282	50
	Sophomore	320	131
	Junior	429	163
	Senior	200	236
Grade school			
Pilot study 2—1959	2	51	0
	3	46	0
	4	55	0
	5	47	0
	6	57	0
	7	52	0
	8	58	0
Pilot study 3—1961	2	46	58
	3	44	53
	4	54	67
	5	57	63
	6	58	57
	7	64	58
	8	53	56
Pilot study 4—1961	2	0	65
	3	26	75
	5	45	48
	7	34	51
Pilot study 5—1961	4	28	59
	6	27	53
	8	29	57
Pilot study 6—1961	4	56	23
	6	72	67
	8	80	120
Pilot study 7—1961	3	53	47
	5	46	50
	7	59	80

Table B.08—Continued

Pilot test	Grade	Middle status	Low status
Pilot study 8—1961	3	39	20
	5	35	20
	7	57	54
Pilot study 9—1961	3	22	21
	4	17	39
	5–6	45	68
	7–8	58	68
Grade school			
Pilot study 10—1961	4	56	25
	6	55	23
	7–8	40	43
Pilot study 11—1961	3	21	17
	4	23	27
	5	20	20
	6	32	24
	7	27	32
	8	29	31
Pilot study 12—1961	3	27	34
	4	0	5
	5	64	59
	8	52	62
Pilot study 13—part A	2	57	0
1961	4	57	0
	6	68	0
—part B	2	28	47
1961	3	28	11
	6	37	31
	7	25	28
Pilot study 14—1962	2	101	118
	3	105	120
	4	107	118
	5	114	109
	6	124	113
	7	101	122
	8	46	57
Supplementary study			
—1964	2	47	50
	3	47	59
	4	59	68
	5	60	77
	6	61	67
	7	61	75
	8	60	25

APPENDIX C

Item Combinations and

Scaling Descriptions

The decision to combine items into indices or scales was based upon two considerations: first, the investigators' intent to deal with certain dimensions; second, the correlation between items or their Guttman scaling properties, which would indicate the degree to which given items were measuring the same dimension.

In addition to making decisions concerning the items to be combined, a series of analyses related to the scoring of these items was undertaken. Here a decision on the manner of scoring "Don't know" responses had implications for the majority of indices of political attitudes. In the questionnaire, all the 5-point scales which measured agreement with an item had presented "Don't know" as the middle alternative on the scale (scored 3). If the responses to these items had been normally distributed at all grade levels, this scoring would have made "Don't know" equivalent to the neutral point on the attitude scale. In fact, however, many responses were skewed toward the "agree" side of the distribution in the early grades and toward the "disagree" side in the later grades. In correlation procedures, "Don't know" responses were therefore acting as more negative responses when given by young children and as more positive responses when given by older children. In addition, in some of the early correlation matrices, items which included the "Don't know" alternative correlated more highly with other items having "Don't know" alternatives than with items whose content was similar. For these reasons it was decided to give "no response" scores to children who responded "Don't know" to more than half of the questions in any index. Those with fewer than half "Don't know" responses were given scores estimated from the questions which they had answered with a content response. (For example, if a child answered 4 out of 5 questions, his score computed from this 4 questions was multiplied by 5/4 to estimate the score he would have received if he had responded to all 5 questions.) The "Don't know" response was eliminated in a similar fashion from all individual items and indices.

254

"Don't Know" Index

A separate "Don't know" Index was formed by summing the number of "Don't know" responses from a large number of questions. The number of "Don't know" responses given to questions in three content areas (partisanship, efficacy, definition of democracy), and to a group of miscellaneous items, were counted to form four "Don't know" subscores. The correlations between these subscores and the total "Don't know" score (in each case subtracting the subscore being correlated) ranged from .53 to .68 for fourth-graders, from .51 to .62 for sixth-graders, and from .42 to .49 for eighth-graders. The magnitude of these correlations justified the summation of all the "Don't know" subscores to form a "Don't Know" Total Score based on responses to 32 items.

Personification of the Government, and Voting as a Symbol of the Government

These indices were constructed to measure the child's conception of the government—the symbol, picture, or objects which are most salient to him in describing or thinking about the government. The score on the Personification Index was computed by adding one point for each of the following choices:

1) Choice of George Washington as "the best picture of the government."
2) Choice of the President as "the best picture of the government."
3) Choice of the President as the one who "runs the country."
4) Choice of the President as making you "the most proud to be an American."

Using all the third-grade students in the large western city and the small midwestern city, a Guttman scaling procedure was performed on these items. The Coefficient of Reproducibility was .90. The ordering of the items was identical in all seven grades; that is to say, the President was chosen more frequently as running the country than he was as the best picture of government, and so on.

Representation of the government by the voting process was indexed by the following choices:

1) Choice of voting as "the best picture of the government."
2) Choice of "Americans can vote for their own leaders" as "what makes you the most proud to be an American."

These items were combined because of their similar content and to complement the Personification Index.

Index of the President's Responsiveness to Individuals

This index assessed the feeling that the President has a personal interest in the child's well-being and ideas. The items which were combined to form this index were:

1) Ratings of the President on the dimension 1—Would always want to help me if I needed it, to 6—Would not usually want to help me if I needed it.
2) Ratings of the President on the dimension 1—If you write to the President he cares *a lot* what you think, to 3—If you write to the President he cares a *little* what you think.

The correlation between these items in the total group of eighth-grade children was .47. The score on this index was formed by summing the responses to these items and reversing the scale so that high scores corresponded to high ratings of responsiveness.

Index of Efficacy

The questions which made up this index were adapted from those used by the Survey Research Center to measure feelings of political efficacy in adults (Campbell *et al.,* 1954). In the present study, a number of items related to this content area were pilot tested, but because of low correlations among some items, only the following were selected for the final instrument:

1) What happens in the government will happen no matter what people do. It is like the weather, there is nothing people can do about it.
2) There are some big, powerful men in the government who are running the whole thing and they do not care about us ordinary people.
3) My family doesn't have any say about what the government does.
4) I don't think people in the government care much what people like my family think.
5) Citizens don't have a chance to say what they think about running the government.

Each statement was followed by a five-point scale with the alternatives: "YES," "yes," "Don't Know," "no," "NO." The correlations among these items ranged from .31 to .43 in the eighth-graders from the large western city and from the small cities in the Midwest and South. Individuals who did not respond or answered "Don't know" on more than two of the five questions received no score on this index. Scores were estimated for children who had no response or a "don't know" response on one or two questions. The alternatives were scored as follows: "YES" received a score of 1; "yes," a score of 2; "no," a score of 3; and "NO," a score of 4. The range of scores was 5 to 20 (rescaled for computer storage as 1 to 16). Since negative responses to these items indicate feelings of higher efficacy, high scores on this index correspond to a greater sense of efficacy.

Index of Participation in Political Discussion

The score on this index consisted of the number of "yes" responses to the following items:

1) I have talked with my mother or father about our country's problems.
2) I have talked with my friends about a candidate.
3) I have talked with my mother or father about a candidate.

Index of Concern with Political Issues

This index was formed from the following list of issues [1]:

1) The United Nations.
2) Giving money to other countries.
3) People who are out of work in our country.
4) Government aid to schools.
5) Taxes.

For each issue, the alternatives were: (1) I have not talked about this; (2) I have talked about this, but I have not taken sides on it; (3) I have talked about this, and I have taken sides on it; (4) I don't know. If the subject omitted or answered "Don't know" on more than two

1. The "space race" was eliminated from the issues scored on this index because in early analysis it showed low correlations with the other issues. The conquest of space is a topic of great interest to children but is apparently not particularly related to political concern.

items, he was not scored on this index. Scores were estimated for children who had no response or "Don't know" on one or two items. The alternatives were scored as follows: "not talked about it" received a score of 1; "talked but not taken sides" received a score of 2; "talked and taken sides" received a score of 3.

Index of Party Stands

The index of the relative contributions of the two parties was composed of the following questions:

1) Who does more for the rich people?
2) Who does most to keep us out of war?
3) Who does most to help people who are out of work?
4) Who does more to protect the rights of citizens?
5) Who does more to help my family?
6) Who does more for the United States?

For each question, the alternatives were: (1) Republicans; (2) Democrats; (3) Both about the same; (4) Don't Know. If the subject omitted or answered "Don't know" on more than two items, he received no score on this index. Scores were estimated for children who had no response or a "Don't know" response on one or two items. The alternatives were scored as follows: "Republican" received a score of 1; "Democrat" received a score of 3; "Both about the same" received a score of 2. The higher the score, the more the respondent attributed positive contribution to members of the Democratic party.

Index of Political Activity

The score on this index was the number of "yes" responses to the following questions:

1) I have worn a button for a candidate.
2) I have helped a candidate by doing things for him—such as handing out buttons and papers with his name on them.
3) I have read about a candidate in newspapers or magazines.

Using all the third- and eighth-grade students in the large western and small midwestern city, these items were Guttman scaled with a Coefficient of Reproducibility of .96.

Index of the Relative Influence of Father and Teacher in Citizenship Training

This index was made up of the ratings given by respondents to father and to teacher on the dimension, 1—teaches me an awful lot about being a good citizen, to 5—doesn't teach me at all about being a good citizen. The score was calculated by subtracting the rating given to teaching from the rating given to father. The score was rescaled to a 1-9 range to eliminate negative scores. The higher the score, the greater the teacher's role in teaching citizenship, relative to the father.

Supplementary
Figures and Tables

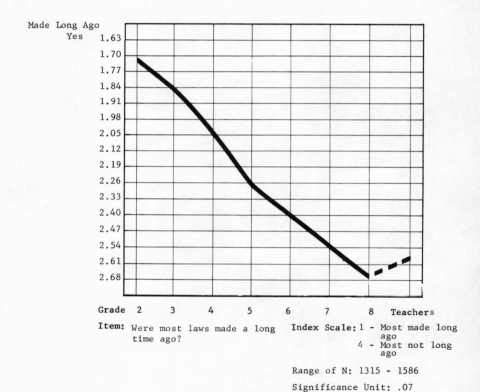

Fig. D.01.
Comparison of means of grades 2 through 8 in belief that
laws were "made a long time ago."

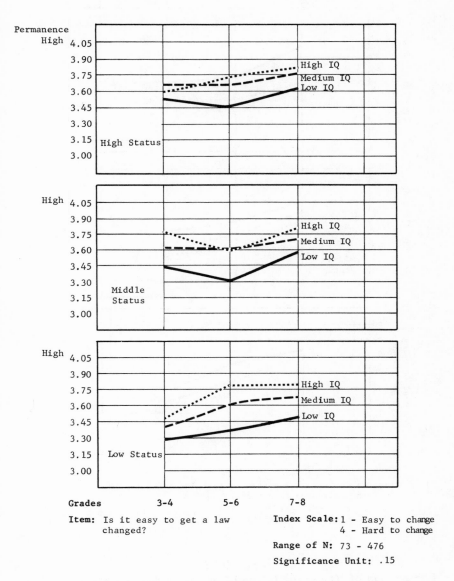

Permanence

Grades   3-4   5-6   7-8

Item: Is it easy to get a law   **Index Scale:** 1 - Easy to change
changed?   4 - Hard to change

Range of N: 73 - 476

Significance Unit: .15

Fig. D.02.
Comparison of means of IQ groups in belief that laws are
permanent, within social status and grade.

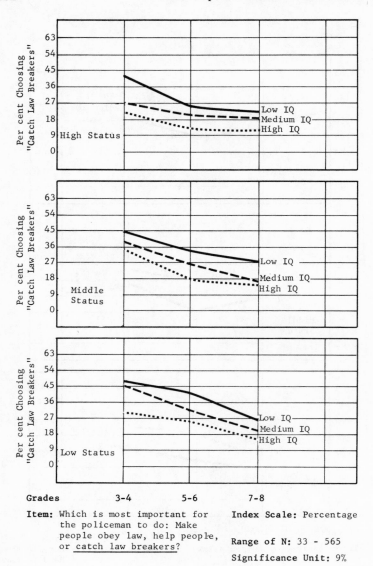

Grades   3-4   5-6   7-8

Item: Which is most important for   Index Scale: Percentage
      the policeman to do: Make
      people obey law, help people,   Range of N: 33 - 565
      or catch law breakers?
                                          Significance Unit: 9%

Fig. D.03.
Comparison of IQ groups in choice of "catch law breakers" as most
important aspects of policeman's role, within social status and grade.

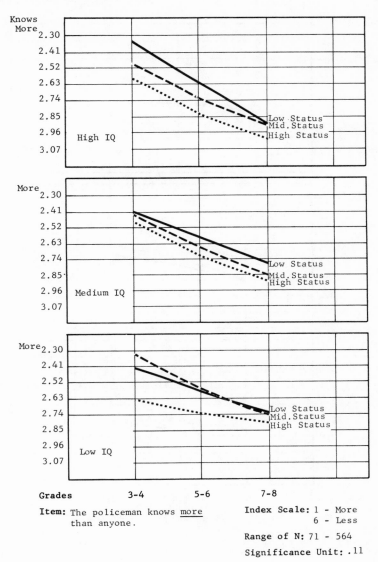

Grades   3-4   5-6   7-8

Item: The policeman knows _more_
      than anyone.

Index Scale: 1 - More
             6 - Less
Range of N: 71 - 564
Significance Unit: .11

Fig. D.04.
**Comparison of means of social-status groups in rating role
performance of policeman (knowledge), within IQ and grade.**

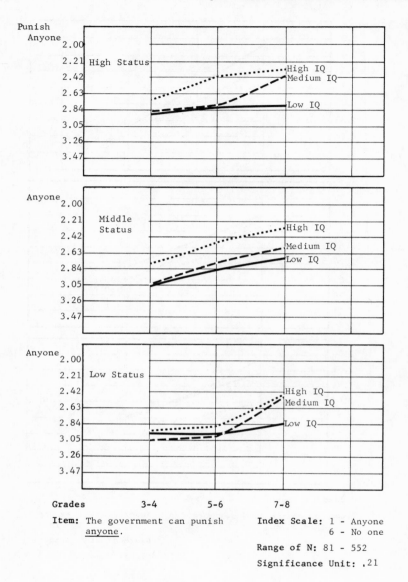

Grades   3-4   5-6   7-8

Item: The government can punish   Index Scale: 1 - Anyone
      anyone.   6 - No one

                                        Range of N: 81 - 552
                                        Significance Unit: .21

Fig. D.05.
**Comparison of means of IQ groups in rating punitive power of
the government, within social status and grade.**

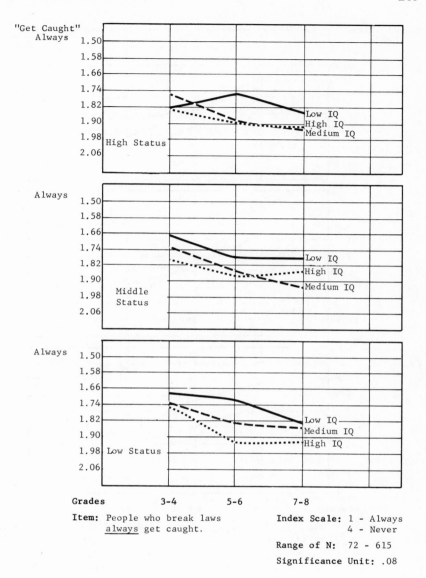

Fig. D.06.

Comparison of means of IQ groups in perception of success of law enforcement, within social status and grade.

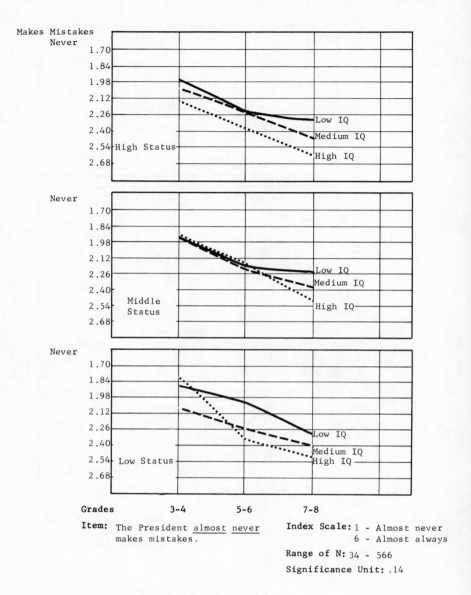

Fig. D.07.
Comparison of means of IQ groups in rating infallibility of President, within social status and grade.

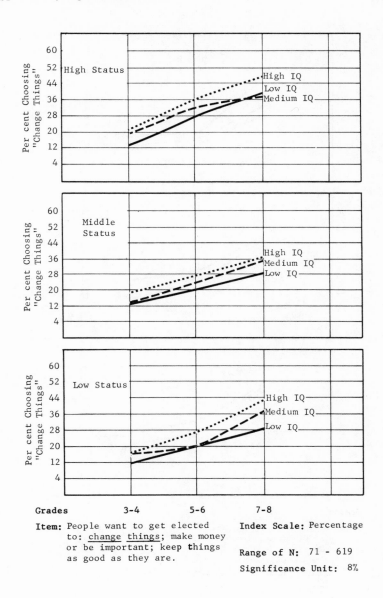

Grades 3-4 5-6 7-8

Item: People want to get elected to: change things; make money or be important; keep things as good as they are.

Index Scale: Percentage

Range of N: 71 - 619

Significance Unit: 8%

Fig. D.08.

Comparison of IQ groups in choice of government reform as reason for seeking office, within social status and grade.

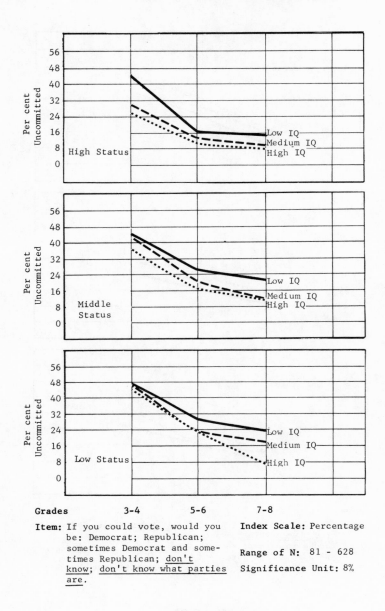

Grades   3-4   5-6   7-8

Item: If you could vote, would you
be: Democrat; Republican;
sometimes Democrat and sometimes Republican; don't
know; don't know what parties
are.

Index Scale: Percentage

Range of N: 81 - 628

Significance Unit: 8%

Fig. D.09.
*Comparison of IQ groups in reporting either that they do not know
which party to choose, or what parties are, within
social status and grade.*

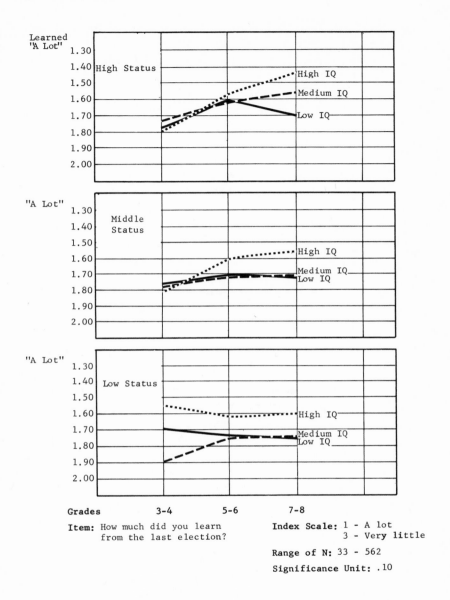

Fig. D.10.

Comparison of means of IQ groups in use of elections as sources of political information, within social status and grade.

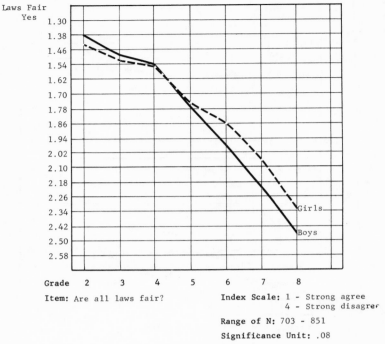

Item: Are all laws fair?   Index Scale: 1 - Strong agree
                                              4 - Strong disagree

                                  Range of N: 703 - 851
                                  Significance Unit: .08

Fig. D.11.
**Comparison of means of boys and girls in belief that laws
are fair, within grade.**

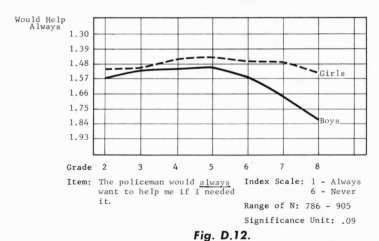

Item: The policeman would <u>always</u>   Index Scale: 1 - Always
      want to help me if I needed   6 - Never
      it.
                                          Range of N: 786 - 905
                                          Significance Unit: .09

Fig. D.12.
**Comparison of means of boys and girls in rating policeman's
responsiveness to individuals, within grade.**

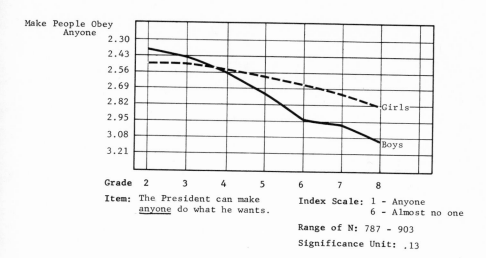

Fig. D.13.

Comparison of means of boys and girls in rating coercive power of President, within grade.

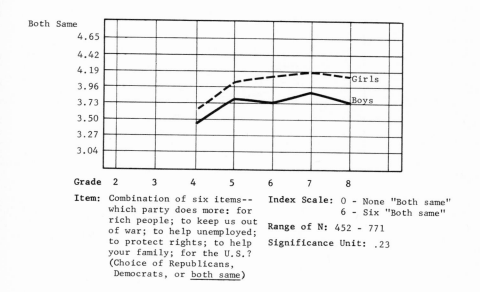

Fig. D.14.

Comparison of means of boys and girls in belief that Democrats and Republicans contribute equally to national welfare, within grade.

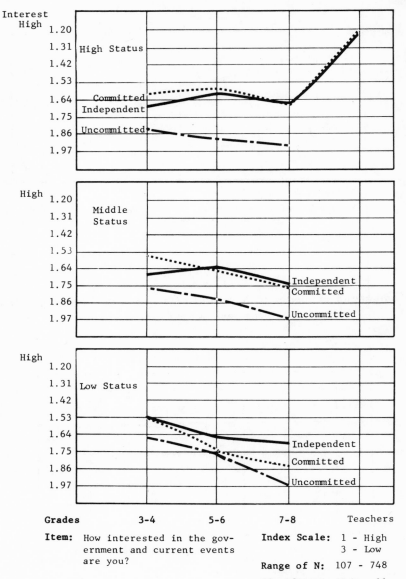

Grades   3-4   5-6   7-8   Teachers

Item: How interested in the gov-   **Index Scale:** 1 - High
ernment and current events   3 - Low
are you?
                                          Range of N: 107 - 748

                                          Significance Unit: .11

Comparison (within social status and grade) of mean
levels of political interest of three groups: 1)those
committed to a political party; 2)those uncommitted;
and 3) independents.

Fig. D.15.
Party commitment and political interest.

Participation

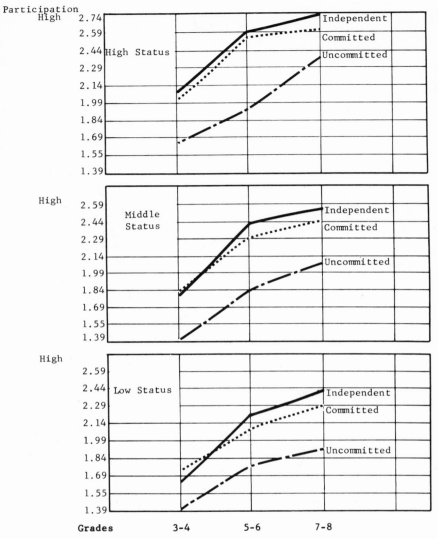

Item: Combination of three items --   Index Scale: 0 - None Discussed
      have you talked: with parents   3 - Three   "
      about candidates; with parents Range of N: 75 - 735
      about country's problems;
      with friends about candidates? Significance Unit: .15

      Comparison (within social status and grade) of mean
      levels of participation in political discussion
      by three groups: 1) those committed to a party; 2) those
      uncommitted; and 3) independents.

Fig. D.16.
Party commitment and participation in political discussion.

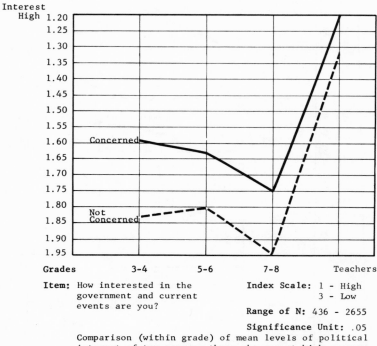

Interest
High

| | 3-4 | 5-6 | 7-8 | Teachers |

Item: How interested in the
government and current
events are you?

Index Scale: 1 - High
3 - Low

Range of N: 436 - 2655

Significance Unit: .05

Comparison (within grade) of mean levels of political
interest of two groups: those who report high concern
about the outcome of the 1960 election, and those who
report low concern.

Fig. D.17.
Concern with election outcome and political interest.

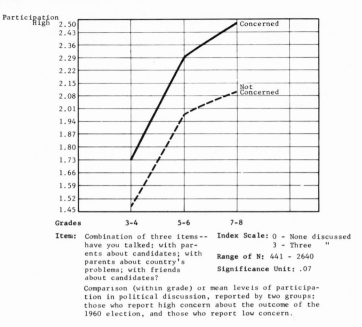

Item: Combination of three items --
have you talked: with parents about candidates; with
parents about country's
problems; with friends
about candidates?

Index Scale: 0 - None discussed
             3 - Three   "

Range of N: 441 - 2640

Significance Unit: .07

Comparison (within grade) of mean levels of participation in political discussion, reported by two groups:
those who report high concern about the outcome of the
1960 election, and those who report low concern.

Fig. D.18.
Concern with election outcome and participation in political discussion.

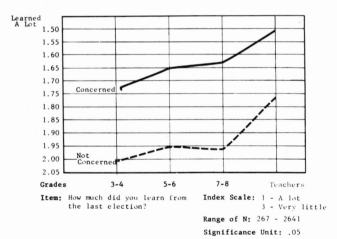

Item: How much did you learn from
the last election?

Index Scale: 1 - A lot
             3 - Very little

Range of N: 267 - 2641

Significance Unit: .05

Comparison (within grade) of mean ratings of the amount
learned from the 1960 election, by two groups: those
who report high concern about the outcome of the election, and those who report low concern.

Fig. D.19.
Concern with election outcome and rating of elections as sources of political information.

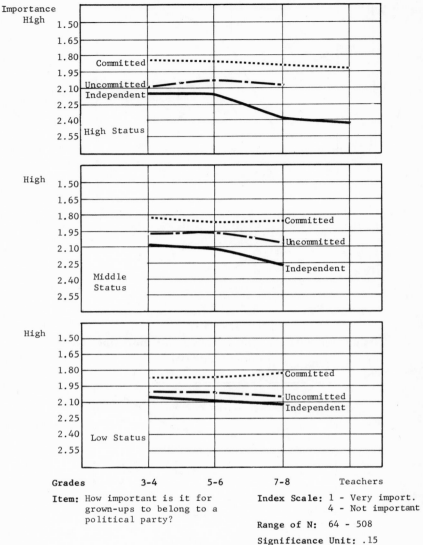

Grades   3-4   5-6   7-8   Teachers

Item: How important is it for   Index Scale: 1 - Very import.
      grown-ups to belong to a   4 - Not important
      political party?
                                     Range of N: 64 - 508

                                     Significance Unit: .15
      Comparison (within social status and grade) of mean
      ratings of the importance of belonging to a party as
      an adult, by three groups: 1)those committed to a
      party; 2)those uncommitted; and 3)independents.

Fig. D.20.
Party commitment and rating importance of party membership.

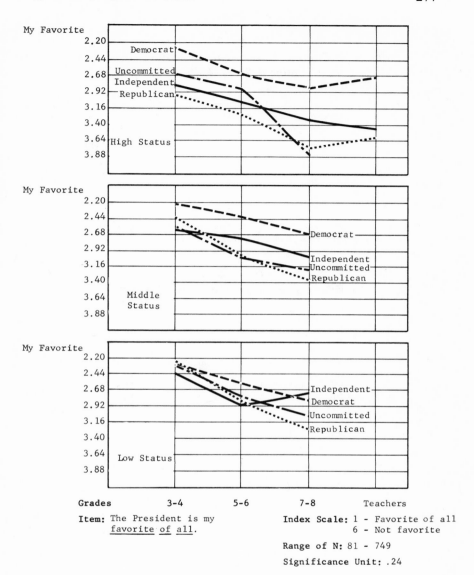

Item: The President is my
      favorite of all.

Index Scale: 1 - Favorite of all
             6 - Not favorite

Range of N: 81 - 749

Significance Unit: .24

Fig. D.21.

**Comparison of means of party preference groups in attachment to
President, within social status and grade.**

Table D.22
Changes by Grade in Correct Identification of President's Political Party Affiliation

Grade level	N	Eisenhower a Republican	N	Kennedy a Democrat
2	46	52.2%	96	68.8%
3	45	82.2	97	86.6
4	55	78.2	119	87.4
5	47	76.6	119	87.4
6	58	91.4	115	96.5
7	52	100.0	122	96.7
8	58	98.3	109	100.0

Note—Item: Which party does the President belong to? Eisenhower data from Pilot Study 2, 1958; Kennedy data from Pilot Study 3, 1961.

Table D.23
Changes by Grade in Rating Importance of Party Membership

Grade level	N	Very important	Important	Not too important	Not important at all
3	1296	39.0%	37.3%	19.5%	4.2%
4	1409	32.6	42.2	20.4	4.8
5	1595	32.8	41.4	21.6	4.1
6	1570	35.9	39.6	20.1	4.3
7	1611	35.7	35.6	22.8	5.8
8	1599	32.6	37.3	23.6	6.4
Teachers	382	25.4	37.2	29.8	7.6

Notes.—Item: How important do you think it is for grown-ups to belong to either the Republican or Democratic party?

Bibliography

AGGER, R. E. Independence and party identifiers: characteristics and behavior in 1952. In E. Burdick & A. J. Brodbeck (Eds.), *American voting behavior*. Glencoe, Ill.: Free Press, 1959.

ALMOND, G. A., & VERBA, S. *The civic culture: political attitudes and democracy in five nations*. Princeton, N.J.: Princeton University Press, 1963.

ANDERSON, I. H., HUGHES, B. O., & DIXON, W. R. The rate of reading development and its relation to age of learning to read, sex, and intelligence. *J. educ. Res.*, 1957, *50*, 481–494.

BACH, R. Father fantasies and father typing in father separated children. *Child Develpm.*, 1946, 17 63–80.

BALDWIN, A. L. Socialization and the parent-child relationship. *Child Develpm.*, 1948, *19*, 127–136.

BANFIELD, E. *The moral basis of a backward society*. Glencoe, Ill.: Free Press, 1958.

———. The political implications of metropolitan growth. *Daedalus*, 1960, *90*, (1), 61–78.

———. *Political influence*. Glencoe, Ill.: Free Press, 1961.

BAURERFEIND, R. Measuring children's strength of response to attitude items. *Educ. psychol. Measmt*, 1955, *15*, 63–70.

BECKER, H. S. *Boys in white: student culture in medical school*. Chicago: University of Chicago Press, 1961.

BELOFF, J., & BELOFF, J. Influence of valence on distance judgments of human faces. *J. abnorm. soc. Psychol.*, 1961, *62*, 720–722.

BERELSON, B., LAZARSFELD, P., & MCPHEE, W. *Voting*. Chicago: University of Chicago Press, 1954.

BERNSTEIN, B. Aspects of language and learning in the genesis of the social process. *J. child Psychol. Psychiat.*, 1960, *1*, 313–324.

———. Social class, linguistic codes and grammatical elements. *Lang. & Speech*, 1962, *5*, 221–240.

———. Family role systems, communication and socialization. Paper read at Cross-nat. Conf. Childh. Adolesc., Chicago, February, 1964.

BLOOM, B. S. *Stability and change in human characteristics*. New York: John Wiley & Sons, 1964.

BRIM, O. G., JR., & WHEELER, S. *Socialization after childhood: two essays*. New York, John Wiley & Sons, 1966.

BRONFENBRENNER, U. Socialization and social class through time and space.

In E. E. Maccoby, T. Newcomb, & E. L. Hartley (Eds.), *Readings in social psychology*. New York: Holt, 1958.

———. Toward a theoretical model for the analysis of parent-child relationship in a social context. In J. C. Glidewell (Ed.), *Parental attitudes and child behavior*. Springfield, Ill.: Charles C Thomas, 1961.

BUCHANAN, W. An inquiry into purposive voting. *J. Polit.*, 1956, *18*, 281–296.

CAMPBELL, A., CONVERSE, P., MILLER, W., & STOKES, D. *The American voter*. New York: John Wiley & Sons, 1960.

———, GURIN, G., & MILLER, W. *The voter decides*. Evanston, Ill.: Row, Peterson, 1954.

CANTRIL, H., & STRUNK, MILDRED. *Public opinion: 1935-1946*. Princeton, N. J.: Princeton University Press, 1951.

CHILD, I. L. Socialization. In G. Lindzey (Ed.), *Handbook of social psychology*. Reading, Mass.: Addison-Wesley, 1954.

CLOWARD, R., & OHLIN, L. *Delinquency and opportunity*. Glencoe, Ill.: Free Press, 1960.

COHEN, J. A coefficient of agreement for nominal scales. *Educ. psychol. Measmt*, 1960, *20*, 37–46.

CRONBACH, L. J. *Essentials of psychological testing*. New York: Harper, 1960.

DAVIES, J. C. Charisma in the 1952 campaign. *Amer. polit. Sci. Rev.*, 1954, *48*, 1083–1102.

DAVIS, A. *Social-class influences upon learning*. Cambridge, Mass.: Harvard University Press, 1948.

DOLGER, LAURA, & GINANDES, JANET. Children's attitude toward discipline as related to socio-economic status. *J. exp. Educ.*, 1946, *15*, 161–165.

DUBIN, ELISABETH R., & DUBIN, R. The authority inception period in socialization. *Child Develpm.*, 1963, *34*, 885–898.

EASTON, D., & HESS, R. D. Youth and the political system. In S. M. Lipset & L. Lowenthal (Eds.), *Culture and social character: the work of David Riesman reviewed*. Glencoe, Ill.: Free Press, 1961.

ELDERSVELD, S. J. The independent voter: Measurement, characteristics and implications for party strategy. *Amer. polit. Sci. Rev.*, 1952, *46*, 732–753.

ERBE, W. Social involvement and political activity: a replication and elaboration. *Amer. sociol. Rev.*, 1964, *29*, 198–215.

EULAU, H. *Class and party in the Eisenhower years*. Glencoe, Ill.: Free Press, 1962.

FISKE, D. W. The constraints on intra-individual variability in test responses. *Educ. psychol. Measmt*, 1957, *17*, 317–337.

FLANAGAN, J. C., & SCHWARZ, P. A. Development of procedures for converting intelligence test scores to a common scale. Mimeographed publication of Amer. Inst. Res., Pittsburgh, 1958.

FRANK, J. *Law and the modern mind*. New York: Coward-McCann, 1949.

FREUD, S. *Civilization and its discontents*. London: Hogarth Press, 1930.

FREY, F. The socialization to national identification: the Turkish peasant. Paper read at Amer. Polit. Sci. Ass., New York, Sept., 1966.

GLANTZ, O. Protestant and Catholic voting in a metropolitan area. *Publ. Opin. Quart.*, 1959, *23*, 73–82.

GOLD, D. The influence of religious affiliation on voting behavior. Unpublished doctoral dissertation, University of Chicago, 1953.

GOULDNER, A. The norm of reciprocity. *Amer. sociol. Rev.*, 1960, *25*, 161–179.

GRASSMUCK, G. L. Sectional biases in Congress and foreign policy. *Johns Hopkins Univer. Stud. Histor. Polit. Sci.*, 1951, Ser. LXVIII, No. 3.

GREENSTEIN, F. I. More on children's images of the President. *Publ. Opin. Quart.*, 1961, *25*, 648–654.

―――. *Children and politics.* New Haven, Conn.: Yale University Press, 1965. (a)

―――. Young men and the death of a young president. In Martha Wolfenstein & G. Kliman (Eds.), *Children and the death of a president: Multi-disciplinary studies.* Garden City, N.Y.: Doubleday, 1965. (b)

GREER, S. Individual participation in mass society. In R. Young (Ed.), *Approaches to the study of politics.* Evanston, Ill.: Northwestern University Press, 1958.

―――. Catholic voters and the Democratic party. *Publ. Opin. Quart.*, 1961, *25*, 611–625.

HARRIS, D. How children learn interests, motives and attitudes. In N. B. Henry (Ed.), Learning and instruction, *Yearb. nat. Soc. Stud. Educ.*, 1950, *49*, Part I.

―――. A scale for measuring attitudes of social responsibility in children. *J. abnorm. soc. Psychol.*, 1957, *55*, 322–326.

HARTLEY, E. L., & KRUGMAN, D. C. Note on children's social role perception. *J. Psychol.*, 1948, *26*, 399–405.

HASTINGS, P. K. The non-voter in 1952: a study of Pittsfield, Mass. *J. Psychol.*, 1954, *38*, 301–312.

HAUSKNECHT, M. *The joiners.* New York: Bedminster Press, 1962.

HAVIGHURST, R., & DAVIS, A. *Father of the man.* Boston: Houghton Mifflin, 1947.

HESS, R. D. The socialization of attitudes toward political authority: some cross-national comparisons. *Int. Soc. Sci. J.*, 1963, *25*, 542-559.

―――, & EASTON, D. The child's changing image of the President. *Publ. Opin. Quart.*, 1960, *24*, 632–644.

―――, ―――. The role of the elementary school in political socialization. *Sch. Rev.*, 1962, *70*, 253–265.

―――, SHIPMAN, VIRGINIA C. Early experience and the socialization of cognitive modes in children. *Child Develpm.*, 1965, *36*, 869–886.

―――, TORNEY, JUDITH V. The development of basic attitudes and values toward government and citizenship during the elementary school years, Part I. Report to U.S. Off. Educ. on Coop. Proj. No. 1078, 1965.

―――, and MINTURN, LEIGH. Authority rules and aggression: a cross-national study of the socialization of children into compliance systems. Unpublished manuscript.

HOFFMAN, L. W. The father's role in the family and the child's peer group adjustment. *Merrill-Palmer Quart.*, 1961, *7*, 98–105.

HOLCOMBE, A. N. *Political parties of today.* New York: Harper, 1924.

HORTON, D., & WOHL, R. R. Mass communication and para-social interaction. *Psychiat.*, 1956, *19*, 215–229.

HUGHES, E. C. Institutional office and the person. *Amer. J. Sociol.*, 1937, *43*, 404–413.

HUGHES, MILDRED C. Sex differences in reading achievement in the elementary grades. *Suppl. Educ. Monogr.*, 1953, (77), 102–106.

HYMAN, H. *Political socialization.* Glencoe, Ill.: Free Press, 1959.

JOHNSON, MIRIAM M. Sex role learning in the nuclear family. *Child Develpm.*, 1963, *34*, 319–333.

JOSEPHSON, E. Political youth organizations in Europe, 1900–1950. Unpublished doctoral dissertation, Columbia University, 1959.

KAGAN, J. Socialization of aggression and the perception of parents in fantasy. *Child Develpm.*, 1958, *29*, 311–320.

————, HOSKEN, BARBARA, & WATSON, SARA. Child's symbolic conceptualization of parents. *Child Developm.*, 1961, *32*, 625–636.

————, & MOSS, H. A. *Birth to maturity: A study in psychological development.* New York: John Wiley & Sons, 1962.

KELLEY, T. L., & KREY, A. C. *Tests and measurements in the social sciences.* New York: Scribner's, 1934.

KEY, V. O., JR. *Political parties and pressure groups.* New York: Thomas Y. Crowell, 1947.

————. *Public opinion and American democracy.* New York: Alfred A. Knopf, 1961.

KOHLBERG, L. Moral development and identification in child psychology. In H. W. Stevenson (Ed.), *Yearb. nat. Soc. Stud. Educ.*, 1963, *62*, Part I.

————. Cognitive developmental analyses of children's sex role concepts and attitudes. In Eleanor Maccoby (Ed.), *The development of sex differences.* Stanford, Calif.: Stanford University Press, 1966.

KOHN, M. L. Social class and the exercise of parental authority. *Amer. sociol. Rev.*, 1959, *24*, 352–366.

————. Social class and parent child relationships. *Amer. J. Sociol.*, 1963, *68*, 471–480.

KORNHAUSER, W. *The politics of mass society.* Glencoe, Ill.: Free Press, 1959.

LANE, R. E. *Political life: why people get involved in politics.* Glencoe, Ill.: Free Press, 1959.

LASSWELL, H. D. *Psychopathology and politics.* Chicago: University of Chicago Press, 1930.

————. *Power and personality.* New York: W. W. Norton, 1948.

LAZARSFELD, P., BERELSON, B., & GAUDET, H. *The people's choice.* (2nd ed.) New York, Columbia University Press, 1948.

LIPSET, S. M. *Political man.* New York: Doubleday, 1959.

LITT, E. Civic education, community norms, and political indoctrination. *Amer. sociol. Rev.*, 1963, *28*, 60–75.

LYNN, D. B. Sex role and parental identification. *Child Develpm.*, 1962, *33*, 555–564.

MAAS, H. S. Some social class differences in the family systems and group relationships of pre- and early adolescents. *Child Develpm.*, 1951, *22*, 145–152.

MACCOBY, ELEANOR, MATTHEWS, R., & MORTON, A. Youth and political change. *Publ. Opin. Quart.*, 1954, *18*, 23–39.

MACCOBY, H. The differential political activity of participants in a voluntary association. *Amer. sociol. Rev.*, 1958, *23*, 524–532.

MELTZER, HELEN. Development of children's nationality preference, concepts and attitudes. *J. Psychol.*, 1941, *11*, 343–358.

MERTON, R. K., & ROSSI, ALICE S. Contributions to the theory of reference group behavior. In R. Merton (Ed.), *Social theory and social structure.* Glencoe, Ill.: Free Press, 1957.

MILLER, D. R., & SWANSON, G. E. *Changing American parent.* New York: John Wiley & Sons, 1958.

MONEY-KYRLE, R. E. *Psychoanalysis and politics: A contribution to the psychology of politics and morals.* New York: W. W. Norton, 1951.

MUSSEN, P., & WYSZYNSKI, ANNE. Personality and political participation. *Hum. Relat.,* 1952, *5,* 65–82.

OESER, O., & EMERY, F. *Social structure and personality in a rural community.* New York: Macmillan, 1954.

OSGOOD, C. E., SUCI, G. J., & TANNENBAUM, P. H. *The measurement of meaning.* Urbana, Ill.: University of Illinois Press, 1957.

PARSONS, T., & BALES, R. F. *Family, socialization and interaction process.* Glencoe, Ill.: Free Press, 1955.

PAUL, I. H. Impressions of personality, authoritarianism, and the fait accompli effect. *J. abnorm. soc. Psychol.,* 1956, *53,* 338–344.

PIAGET, J. *The psychology of intelligence.* London: Routledge and Kegan Paul, 1947.

REMMERS, H. H., & RADLER, D. H. *The American teen-ager.* Indianapolis, Ind.: Bobbs-Merrill, 1957.

REMMERS, H. H., & WELTMAN, N. Attitude interrelationships of youth, their parents and teachers. *J. soc. Psychol.,* 1947, *26,* 61–68.

RIBMAN, R. B., & RIBMAN, S. M. The poor man in the scales. *Harper's,* 1964, *228* (1367), 150–158.

ROSE, A. M. Attitudinal correlates of social participation. *Soc. Forces,* 1959, *37,* 202–206.

———. Alienation and participation: A comparison of group leaders and the mass. *Amer. soc. Rev.,* 1962, *27,* 834–838.

ROSEN, B. C. Race, ethnicity, and the achievement syndrome. *Amer. soc. Rev.,* 1959, *24,* 47–60.

SCHACHTEL, E. G. On memory and childhood amnesia. *Psychiat.,* 1947, *10,* 1–26.

SCHAEFER, E. S. Converging conceptual models for maternal behavior and for child behavior. In J. C. Glidewell (Ed.), *Parental attitudes and child behavior.* Springfield, Ill.: Charles C Thomas, 1961.

SCHRAMM, W., LYLE, J., & PARKER, E. B. *Television in the lives of our children.* Stanford, Calif.: Stanford University Press, 1961.

SCOBLE, H. M., & EPSTEIN, L. D. Religion and Wisconsin voting in 1960. *J. Polit.,* 1964, *26,* 381–392.

SCOTT, L. Social attitudes of children revealed by responses to television programs. *Calif. J. elem. Educ.,* 1954, *22,* 176–179.

SCOTT, W. A. Conceptualizing and measuring structural properties of cognition. In O. J. Harvey (Ed.), *Motivation and social interaction.* New York: Ronald Press, 1963.

SEWELL, W. H. Some recent developments in socialization theory and research. *Ann. Amer. Acad. Polit. Soc. Sci.,* 1963, 349.

SMITH, M. B., BRUNER, J. S., & WHITE, R. W. *Opinions and personality.* New York: John Wiley & Sons, 1956.

STARK, P. Some determinants of political activity among liberals. Unpublished doctoral dissertation, Columbia University, 1957.

STILLMAN, JANE G., GUTHRIE, G. M., & BECKER, S. W. Determinants of political party preference. *J. soc. Psychol.,* 1960, *51,* 165–171.

STRICKLER, G. The use of the semantic differential to predict voting behavior. *J. soc. Psychol.,* 1963, *59,* 159–167.

TILLER, P. O. *Father absence and personality development of children in sailor families.* Copenhagen: Enjar Munksgaards Forlag, 1958.

TORNEY, JUDITH V. Structural dimensions of children's political attitude-concept systems: a study of developmental and measurement aspects. Unpublished doctoral dissertation, University of Chicago, 1965.

———, HESS, R. D., & EASTON, D. The child's idealization of authority. Unpublished paper read at Amer. Psychol. Ass., St. Louis, September, 1962.

TRUMAN, D. B. *The congressional party.* New York: John Wiley & Sons, 1959.

———. *The governmental process.* New York: Alfred A. Knopf, 1963.

TUTTLE, H. S. Obedience: A necessary convenience. *Elem. Sch. J.,* 1943, *43,* 343–346.

VERBA, S. *Small groups and political behavior.* Princeton, N. J.: Princeton University Press, 1961.

WARNER, W. L. *The living and the dead.* New Haven, Conn.: Yale University Press, 1959.

———, MEEKER, M., & EELLS, K. *Social class in America.* Chicago: Science Research Associates, 1949.

WEBER, M. *Max Weber, Essays in sociology.* H. Gerth & C. W. Mills (Eds.), New York: Oxford University Press, 1946.

WEINSTEIN, E. A. Development of concept of flag and sense of national identity. *Child Develpm.,* 1957, *28,* 167–174.

WERNER, H. *Comparative psychology of mental development.* New York: International Universities Press, 1957.

———, & KAPLAN, EDITH. The acquisition of word meanings: a developmental study. *Soc. for Res. child Develpm. Monogr.,* 1950, *15,* No. 1 (Whole No. 51).

WESLEY, E. B., & ADAMS, M. A. *Teaching social studies in elementary schools.* Boston: D. C. Heath, 1952.

WHYTE, W. *Street corner society.* Chicago: University of Chicago Press, 1943.

WOODWARD, J. L., & ROPER, E. Political activity of American citizens. *Amer. polit. Sci. Rev.,* 1950, *44,* 872–885.

ZIMMER, B. G., & HAWLEY, A. H. The significance of membership in associations. *Amer. J. Sociol.,* 1959, *65,* 196–201.

Index

285

ALSO FROM ALDINE

Sibylle K. Escalona

THE ROOTS OF INDIVIDUALITY

An exploratory study of infant behavior based on twenty years research, this book presents a general theory of early developmental processes, formulated from an analysis of behavior patterns in normal infants between the ages of 4 and 32 weeks. Sibylle K. Escalona is Professor of Psychiatry (Psychology), Albert Einstein College of Medicine, Yeshiva University. Modern Applications in Psychology.

Seymour Warkov, with a chapter by Joseph Zelan

LAWYERS IN THE MAKING

A study of the legal profession as it is mirrored in the eyes of prospective members, based on an extensive survey of college graduates entering the study of law and planning legal careers. Introduction by Louis A. Toepfer. Seymour Warkov is Senior Study Director, National Opinion Research Center, and Assistant Professor of Sociology in the University of Chicago. NORC Monographs in Social Research No. 7. 181 pp.

James A. Davis

UNDERGRADUATE CAREER DECISIONS:
Correlates of Occupational Choice

A study of the way in which undergraduates formulate — and change — their career plans during their college years, correlating family background, academic achievement and values with career choice. The author is Senior Study Director, National Opinion Research Center, and Associate Professor of Sociology, University of Chicago. NORC Monographs in Social Research No. 2. 307 pp.

Ronald Freedman, editor

POPULATION: The Vital Revolution

A useful and readable summary of contemporary population trends and problems that analyzes both increases—the "population explosion" and its significance in the United States and abroad—and decreases in population to give an accurate, comprehensive and meaningful explanation of the world population picture. Ronald Freedman is Professor of Sociology and Director, Population Studies Center, University of Michigan. 274 pp.

Karl E. Taeuber and Alma F. Taeuber, editors

NEGROES IN CITIES: Residential Segregation and Neighborhood Change

A systematic and highly original description of the patterns of Negro residential segregation and the processes of urban neighborhood change. The editors are Associate Professor, and Research Associate, respectively, in the Department of Sociology, University of Wisconsin. Population Research and Training Center Monographs.

John W. C. Johnstone and Ramon J. Rivera

VOLUNTEERS FOR LEARNING

A broad study of the educational pursuits of American adults, including a detailed analysis of why adults take courses, what they get from them, and how adult education is viewed across the social spectrum. NORC Monographs in Social Research No. 4. John W. C. Johnstone is Senior Study Director, National Opinion Research Center, and Assistant Professor of Sociology, University of Chicago. Raymond J. Rivera is Senior Study Director, National Opinion Research Center. 626 pp.

Gerald Handel, editor

THE PSYCHOSOCIAL INTERIOR OF THE FAMILY: A Sourcebook for the Study of Whole Families

An interdisciplinary series of readings — drawing upon findings in anthropology, psychiatry, social psychology, and sociology — providing a composite study of whole families and the complex interplay between self and family. The editor is Senior Research Associate with the Center for Urban Education in New York. 572 pp.

James A. Davis

**GREAT ASPIRATIONS: The Graduate School Plans
of America's College Seniors**

A careful analysis of the post-graduate plans of 34,000 students
who graduated from college in June, 1961, with special attention
given to recruitment into graduate study and into specific occupations. The author is Senior Study Director, National Opinion Research Center, and Associate Professor of Sociology, University
of Chicago. NORC Monographs in Social Research No. 1. 319 pp.

Robert D. Hess and Roberta Meyer Bear, editors

EARLY EDUCATION: Current Theory, Research, and Practice

This authoritative and stimulating set of original essays provides
an up-to-date sourcebook on what has been done in the field of
early education, presents a comprehensive evaluation of contemporary theories and teaching techniques, and offers a wealth of
suggestions for the course of future research and practice. Robert
D. Hess is Lee Jacks Professor of Child Education, School of
Education, Stanford University, and Roberta Meyer Bear is
Research Associate, Committee on Human Development, University of Chicago. 352 pp.

W. Sluckin

IMPRINTING AND EARLY LEARNING

A comprehensive review of research and theory dealing with
imprinting in relation to conditioning and early learning and in
terms of its implications for educational, social, and abnormal
psychology. The author is Reader in Psychology, University of
Leicester. Clothbound 147 pp., or Paperbound (available in quan-
tities of 5 or more only).

C. Arnold Anderson and Mary Jean Bowman, editors

EDUCATION AND ECONOMIC DEVELOPMENT

An interdisciplinary survey — economic, sociological, historical
and pedagogical — of the problems and processes of education as
a crucial factor in stimulating and maintaining economic development. C. Arnold Anderson is Professor of Education and Sociology and Director of the Comparative Education Center, and
Mary Jean Bowman is Research Associate Professor of Eco-
nomics, both in the University of Chicago. 448 pp.

Peter H. Rossi and Bruce J. Biddle, editors

THE NEW MEDIA AND EDUCATION:
Their Impact on Society

Mass instruction for individuals or individual instruction for the masses? In a multifaceted investigation of the role of the new media in contemporary education, the papers in this volume discuss the complete spectrum of education today, from architecture to social organization, and present a sophisticated, detailed handbook for educators and sociologists on the use and effects of television, tape recordings, programmed instruction material, new teaching aids, films, and other new media. Peter H. Rossi is Chairman, Department of Social Relations, Johns Hopkins University; Bruce J. Biddle is Professor of Sociology and Psychology and Director of the Center for Research in Social Behavior, University of Missouri. NORC Monographs in Social Research No. 12. 448 pp.

Muzafer Sherif and Carolyn W. Sherif, editors

PROBLEMS OF YOUTH: Transition to Adulthood
in a Changing World

A collection of 13 essays by leading American theorists and practitioners outlining current thought and research into the problems of youth today, including a major, previously unpublished report by the editors on adolescent attitudes, goals and behavior. Muzafer Sherif is Professor of Sociology, and Carolyn W. Sherif is Associate Professor of Psychology, both in Pennsylvania State University. Modern Applications in Psychology. 352 pp.

D'

F